SELECTED WORKS

OF

CICERO

A New Translation

Introduction by Harry M. Hubbell

Published for the Classics Club by

WALTER J. BLACK · ROSLYN, NEW YORK

CONTENTS

EDITOR'S NOTE: *The translations here presented, based in part on older translations, and the introductions to the various parts, are the work of Isabelle K. and Antony E. Raubitschek, with the assistance of Louise R. Loomis.*

INTRODUCTION

MARCUS TULLIUS CICERO, the greatest of Roman orators, was born at Arpinum on January 3, 106 B.C., and was murdered by henchmen of Mark Antony at Astura, on December 3, 43 B.C. His life covered a period which was marked by turmoil, civil war, anarchy, and the overthrow of the Roman republic. The brilliance of his oratory gave him a distinguished and dangerous position in this time of confusion, and he finally fell a victim to the hatred which the sharpness of his tongue aroused.

His family was of the equestrian order, that is, they possessed moderate wealth, derived from business; but they had never taken part in politics. Cicero received the usual training in oratory, which was designed to produce lawyers and statesmen. His active mind, however, took him beyond the ordinary curriculum, and he was well versed in the theory of Roman law and in Greek philosophy. Prolonged study both at Rome and in Greece with the best teachers of oratory and philosophy, combined with his great natural endowments, soon made him the leader of the Roman bar, and gave him a lucrative practice.

Every ambitious lawyer in that time entered politics. Cicero rose through the minor offices of quaestor, aedile, and praetor —winning his elections easily; a popular young lawyer, whose prosecution of Verres (see p. 18) for plundering the province of Sicily had marked him as a liberal reformer. The climax of his political career came in the year 63, when he held the office of consul.

Cicero's position at this time can be explained only by reference to the general political situation. Political power and control over elections was nominally in the hands of the people, but in practice the elections were manipulated by a small clique of senators—a clan who derived their wealth from land and the plunder of conquered territory. This class resisted—successfully for the most part—the intrusion of any new members into the consulship. Opposed to the Senate was, first, Cicero's own group, the equestrian order, composed of merchants and tax-farmers, who felt that their economic importance entitled them to a larger share in the government, and, second, the propertyless proletariat, which furnished material for revolutionary movements under a series of demagogues. Cicero owed his election to the consulship partly to his popularity with the equestrians and the people, but also to the desire of the senatorial oligarchy to choose between him and Catiline, who was suspected of revolutionary designs. The liberal-minded, honest Cicero, though a "new man," seemed preferable to an agitator. The threatened conspiracy broke out in Cicero's year of office, and he was vigorous in suppressing it (see *Against Catiline*, p. 103). In an excess of zeal, however, he consented to the execution of some of the conspirators without a trial, justifiably, perhaps, but certainly illegally.

The suppression of the conspiracy was the turning point in Cicero's career. Thereafter he was aligned with the senatorial clique, without ever being received as a member in full standing by the ruling aristocracy. His political enemies seized on the illegal execution of the conspirators as a good pretext for exiling him from Italy (March, 58–August, 57). On his part, Cicero forever afterward fancied himself as the greatest man in Rome, the savior of the republic, and when the turn of events put the power into other hands, he retired to private life to nurse his feeling of injured dignity.

This turn of events was the formation of the First Triumvirate, a politico-military cabal, composed of Caesar, Pompey,

8

and Crassus. Their purpose was to control elections and break the power of the Senate. Cicero was invited to work with the Triumvirate, but was unwilling to take a subordinate position, and too scrupulous to lead in a period when rioting and force of arms were superseding orderly political processes. The Triumvirate broke up in the Civil War between Caesar and Pompey, in which Cicero gave half-hearted support to Pompey. He was pardoned, however, by Caesar after the victory of Caesar's army at Pharsalus and remained quiescent until the 15th of March, 44, when Caesar's assassination called him again into political activity. In a series of violent speeches (see *Philippic I*, p. 296) he opposed Antony, the virtual successor of Caesar, and supported the young Octavian, Caesar's great-nephew and designated heir, in the hope that Octavian would restore the power of the Senate. In the end, Antony and Octavian combined with Lepidus to form the Second Triumvirate; a proscriptum or purge of opponents followed, and Cicero was sacrificed to the hatred of Antony. Plutarch records that many years later, Octavian, then Emperor Augustus, discovered his grandson reading one "of Cicero's works. The frightened boy tried to conceal the book under his robe, but Augustus took it, read for a long time, and said, 'An eloquent man, my boy, eloquent and patriotic.' "

The historian Velleius Paterculus, writing in the reign of Tiberius, thus sums up the achievements of Cicero (Book ii, chap. lxvi): "When Cicero was beheaded by the crime of Antony, the voice of the people was silenced, for no one raised a hand in defense of the man who for so many years had defended the interests both of the state and of the private citizen. But you accomplished nothing, Mark Antony. . . . You took from Cicero a few anxious days, a few aging years, a life which would have been more wretched under your rule than was his death in your triumvirate. Far from robbing him of his fame, the glory of his deeds and words, you really enhanced them. He lives and will continue to live in the memory of the ages, and so long as this universe shall endure—this universe which, whether created by chance, or by divine providence, or by whatever cause, he, almost alone of all the Romans, saw with the eye of his mind, comprehended with his intellect, illumined with his eloquence—so long shall it be accompanied throughout the ages by the fame of Cicero. All posterity will admire the speeches that he wrote against you, while your crime against him will call forth their execrations, and the race of man shall sooner pass from the world than the name of Cicero be forgotten."

As a statesman, it must be confessed that Cicero was a failure; but he failed because he was an idealist who attempted to maintain his ideals of orderly constitutional government in the midst of power politics. Unable by temperament to be a leader at such a time, he was compelled to choose between two dictatorships, that of Caesar on the one hand and of Pompey and the senatorial aristocracy on the other. He gave half-hearted support to Pompey because, though incompetent, he seemed to offer the only chance of preserving the old constitution. Too late Cicero learned that both sides were bent on destroying the constitution. His later choice of Octavian over Antony was dictated by the same hope, that Octavian would restore the old order. He lived to see the extinction of all his hopes, and died a failure, but to the last an honest man, true to his ideals.

As an orator, Cicero brought Roman eloquence to its zenith and fixed forever a prose style which is known as Ciceronian. As popularly understood, this style is characterized by the long, rhythmical, periodic sentence, best represented in English by the stylists of the eighteenth century, notably Burke and Gibbon. But Cicero was equally proficient in all styles—the quiet manner of *In Defense of Archias* (p. 142) or the short, crisp sentences of the opening of Catiline I, which ring like blows on an anvil. His breadth of reading in philosophy and history gave his speeches a richness of content which few orators have equaled, and emotion lent the fire which true oratory requires. In reading his speeches, particularly the private orations (e.g. *In Defense of Caelius*, p. 161), one should remember that Cicero was always an advocate, bent on winning his case at all odds; that Roman jurisprudence allowed an advocate much wider liberty of statement than is permissible in British or American courts, and that "scandal was the proper element of Roman oratory." Cicero's speeches are not to be used as historical documents, unless properly corroborated.

His philosophical works we owe to his years of retirement, when, as he said, "If no one will employ us, let us write and read Republics." They make no pretense to originality (Cicero said he provided only the language), but are graceful presentations of current philosophical thought. Their charm of style has preserved them when other more original, and perhaps more worthy, works have perished.

The letters are real letters—not literary epistles like those of Pliny—and were written without thought that they would ever be published. They were collected after Cicero's death by his faithful secretary, Tiro, and are invaluable revelations of the mind of the author and of the political life and intrigues of the time. This is particularly true of those addressed to Atticus, his most intimate friend, to whom he spoke without reserve.

Some useful books about Cicero and his times:
Boissier, Gaston, *Cicero and his Friends*, tr. by A. D. Jones, 1865.
Church, Alfred John, *Roman Life in the Days of Cicero*, 1883.

Haskell, Henry Joseph, *This Was Cicero; Modern Politics in a Roman Toga*, 1942.

Petersson, Torsten, *Cicero: A Biography*, 1920.

Richards, George Chatterton, *Cicero, A Study*, 1935.

Rolfe, John Carew, *Cicero and his Influence*, 1923.

Sihler, Ernest Gottlieb, *Cicero of Arpinum*, 1914.

Beesly, Edward Spencer, *Catiline, Clodius, and Tiberius*, 1878.

HARRY M. HUBBELL

SECOND SPEECH AGAINST VERRES

Cicero was always extremely proud of his record as a defense attorney, but in his three most famous sets of speeches he functioned as a prosecutor, each time attacking a powerful personage whom he abhorred as a dangerous enemy of the Roman republic: Verres, Catiline, Mark Antony. The three groups of speeches mark the beginning, the climax, and the end of his own political career. When he undertook the prosecution of Verres, he was himself only a moderately well-known lawyer, who had served some years before as a quaestor or treasury agent in western Sicily (75 B.C.). Although now a senator, he was not only still young but also the first member of his undistinguished family to sit in the Senate (*homo novus*). He had, however, already seen enough to be sincerely disturbed and shocked by the republic's exploitation of its conquered provinces. He was also well aware of the publicity value of the opportunity offered him, when some Sicilians, who had suffered from Verres' outrageous extortions during his term as governor of their island, requested him to initiate a suit on their behalf for redress.

The case against Verres turned out to be particularly significant, because it advertised the scandals of Roman provincial administration at a time when Rome was facing also a severe internal crisis. Moreover, it concerned Sicily, the oldest of the Roman provinces, whose government up to that time had been regarded as a pattern for provincial administration.

Rome had acquired Sicily after the First Punic War, though it was not until the end of the Second Punic War (202 B.C.) that the island had been definitely organized as a province. As such its inhabitants were under Roman protection, though

13

not Roman citizens, and the administration of the territory was in the hands of the Roman consuls and praetors, who served as chief executive and judicial officials, and Roman quaestors. A large part of Sicily had previously been dominated by Carthage; hence there was little resistance to the Roman occupation, the inhabitants quietly exchanging one overlord for another. The fertile soil of the island made it the chief breadbasket of Rome, until Egypt and other rich Eastern provinces were added to the empire. The urban population of Sicily was, however, predominantly Greek, and looked back to a cultural past far superior to that of either Carthage or Rome. Rome was conscious of this proud Sicilian heritage and early conferred on many of the cities special privileges and a preferred status.

Yet during the second century B.C., as Rome continued to add new subject territories to her dominions, both the Sicilian and all other provincial administrations had become increasingly oppressive and corrupt. The consuls and praetors at Rome had to occupy their attention more and more at home, and were compelled to delegate their authority abroad to subordinates, on whose behavior they kept little check, satisfied if they received what they thought an adequate share of the financial profits of government each year. Sulla, during the period when he was in control of affairs, had tried to improve the situation by putting through a law to the effect that the government of the provinces should be the business of ex-consuls and ex-praetors, at the termination of their services in Rome. Each should then go out to administer in person for a year a province assigned to him by the Senate.

But the change failed to bring relief to the provinces. Too many ex-magistrates now looked on their year of governorship as a chance to pay off old debts and enrich themselves and their followers for the rest of their lives. There was no superior authority to whom they had to give an accounting. The only check on misconduct, the only power to whom provincials might appeal, was the court of trials for extortion at Rome, before which a governor might be called on his return from his province at the end of the year. Such trials had been held at the instance of the suffering provincials with increasing frequency as time went on. The juries in these trials had thus far been composed of senators, of men, that is, who either were themselves ex-magistrates and so had already been provincial governors, or were anticipating appointment to such an office in the future and were therefore likely to be strongly prejudiced in favor of the defendant. But in the year in which Verres faced his trial a change was being advocated, namely, a limitation of the number of senators on these juries to one-third of the panel. By the end of the year the change was actually carried out, hastened, it is said, by the notorious case of Verres.

The year of Verres' trial saw also momentous events in Roman internal politics. Pompey and Crassus were consuls, the one after a victorious campaign in Spain, the other after the successful suppression of a revolt in Italy. Now that these two powerful men held the highest office in the state, they were attempting to remodel the republic to their liking. A principal point in their program was the discrediting and abolition of Sulla's system of senatorial control of government, of which the system of provincial administration had been a part. It seems, therefore, that Cicero's action against the scandalous Verres was in line with the policy then being followed by Pompey, and the preliminaries of this trial probably brought about the first close contact between Cicero and Pompey.

The trial of Verres then was one test case in a complicated struggle of principles, but it was not without its personal significance. Verres belonged to an aristocratic senatorial family;

15

his father was in the Senate and he himself had been a member of that body since 83 B.C., and had served in various administrative positions in the East and in Rome. All the information that we have about his record there and as praetor in Sicily (73–70 B.C.) is derived from Cicero's orations, which surely are not unbiased. But it is certainly true that once Cicero commenced to submit publicly the evidence of his activities in Sicily, Verres preferred to leave Rome forever and retire to Marseilles. He died there in 43 B.C., one of the victims of Antony's proscription, soon after hearing that his adversary, the "new man," Cicero, had met a similar fate.

Yet, up to the actual opening of the trial, in August of 70 B.C., both Verres and his famous lawyer, Hortensius, were confident that Cicero would fail to secure a conviction. They relied primarily on a delaying action, which would have extended the trial into the year 69 B.C., when friends of Verres would have held most of the important positions, including the presidency of the court of extortions. Under ordinary circumstances the lengthy rhetorical harangue, for which Cicero was famous, would have consumed so much time as to favor Verres' plan. But Cicero dispensed with his customary display of sheer oratorial talent, and, after a short introduction, began presenting the hard facts through the testimony of unimpeachable witnesses. This unusual procedure promptly decided the case, but the very speed of the sentence left the victorious prosecutor with a mass of unused data on his hands. We are grateful to him for having published most of this material in the form of speeches, which in fact he never had a chance to deliver. The speech translated here, the second book of the *Second Speech Against Verres*, belongs in this group.

Aside from the accusations against Verres for criminal perversion of justice, abuses in methods of procurement of food supplies for the city of Rome, and support of Crassus in suppressing the revolting slaves in Italy, there is also an entire speech devoted to his activities as an art collector. The account of the art treasures Verres acquired, not only in Sicily but even earlier, in the East, is a valuable record of the survival of ancient Greek art in those regions and a testimony to the lively interest the Roman upper class was then taking in fine antiques. Cicero must have made a special study of the subject to present the case in such great detail. Even more than his broad education and first-hand experience in Sicilian affairs would lead us to expect, he reveals in these orations against Verres an astonishing skill in collecting and organizing pertinent evidence of every sort. Much of it, to be sure, may have come to him second hand, but most of it he seems to have collected himself during his seven-weeks' visit of investigation in Sicily, which he undertook in spite of threats to his personal safety.

SECOND SPEECH

VERRES

Book Two
[In Verrem, II, 2]

I MUST necessarily pass over a great deal, gentlemen of the jury, in order to be able at last to say something on the business entrusted to me. For I have undertaken to plead the cause of the province of Sicily. When I assumed this burden, I saw before me a much larger task; for I was also taking on myself the task of speaking in behalf of the whole senatorial order and of the republic itself. And I thought we should have a proper trial, if both the guilty defendant and an ardent and vigorous plaintiff appeared in court. I must, then, come to the point as soon as possible, and leave out all mention of the defendant's other trespasses and outrages, to save my strength and economize on the time allotted me.

But before describing the misfortunes that have befallen Sicily, I must say a few words about the noble past and the present value of the province. For although you should show some concern for all our allies and provinces, you have a special obligation to Sicily, gentlemen, since Sicily was the first foreign country to ally herself in friendship with the Roman people. She was the first to be called a province, the jewel in the crown of our empire. She was the first to teach our ancestors the glory of ruling over foreign nations. She alone has dis-

18

played such loyalty towards the Roman people that her cities, when once they became our allies, have never afterward revolted, and many of her most famous towns have remained always firm in their allegiance. Our ancestors, accordingly, made this province the stepping-stone for imperial expansion into Africa. The mighty power of Carthage would not have fallen so easily, if Sicily had not been open to us as a granary for our armies and a harbor for our fleets.

For these reasons, after the defeat of Carthage, Scipio [1] filled the cities of Sicily with magnificent statues and monuments, for he thought that those who had the best cause for rejoicing in the Roman victory should receive the most memorials of his triumph. Marcus Marcellus [2] made a name for himself in Sicily by his vigorous measures against the enemy, his mercy to the conquered, and his loyalty to the rest of Sicily. Throughout the war he acted to safeguard our allies, and yet treated the defeated enemy with moderation. By his strategy he succeeded in capturing beautiful Syracuse, a city protected both by her strong fortifications and by her natural defenses against attacks by land and sea. And after his victory, Marcellus not only left Syracuse unharmed but even embellished her, to stand as a monument to his victory, his clemency, and his moderation; that all might see what he had conquered, to whom he had been merciful, and how he had dealt with the city. He respected the position of Sicily so deeply that he did not think it right to destroy even a hostile city in allied territory.

Furthermore, our attitude towards this province has always been to consider the fruits of her toilers not as foreign im-

---

[1] Scipio Africanus, the Elder (237–183 B.C.), won the decisive victory of Zama over Hannibal in 202, that brought the end of the Second Punic War.

[2] Marcus Marcellus was another famous general in the war with Hannibal. He captured Syracuse in 212.

19

ports, but as home produce. And has it ever happened that the grain she was bound to deliver did not arrive on time? Has she ever failed to promise, of her own accord, what she thought we needed? Has she ever refused any demands? With good reason, therefore, did Cato call Sicily the breadbasket of our republic, and the provider of the people of Rome.

We discovered also, during the long and difficult Social War,[3] that Sicily was not only our breadbasket but also our storehouse, left well-filled by our ancestors. With no expense whatever to us, the island supplied us with leather, garments, and grain, and thus clothed, fed, and armed our mighty forces. I wonder if we realize the extent of its contributions.

Many of our citizens, too, build up their fortunes in this loyal and productive province nearby, to which they may easily travel and where they may freely conduct their business. Some of them return here with stocks of profitable merchandise; some stay on there as farmers or cattle raisers, or engage in some other occupation, and decide finally to settle down. It is no small advantage to our republic that so many Roman citizens can find profitable enterprises so near home. And since the tax-paying provinces are like farms for the Roman people, which we value the more the nearer they are to us, the close proximity of this province makes it especially advantageous.

The inhabitants themselves, in their endurance, kindliness, and morality, conform to the old Roman standard rather than to the manners of our day. They are not like other Greeks, indolent and extravagant. On the contrary, they are extremely industrious and thrifty, and used to working hard in public

---

[3] The so-called Social War (90–88 B.C.) was fought by Rome against most of her allies in central and southern Italy. It was caused by her refusal to extend the rights of Roman citizenship to their populations. Rome put down the rebellion but soon afterward admitted all citizens of Italy to citizenship.

as well as in private enterprises. They are so attached to the Romans, too, as to be the one people with whom not even our tax collectors or businessmen are unpopular. They have endured the iniquities of many of our magistrates, and never until now appealed to our justice in order to gain your protection. Yet the misery of one year through which they lived would have crushed them completely, had not Gaius Marcellus fortunately come to their aid, becoming thus the second member of his family to save the fortunes of Sicily.[4] Later they suffered the boundless tyranny of Mark Antony,[5] for they had inherited from their ancestors the conviction that Rome's services to them had been so great that even our outrages must be patiently borne.

Never until now have the communities of Sicily entered a formal complaint against anyone. They would have endured even Verres, if he had confined his crimes to any of the normal and customary misdemeanors. But they could not put up with extravagance, cruelty, avarice, and insolence all at once. This one man's brutality and cupidity were depriving them all of the advantages and privileges bestowed on them by the Senate and the Roman people. They have therefore declared that you must prosecute and punish this criminal; or else, if you judge them unworthy of help, they will abandon their cities and their homes, since already they have been driven from their fields by Verres' iniquitous treatment.

Deputations from them presented this alternative to his successor, Lucius Metellus, and begged him to come to Sicily as soon as possible. In the same despairing spirit, they rehearsed their miseries again and again to their patrons. Impelled by their grievances, they besieged the consuls with demands that sounded like indictments of Verres for his crimes. Their tears

---

4 Marcellus was governor of Sicily in 79 B.C.
5 The father of the famous Mark Antony.

actually succeeded in persuading me to give up my life's work and, much against my reason and desire, become spokesman for their accusations; for they knew my sense of duty and propriety. It looks, however, as if what I had undertaken was a defense rather than an accusation. Finally, the leading men of all the province came forward both officially and in private, and every large and important city of the island sent representatives to protest violently against the injuries done them.

But how have these men fared in Rome? I think now I must speak to you on behalf of these Sicilians more freely than they might wish, because I shall speak for their best interests, rather than to please them. Do you think any provincial criminal was ever so powerfully and zealously protected in his own absence from an investigation? The quaestors of both provinces who had held office while he was praetor were in Sicily with lictors to oppose me. Their successors, very zealous for Verres' interests, since they were being generously supplied from his resources, were no less bitter against me. You see the power of the man—able to enlist four quaestors in one province as fierce defenders and champions of his cause! Even the praetor and his whole army were devoted to him! It was obvious that they did not consider impoverished and persecuted Sicily as their responsibility but rather Verres himself, who had walked off with the booty. They warned the Sicilians not to send any deputations to Rome to testify against Verres. They threatened those that had already gone. They made liberal promises to any who would say a good word for him. They detained by force the star witnesses to his private acts, whom we had subpoenaed.

In spite of all their machinations, only the city of Messina sent an official delegation to speak in his favor. Yet you heard the head of that delegation, the leading citizen of Messina, Caius Heius, say under oath that Verres had built one of his large transport boats at Messina at the city's expense. The same man, while praising Verres, testified that his own house had been plundered, and various sacred objects, including the statues of his ancestral gods, taken away. A fine recommendation, when a delegation at one and the same time praises a man and requests the return of what he has stolen! Moreover, the reason for Messina's devotion to Verres will be told in its proper place, and you will discover that the cause of this devotion is in itself ground sufficient for Verres' conviction.

But the power of his office, though it had no great influence on whole cities, did move a few individuals. Hence, some insignificant persons from small, poor communities were willing to go to Rome for him, even without authorization. And others who were commissioned to testify against him and provided with official evidence were detained at home by force or threats. I was not disturbed when this happened in a few instances, for the testimony of all the other Sicilian cities, including the greatest, will have the more weight with you. And you will realize that no threat of danger could prevent them from finding out whether or not you would heed the complaints of your oldest and most loyal ally. Some of you may have heard that Verres was given a public eulogy by the Syracusans, but in your first session you learned from the testimony of the Syracusan Heraclius what kind of praise that was. Later on, the whole matter of that city will be clarified. You will then realize that no man was ever so hated by anybody as Verres is and has been hated by the Syracusans.

You may perhaps be imagining that only the native Sicilians are against him, while the Roman citizens doing business in Sicily defend him, love him, and work for his interests. Even if that were the case, you should still listen to the complaints of our allies, since this trial for extortion is conducted on their behalf, and based on their legal rights. But you may have observed, in the first session, that many respectable Roman citizens living in Sicily gave important evidence of injuries done to themselves, or inflicted on their acquaintances. I shall tell only what I know personally. Apparently I have endeared myself to the Sicilians by exposing myself to enmity and danger while trying to right their injuries. I am sure that our fellow citizens likewise appreciate my efforts, in the belief that the preservation of their rights, their liberty, and their possessions depends on the conviction of Verres. When you have heard my story of his Sicilian praetorship, you may acquit him, if you find his acts approved by either the Sicilians or the Roman citizens there, by either the farmers and the cattle-raisers or the merchants. You may acquit him if he did not maltreat and plunder all these groups; if, finally, he ever showed any pity to anyone.

As soon as Verres had been allotted Sicily as his province, he began immediately, while still in Rome, to scheme and consult with his friends how he might make the most possible money out of the province in one year. Although not inexperienced in provincial government, he was not willing to learn only through practice but wanted to come thoroughly prepared to loot Sicily. A strange omen for that province was reported in rumor and gossip—men jestingly prophesying from his name how Verres [6] would act on his arrival there. When one recalled his negligence and dishonesty as a quaestor, and remembered his plundering of towns and temples as an ambassador, and saw in the Forum his acts of piracy as a praetor, who could doubt what would be the outcome of the fourth act in his wicked career?

You should realize that he informed himself at Rome not only about what he was going to steal but from whom. Here

[6] Cicero implies that the name *Verres* was derived from the verb *verrere*, to sweep.

is a piece of clear evidence that will enable you easily to form some judgment of his methods. The very day he reached Sicily he at once sent a letter from Messina to Halesa,[7] which I suppose he had written while still in Italy. You see he came, true to his name, prepared to carry off everything. As soon as he disembarked he instantly sent a summons to Dio of Halesa on the ground that he wished to inquire about a legacy that had come to Dio's son from a relative, Apollodorus Laphiro. It was a very large sum of money. This Dio, with the help of Quintus Metellus, has now become a Roman citizen.

At our first session it was proved to your satisfaction, by trustworthy witnesses and records now available, that, although the will was quite legal, a clear million sesterces [$50,000] were paid out merely to obtain Verres' approval. Dio's thoroughbred mares, too, were driven away, and all the plate and embroidered robes in his house carried off. Thus Quintus Dio lost a million sesterces merely because he had received a legacy, and for no other reason. Who was the praetor when this legacy first came to Dio's son? Gaius Sacerdos, the same man who was in office when bequests were left to Annia, daughter of the senator Publius Annius, and to the senator Marcus Ligus. At that time neither Dio nor Ligus was molested. Who then brought the matter to Verres' attention? Nobody, unless you suppose that informers were waiting for Verres at the straits of Messina.

It was while Verres was still in Rome that he heard that a Sicilian named Dio had come into a large inheritance, and that as the heir he was supposed to erect statues in the forum, or else pay a penalty to the sanctuary of Venus on Mt. Eryx.[8]

---

[7] Halesa was a town on the northern coast of Sicily, not far from Messina. It is now nothing but a ruin.
[8] Eryx was the ancient name of a mountain in northwest Sicily, now known as Monte San Guiliano. A famous temple to Venus stood there.

Although the statues had already been erected in compliance with the will, Verres thought, since the name Venus was mentioned, he could find some pretext for making money out of that. He therefore produced somebody who claimed the whole legacy for the sanctuary of Venus Erycina. The demand was not made, as would have been customary, by the quaestor to whose province Mt. Eryx belongs, but by a straw-man of Verres, a certain Naevius Turpo, who was not only the worst of a gang of informers but had been convicted while Gaius Sacerdos was praetor. But Dio's record was so clear that Verres was unable to find any more honest person to bring the accusation. Verres thereupon freed Dio from the obligation to pay the money to the sanctuary, but condemned him to pay it to himself. He preferred, one might say, to have men do wrong rather than the gods. He would extort the money from Dio rather than let Venus take anything not due to her.

There is no need for me to repeat the evidence given by Sextus Pompeius Chlorus, who pleaded Dio's case and was familiar with the whole business. This honest man remains one of the leading Sicilians, and long ago received Roman citizenship in recognition of his excellent character. Nor shall I repeat the testimony of good Quintus Caecilius Dio himself, or of Lucius Ligus, or of Titus Manlius and Lucius Calenus. By their evidence the problem of Dio's legacy was completely solved. They were supported by Marcus Lucullus, an old friend of Dio, who said he had long known all about his troubles. And how does it happen that Lucullus, who was then in Macedonia, knew more about these matters than you, Hortensius,[9] who were at Rome? Did not Dio come to you for help, and did you not write to Verres complaining of his unjust treatment of Dio? There is nothing here new and sur-

---

[9] Hortensius was the eminent lawyer Verres had engaged for his defense.

prising to you, for you heard about it from Dio, and from your own mother-in-law, the lady Servilia, an old friend of Dio. My witnesses are ignorant of many of the circumstances with which you are familiar. And if I cannot use you as a witness, this is because the law forbids it, not because your client is innocent. Let us hear now the testimony of Marcus Lucullus, of Chlorus, and of Dio.

This libertine, who went to his province from the arms of his mistress Chelidon, seems indeed to have got a tidy sum by invoking the name of Venus. Listen now to another of his brazenly false charges in a case where a smaller sum was involved. The brothers Sosippus and Philocrates were natives of the town of Agyrium; [10] their father died twenty-two years ago. If any provision of his will were not properly carried out, a fine was to be paid to the sanctuary of Venus. Twenty years later, though there had meanwhile been numerous praetors, quaestors, and sycophants in the province, a claim to their inheritance was suddenly entered in the name of Venus. Verres took charge of the case, and through Volcatius collected about 400,000 sesterces [$20,000] from the two brothers. You have already heard the testimony of a number of witnesses. The brothers of Agyrium contested the case, but they left the court destitute.

It is said, however, that Verres never got this money. What does this mean? Is it a part of the formal defense or merely a trial balloon? For it is all strange to me. Verres furnished the sycophants, arranged for the trial, presided over it, and issued the sentence. A large sum of money was paid over. Those who received it won the case; yet you argue in defense that the money was not paid to Verres. Well, I can help you there. My witnesses too say the same thing; they say that they paid it to

---

[10] The ancient Sicilian town now called San Filippo d'Argiro.

27

Volcatius. But how did Volcatius acquire enough power to get 400,000 sesterces from the two men? No one would have given Volcatius a penny if he had stood only on his own authority. Let him appear now; let him try to repeat his extortion; no one will pay the least attention to him.

But I go further. I assert that you, Verres, have illegally possessed yourself of four million sesterces, though I do not say that any of the money was paid to you personally. Since, however, the money was paid as a result of your official acts and decisions, one should ask not into whose hands it was paid, but who was responsible for the extortion. The agents you selected —the prefects, secretaries, attendants, doctors, diviners, and heralds—served merely as your hands. The closer connection between you and any one of them, the more he was understood to be acting as your agent. Your whole retinue, that worked more harm to Sicily than a hundred bands of runaway slaves, unquestionably acted on your orders. We must therefore assume that whatever any one of them received was passed on to you, actually paid into your hand.

If one should accept as excuse the statement that Verres did not himself receive the money, no prosecution for extortion would ever be possible. For no defendant would parade his guilt so openly that the same defense could not be put up for him, especially since any criminal in the future, wicked as he may be, will seem as innocent as Quintus Mucius Scaevola [11] when compared with Verres, who is now making use of this plea. Even in his case, the plea is put up not so much to defend him as to establish a precedent. You must therefore, gentlemen, be very careful, because it is a matter of grave importance to the republic. The reputation of the Senate is involved, as well as the welfare of our allies. For if we wish to

---

[11] This Scaevola was a lawyer, statesman, and provincial governor of high reputation.

be thought above reproach, we must show not only that our own characters are blameless, but also that our colleagues are the same kind of men.

First of all, we must select as our companions men who will enhance our personal reputation, or if our chosen friends turn out to be worthless, we must penalize them by letting them go. We must always be ready to account for our acts. Generosity is admirable, provided it does not damage our reputation. Scipio Africanus, a most generous man, was of this mind. When challenged by an old friend and follower, whom he had refused to take with him to Africa as his prefect, he said: "You need not be surprised at not receiving this appointment as a favor from me. I have long been begging a man who, I understand, thinks well of me, to go as my prefect, and I have not yet succeeded!"

Indeed, if our success and reputation mean anything to us, we must ask men to accept service under us in the provinces, not hand appointments around as favors. But you, Verres, invited your friends to consider your province as a hunting ground, and either joined them in plundering it or let them do it for you, and presented them in public with gold rings. Did it never occur to you that you might have to account not only for your own actions, but also for those of your friends?

The court trials which Verres staged and carried through with his retinue brought him huge sums. Later, he discovered rich sources for further extortion. We all know that the safety of private property depends on those who control the courts and their decisions. We all know that none of us can keep possession of his house, his farm, or his inheritance, if someone else has a claim to them. Now a dishonest praetor, whose actions cannot be challenged, can instruct a corrupt judge to give whatever sentence he bids him. The situation is still worse if the praetor arranges the trial in such a way that even an experienced judge, like Lucius Octavius Balbus, has the decision forced on him; as when, for instance, the writ goes: "Let Lucius Octavius be the judge. If it is proved that the disputed farm at Capena legally belongs to Publius Servilius, that farm must in fact be restored to Quintus Catulus." Is not Lucius Octavius then bound, as judge, to compel Publius to restore the farm to Quintus Catulus, and thus decide in favor of the wrong man? All legal procedure in Sicily was like this for three years, while Verres was praetor. For example: "If a man will not accept what you assert is the amount of your debt to him, indict him; if he sues you, put him in prison." This very thing happened to Caius Fuficius, to Lucius Suettius, and to Lucius Racilius. The composition of the courts was equally illegal. Roman citizens functioned as jury, when, according to the laws, Sicilians ought to have done so; and vice versa.

But in order to appreciate the character of these trials, you must first know the laws of the Sicilians, and, secondly, how Verres handled them. In Sicily the legal procedure is as follows. Disputes between citizens of the same community are decided locally according to local law. In disputes between Sicilians of different communities the Roman praetor selects the jury according to the Rupilian Law, which is based on the findings of ten commissioners. In disputes between entire communities and private individuals, the senate of some other city furnishes the jury, since the magistrates of the cities involved are disqualified. If a Roman citizen sues a Sicilian, a Sicilian judge is appointed; if a Sicilian sues a Roman citizen, a Roman citizen is appointed to judge. In all other cases the jurymen are selected from resident Roman citizens. In lawsuits between farmers and tax-collectors, trials are regulated by the grain law, known as the Hieronic Law. While Verres was praetor, however, all these rules were not merely infringed, but were openly ignored, in cases involving both Sicilians and Roman citizens.

First of all, as regards the local Sicilian laws, in disputes between Sicilians, Verres appointed as judge whomever he pleased, his own herald, soothsayer, or physician. If a local court had already been set up by law, the Sicilian judge was not permitted to decide freely. And listen to this edict of Verres, by which he took over control of all legal procedure: "Any wrong decision will be re-examined by Verres himself, who will then fix the penalty." In this way every judge was made aware that his decision would be reviewed, and that he himself might be penalized. He would therefore court the favor of the one who might presently be judging him.

Jurymen were not taken from Romans resident in Sicily, nor from Roman merchants. They all came from the retinue of Gaius Verres, and were no friends of Quintus Scaevola, who did not use this method! You may imagine the character of the retinue, with Verres at its head! You may also read in the edict: "If the senate makes a wrong decision. . . ." But I shall prove to you that even the few senators who ever served as jurymen were forced to give decisions contrary to their own opinions. The Rupilian Law was never obeyed, unless Verres had no interest at all in the case. The many tribunals provided by the Hieronic Law were all abolished by a single edict. No juries were chosen from Roman residents or businessmen.

You have seen Verres' power; now hear how he used it! Heraclius, son of Hiero, one of the leading citizens of Syracuse, was, before Verres came as praetor, one of the wealthiest men of the city, but is now quite destitute, all through Verres' criminal cupidity. He had inherited from a relative named Heraclius at least three million sesterces [$150,000], and a house full of exquisitely engraved silver plate, embroidered robes, and valuable slaves. Everybody knows Verres' interest in

31

this kind of property. It was common knowledge that a great sum of money had been left to Heraclius, and that he was rich and well supplied with furniture, silver, robes, and slaves.

When Verres heard of this, he first tried a mild kind of ruse, and asked Heraclius to lend him some of his property for inspection, planning, of course, never to return it. But afterwards he got advice from some Syracusans, Cleomenes and Aeschrio, who were practically relatives of his, since he was intimate with their wives. You may deduce their bad influence from the subsequent accusation. These two men, as I say, described Heraclius' property as handsome and well equipped, and Heraclius as an inactive old gentleman who could appeal for help only to his patrons, the Marcellus family. Furthermore, they declared that the will in question required the heir to erect some statues in the gymnasium. They said, "We shall get the officials of the gymnasium to deny that the statues have been erected according to the terms of the will, and they will then claim the whole inheritance for the gymnasium." The idea pleased Verres, since he foresaw that there would surely be something for him in it, if once the legality of the inheritance were questioned in court. In approving the plan, he suggested that the elderly and peaceable Heraclius be attacked as promptly and as violently as possible.

The suit against Heraclius was initiated. At first everyone was amazed at the insolence of the accusation. But after a time, those acquainted with Verres either suspected or knew that he had cast his eyes on the estate. The appointed day arrived on which Verres was to select the jury at Syracuse according to the procedure established by the Rupilian Law. He came all ready to name the jurymen for the trial. At that point, however, Heraclius objected, because the Rupilian Law does not permit the nomination until thirty days after the notice of action has been filed, and the thirty days had not yet elapsed. Heraclius was hoping to postpone the date so that Quintus Arrius, whom Sicily was eagerly expecting, might arrive in time to do the selecting. Verres then postponed the selection, but only until the earliest legitimate date.

When that day came, he announced his intention to start making the nominations. Heraclius, accompanied by his lawyers, demanded that he and the officials of the gymnasium, representing the people of Syracuse, should be treated as equals before the law. His opponents contended that in this case the jury should come from the other cities whose citizens normally served in the Syracusan courts. A jury of Verres' choice was in fact appointed. Heraclius in objecting said that the jury should be appointed according to the Rupilian Law; that they should adhere to the customs of their ancestors, the findings of the senate, and the prerogatives of all Sicilians.

Do you need further evidence of Verres' wicked maladministration of justice? Who of you does not remember his praetorship in Rome, when no one could get any legal action against the wishes of his mistress, Chelidon? His province did not corrupt him, as it has corrupted some men; he was the same man there that he had been in Rome. Heraclius pointed out a fact, already commonly known, namely, that the Rupilian Law covers suits between Sicilians. The law was formulated by the consul, Publius Rupilius, on the basis of the findings of ten commissioners, and every praetor and consul in Sicily until then had always observed it. Verres, on the other hand, refused to appoint the jury according to the Rupilian Law, and chose five men agreeable to him. What can be done with such a man? Is any punishment severe enough for his lawlessness? The rule for appointing juries among Sicilians was laid down for you, Verres, by a law based on the ruling of a commanding general, the authority of ten well-known commissioners, and a decision of the Senate. By this decision,

Publius Rupilius was to use the findings of his commission to set up laws for Sicily. Before you came as praetor, everyone had strictly observed these Rupilian Laws in all cases, especially in the matter of the composition of the courts. How did you dare override this solemn tradition to get booty for yourself? Do the laws not exist for you? Had you no scruples, no care for your reputation, no dread of judgment? Had you no regard for authority? Was there no rule for you to follow?

However, as I was saying, once the five jurymen were illegally appointed according to Verres' caprice, not to give a considered verdict but a foreordained dictum, on that day nothing more was done. The parties were ordered to appear the next day. Meanwhile Heraclius realized that Verres was scheming to get hold of his fortune, and taking the advice of friends and relatives not to show himself in court, he left Syracuse the same night. The next morning Verres got up earlier than ever before and ordered the jury summoned. On learning then that Heraclius had gone, he started to insist that Heraclius should be condemned in absentia. The jury pleaded with him to adhere to his own ruling and not force a verdict before afternoon against an absent defendant in favor of the party present. He made this concession.

In the meantime, both he and his friends and counselors were much disturbed at Heraclius' departure. They thought that a condemnation in absentia, where so much money was involved, would be far more scandalous than if Heraclius had been present at his trial. Moreover, as the jury had not been appointed according to the Rupilian Law, the whole affair would look even more flagrant and shocking. So he then tried to correct that error and made his greed and dishonesty thereby even more obvious. For he dismissed those five jurymen, and ordered both Heraclius and the plaintiffs to be sum-

moned, which, of course, he should have done at the beginning, by the terms of the law.

Verres next declared that he would select the jury by lot,
according to the Rupilian Law, the action which Heraclius had
been unable to obtain from him on the day before, in spite of
his pleas and entreaties. Now, one day later, he suddenly decided that the panel should be chosen legally. He drew three
names out of an urn. He then ordered the jury thus selected
to condemn Heraclius in absentia, and, consequently, they
condemned him. What senseless procedure! Did you believe,
Verres, that you would never have to account for your act?
Did you think the Senate would never hear of this affair? Can
an inheritance be claimed unlawfully, merely to fall into the
hands of the praetor? Is the good name of a city to be stained
and the role of false accuser foisted on an honorable state? Is
a whole trial to be conducted without even the slightest pretext of justice? Immortal gods, what difference does it make
whether a praetor forces one to hand over his property directly, or contrives a court verdict by which the accused loses
his whole fortune?

For indeed, Verres, you cannot deny that you should have
chosen the jury according to the Rupilian Law, especially since
Heraclius demanded it. If you say you had Heraclius' consent
to ignore the law, you will be contradicted by your own defense. For why did Heraclius refuse to appear, if the jury was
chosen as he demanded? And then why did you choose the
new panel by lot, after Heraclius had gone, if the jury you first
selected was acceptable to both parties? Finally, in all other
cases, the jury was publicly selected by the quaestor, Marcus
Postumius; only in this case did you happen to appoint it.

Yet someone will argue that Verres after all bestowed
Heraclius' inheritance on the people of Syracuse as a gift. Even
if I admitted such a defense, still you would have to condemn

him, for we must not lightly give one man something we have taken from another. But you will find out that he made brazen use himself of the inheritance, while the people of Syracuse received as their share no money but only disgrace. The few Syracusans here who say they have come as official witnesses for Verres, did, to be sure, participate in the plunder. They are here now not to defend him so much as to determine the amount of the fine they must pay.

After Heraclius was condemned *in absentia*, the gymnasium, that is, the people of Syracuse, did receive the title not only to the disputed inheritance, worth three million sesterces, but also to all of Heraclius' possessions of similar value. But what kind of government is this? You take away a man's lawful inheritance, willed to him by a relative. If the man who made the will leaving Heraclius the full use and ownership of his property had died before your praetorship, no question about it would ever have arisen.

Be that as it may. Deprive people of their family inheritances and give them to officials of gymnasiums! Plunder other people's property in the name of the state! Violate laws, wills, the wishes of the dead, the rights of the living! Still, did you have to deprive Heraclius even of his inheritence from his father? Yet his whole property was seized as soon as he fled, an act of outrageous brutality, disastrous to Heraclius, profitable to Verres, disgraceful to the Syracusans, and obnoxious to the rest of mankind. First, all Heraclius' engraved silver plate was brought from his house to Verres, and all his Corinthian vessels and carpets. No one doubted, after the plunder of that estate, that the riches of the entire province would inevitably be assembled in the house of Verres. He then took the slaves he wanted, and the rest he gave away. An auction was held in which his invincible troops had places of advantage.

But, best of all, the Syracusans in charge of the collection, or rather the distribution, of Heraclius' property gave an account of their activity in their senate. They testified that many pairs of goblets, many costly silver pitchers, many carpets, and many valuable slaves had been turned over to Verres. They stated too how much money each one had received on Verres' orders. The Syracusan senators groaned, but did nothing. When, however, suddenly the item was read that one man had received 300,000 sesterces [$15,000], a loud exclamation arose from everyone. Not only decent men, who had always opposed illegal seizure of private property in the name of the people, but even the instigators of the crime and the accomplices in the plundering began protesting that a person had a right to his own inheritance. So great an uproar broke out in the senate house that a crowd gathered.

The story spread immediately among the populace, and Verres was informed of it at his house. He was enraged with the men who had read the accounts, and with all who had raised the outcry. He blazed with fury, and went almost out of his mind. You know his boldness, his effrontery; yet at that moment he was seriously perturbed by the clamor of the populace, and by the fact that his trickery had become common knowledge. As soon as he had collected his wits, he called for representatives of the Syracusans. He could not deny that the money had been spent, and he did not look far afield, which would have been difficult, but told them that one of his most intimate friends, a sort of second son, had stolen the money. He declared he would force him to return it. As soon as the young man heard of the accusation, he attempted to save his good name and position by declaring before the senate that he had had nothing to do with the whole matter. Nor did he mince words in speaking of Verres, since everyone knew the facts. So the Syracusans later erected a statue in his honor.

He himself left both Verres and the province as soon as he could.

Yet Verres is always, they say, complaining that he suffers less from his own errors than from the crimes of his associates. Look at the record! You kept the province for three years; your prospective son-in-law, who is a fine young man, stayed with you but one year. Your staff, a group of efficient men, left you after the first year. Publius Tadius, the only one who remained, saw little of you. If he had been constantly in your company, he might, by dint of great effort, have saved your reputation, and, even more, his own. But what evidence have you to warrant your laying the blame on others? If you cannot put the entire blame on them, what makes you think you can compel them to share in your responsibility? The three million sesterces were awarded to the Syracusans, but I shall produce documents and witnesses to show how this same money returned to Verres by the back door.

Many a Syracusan grew rich on his dishonesty, against the will of the people and of the Syracusan senate. Other crimes were committed by Theomnastus, Aeschrio, Dionysodorus, and Cleomenes, much against the city's will. To begin with, the whole city was plundered, but of this I shall have to speak further at another time. With the connivance of the above-mentioned men, Verres removed from the sacred temples all the statues, all the ivories, all the paintings, and even all the cult-figures he pleased. In the senate house at Syracuse, known as the Bouleuterion, which to the citizens is a symbolic building, there stands a bronze statue of Marcus Marcellus, who, instead of destroying the building, as by the rules of war he might have done, preserved and restored it to the city. Gilded statues of Verres and his son were erected there to bring bitterness and sorrow to the Syracusan senate as long as the memory of him should last.

Then, supported by these same men, who shared crimes and wives with him, he ordered the festival of Marcellus at Syracuse to be abolished, a heavy blow to the citizenry, who celebrated that day in remembrance of the recent good services of Gaius Marcellus, and in commemoration of the earlier benefactions of the whole Marcellus family. Even Mithridates,[12] when he conquered the whole of the province of Asia, did not abolish the festival celebrated there in memory of Mucius Scaevola. Mithridates was a ferocious and uncivilized enemy, yet he would not insult the sacred memory of a great man. But you forbade the Syracusans to celebrate a single day in honor of the Marcellus family, who made possible for them the enjoyment of all their other festivals.

Instead, you granted them another holiday to be celebrated in honor of Verres, and you supplied them with means for celebrating that day with sacrifices and banquets for many years to come. Yet, in spite of this incredible arrogance, it may be best to pass over certain of these details, lest we overstress the point, and appear to be motivated solely by indignation. Time and strength would fail me were I to enlarge on the preposterous act, requiring a people who were utterly ruined by him to celebrate a festival day in his honor! A wonderful holiday indeed! Everywhere you went you forced people to remember the day of your coming. Actually, you never visited a house, a city, or even a shrine without leaving it ruined and plundered. Let this festival, then, be appropriately called the Verric, not, however, in honor of your name, but as a memento of your rapacious character!

You see, gentlemen, how easily injustice and the habit of

---

12 Mithridates (c. 132–63 B.C.), king of Pontus in Asia Minor, was one of the most formidable enemies ever encountered by the expanding Roman state. He conquered the Roman provinces in Asia, and fomented a Greek revolt against Roman domination.

doing wrong creep into a man's character, and how difficult it is to check them. Bidis is a small town not far from Syracuse; its outstanding citizen was Epicrates. This man received a legacy of 500,000 sesterces [$25,000] from a female relative, so closely related to him that, according to the laws of Bidis, he would have been her legal heir, even if she had died intestate. But people remembered the case of Heraclius of Syracuse, who lost his whole property, as I have just told you, because he came into an inheritance. Epicrates too, as I have said, came into an inheritance. His enemies therefore conceived the idea that he also might be easily deprived of his property, with the help of the same praetor who had brought about the loss of Heraclius' possessions.

They plotted secretly and through his agents informed Verres. A case was made up in such a way that the officials of the gymnasium at Bidis claimed Epicrates' legacy, just as it had happened to Heraclius in Syracuse. No praetor ever showed so much interest in sports! Our ardent champion of the gymnasium was well greased when he left the court. As soon as he understood the situation, he ordered 80,000 sesterces [$4,000] given to one of his friends. But the scheme could not be kept entirely secret. Epicrates was informed by a man concerned in the plot. At first he was inclined to ignore the report, for there was no lawful basis whatever for the claim. Afterwards, when he recalled the fate of Heraclius and the greed of Verres, he thought it best to leave Sicily secretly. He did so and went to Reggio.

When his departure was known, the men who had paid out the 80,000 sesterces became anxious, supposing that nothing could be done while Epicrates was away. For Heraclius had been present when the first jury was appointed for his case, while Epicrates had departed before the suit was filed, even before there was any mention of legal action. The men then went to see Epicrates in Reggio, and told him what he already knew, that they had paid out 80,000 sesterces. They begged him to reimburse them, taking any security he wanted, and promised that none of them would make any further move against him over his inheritance. Epicrates reproached the men at length and sent them away. On their return from Reggio to Syracuse, they complained openly, as was only natural, that they had paid out 80,000 sesterces for nothing. The affair became the topic of everyone's conversation.

Verres then repeated his old Syracusan trick. He declared that he wanted to investigate this payment that had been made. He summoned many people for questioning. Those questioned admitted that they had given the money to Volcatius, without adding that they had done so at Verres' own order. Volcatius was summoned and ordered to return the money. He had nothing to lose and calmly returned the money in the presence of many onlookers, and the citizens of Bidis who had paid it to him carried it away.

Someone now will ask: "What fault then do you find with Verres? He did not steal the money himself, nor permit anyone else to steal it." Listen, and soon you will understand how this money, which left Verres' house by the front door, returned by the back. I ask you what should he, as praetor, have done, when he learned officially that one of his associates had taken a bribe to influence a legal decision, especially when, as in this case, the praetor's own reputation and standing as a citizen were endangered by the bribery committed by these men of Bidis? Should he not have punished both the man who accepted the money and those who gave it? You, Verres, have punished jurymen for wrong decisions, even though they often went wrong out of mere ignorance. You should never have left these men unpunished, who used bribery to

41

influence your official decisions. And Volcatius, a Roman knight, remained with you after his shameless behavior!

What is worse ignominy for a nobleman, or even for a humble freeman, than to be compelled publicly to return stolen money? If Volcatius had had the decency of a Roman knight, or even of a free citizen, he could not have looked you in the face after all that. He would have been your enemy, unless indeed he acted in collusion with you, and served your purposes rather than his own. But he did remain your friend, as long as he was with you in the province, and he is now still your friend, when all the rest have deserted you. You know this, and we too can surmise it.

The fact, however, that Verres himself was implicated in the crime was not his only reason for leniency toward Volcatius and the men of Bidis. The best proof of his guilt was his attitude towards these citizens of Bidis, with whom he should have been indignant because of their attempt at bribery, and because legally they had no right to attack Epicrates, even if he had been there. Yet Verres conferred on these men not only the legacy which had come to Epicrates, but all his other private possessions, just as he had done in the case of Heraclius of Syracuse. This case, however, was even more flagrant than the other, because no formal action had even been brought against Epicrates. Verres showed thereby that he would, contrary to all precedent, accept suits against persons in their absence.

That is what he did when the men of Bidis appeared and claimed Epicrates' legacy. The lawyers of Epicrates demanded that the case be tried according to local law, or by the terms of the Rupilian Law. The accusing party did not dare put their opposition into words and no compromise was proposed. They, however, charged that Epicrates had fled for the purpose of cheating them, and so demanded permission to take over his property. But Epicrates owed not a penny to anyone, and his friends said that if anyone presented a claim, they would stand trial for him, and would obey any court injunctions on his behalf.

When interest in the case had slackened, the accusers began, on Verres' advice, to hint that Epicrates had tampered with the public records, which, of course, was never the truth. Yet the charge was brought into court. Epicrates' friends protested that no legal action affecting his reputation should be taken in his absence, and at the same time demanded that the whole case be referred to a local court. Verres, however, took advantage of the fact that here was a point on which the friends of Epicrates could not appear on his behalf, and insisted that this point be taken up first. It then transpired that Verres had not only taken the money which he had supposedly returned, but had later taken much more, and the friends of Epicrates ceased to argue. Verres accordingly ordered the men of Bidis to seize all Epicrates' property, and keep it for themselves. In addition to the legacy of 500,000 sesterces [$25,000], there was his own private fortune of 1,500,000 sesterces [$75,000]. Now I ask you, was the affair planned this way from the beginning or did it accidentally end up this way? The sum involved was no trifle, nor is it likely that Verres exerted himself so hard for nothing.

There is little more to hear about those unfortunate Sicilians. Both Heraclius of Syracuse and Epicrates of Bidis, after losing all their property, came to Rome. They lived here for nearly two years in mourning and misery. When Lucius Metellus received Sicily as his province, they both went back with him as welcome companions. As soon as Metellus reached Syracuse, he at once rescinded the verdicts against both Epicrates and Heraclius. But all their property had disappeared, except what could not be moved.

43

At the outset Metellus acted admirably, declaring void as many of Verres' criminal acts as he could. Although his attempts to restore Heraclius' property were unsuccessful, all the Syracusan senators whom Heraclius denounced were sent to prison, and there were many of them. Epicrates' estate was returned to him at once. Similar unjust sentences in Lilybaeum,[13] Agrigentum, and Palermo were rescinded. Nor did Metellus pay any attention to the census taken while Verres was praetor. He declared that he would farm out the taxes in kind according to the Hieronic Law, which Verres had violated.

But in all these acts Metellus seemed to be simply undoing the harm Verres had done, rather than following an independent policy of his own. And as soon as I arrived in Sicily, his behavior changed. Two days earlier, one Letilius, a man of much literary cultivation, had come to act as his secretary. Letilius had brought Metellus many letters, one of which, from Rome, altered his whole attitude. Suddenly he began to approve of everything Verres had done, and spoke of him as an intimate friend. Everyone was amazed that this thought had not occurred to Metellus until after he had done so much to undo what Verres had done. Some thought that Verres had sent Letilius in order to remind Metellus of their relationship. From that time on the cities were called upon for testimony favorable to Verres. Witnesses of a different sort were not only threatened but even held back by force. After my arrival, I tried to put some check on these activities of Metellus and to carry on the fight for the Sicilians even without assistance from him. But if I had not been aided by the law and the let-

---

[13] The modern port of Marsala stands on the site of the ancient Lilybaeum. Agrigentum was one of the largest and richest cities on the southern Sicilian coast. Ruins of its beautiful temples, four hundred years old in Cicero's time, are still to be seen there.

ters of Glabrio, I should not have been able to bring so many witnesses to this stand.

But, as I said at the beginning, you must hear the story of your unfortunate allies. Heraclius, of whom I have spoken, and Epicrates came a long distance with their friends to meet me. When I reached Syracuse, they thanked me with tears, and said they were anxious to go back with me to Rome. Since I still had several other towns to visit, I arranged with them to meet me on a certain day at Messina. But on my arrival there I was informed by messenger that they were being detained by the praetor, Metellus. I subpoenaed them and asked Metellus for their release, but though they were most eager to come to report the injuries they had suffered, they have not yet appeared. Their rights as allies do not empower them to complain of personal mistreatment.

You have already heard the testimony of this noble young man, Heraclius of Centuripa. He was blackmailed for 600,000 sesterces [$30,000]. Verres succeeded in extorting 400,000 [$20,000] from him in penalties and bail. When a local court decided in favor of Heraclius and released him from bail, Verres declared the verdict void. He deprived Heraclius too of his seat in the senate and forbade him to appear in public. He announced finally that any injury done to Heraclius would not be a cause for prosecution, that any claim against him would be decided by a judge of Verres' own choice, and that Heraclius himself would not be permitted to take action. Yet Verres' influence in the province was so small that no one molested Heraclius, even when the praetor himself permitted or rather encouraged it; nor were any claims entered against him, although Verres had officially opened the door to false accusations. Heraclius, however, was in bad standing as long as Verres remained in the province. Once the courts had been intimidated in this unprecedented way, all suits in Sicily were

patently decided according to Verres' whims. And he intended not only to strip Heraclius of his possessions, in which
he succeeded, but also to bring everyone's property under his
sole control, through pretenses at judicial procedure; that was
to be his real booty.

I will not rehearse each separate case of criminal court action, but select the most glaring instances of dishonest procedure. There was Sopater of Halicyae, a rich and honest man
and one of the leading citizens of his community. His enemies
had accused him on a capital charge before the praetor Gaius
Sacerdos, but he easily got his acquittal. When Gaius Verres
succeeded Sacerdos, the same enemies filed the same charge
with him. It seemed a trifling matter to Sopater, who relied
on his own innocence, and also thought that Verres would
never dare overrule Sacerdos' decision. The defendant was
summoned and the case heard at Syracuse. The charges made
by the plaintiffs had been previously disproved by the defense, and rejected by the court. Sopater was defended by a
Roman knight, Quintus Minucius, whom you all know as an
upright and thoroughly honest man. Sopater had no reason
to fear or even to doubt the outcome of the case.

Meantime however, Timarchides went to Sopater and
warned him not to put too much confidence in Sacerdos' decision and the righteousness of his cause. (Timarchides, a
former slave of Verres, was, as you learned from many witnesses at the first trial, his agent and manager in all affairs of
this kind.) He told Sopater that his enemies were thinking
of bribing the praetor, but, he said, Verres would prefer to
acquit Sopater, especially as he did not want to be forced to
overrule a decision of his predecessor. Sopater was completely
surprised and greatly distressed by this information, and unable to reply immediately to Timarchides. He said, however,
that although he was in great financial difficulties, he would

think it over. When he reported the incident to his friends, they advised him to buy an acquittal. He accordingly went to Timarchides, explained his difficulties, cut the man down to 80,000 sesterces [$4,000], and paid that amount in cash.

When the case was tried, the counsel for Sopater had no fear or even any anxiety. No crime had been committed; the matter had been decided before; Verres had been bribed. Could anyone doubt how it would turn out? But the trial was not completed on the first day, and the court was adjourned. Timarchides went again to Sopater to say that the plaintiffs had offered the praetor much more than Sopater had given, and that if he were wise he would know what to do. Although Sopater was only a defendant and a Sicilian, that is, legally at a disadvantage, he still could no longer endure listening to Timarchides. "Do what you please," he said; "I will pay no more." His friends and legal advisers supported him in this decision, especially since Verres, in spite of his personal behavior, still had on the bench with him several honest Syracusans, who had served under Sacerdos when Sopater had been acquitted. Sopater's advisers, therefore, thought it absolutely impossible for the same men who had formerly acquitted Sopater, to condemn him now on the same charge, supported by the same witnesses. Relying on these facts, they faced the trial. The defendants appeared, and the same judges as before took their seats. Sopater's hope lay in their integrity and honesty, since, as I have already said, they had once before cleared him of the same accusation.

But now you shall see Verres' dishonesty and insolence, which were here revealed with no pretense at dissimulation. He ordered one of the judges, the Roman knight, Marcus Petilius, to go and preside over a private case. Petilius, however, refused to go and leave behind on the bench with Verres certain friends whom he desired to take with him. Verres generously offered to release anyone who wanted to join Petilius. Since none of the other judges wanted to stay, they all departed with Petilius, saying that they had to appear on behalf of one party or the other in Petilius' case. And so Verres and his clique were left alone. Minucius, who was defending Sopater, thought that since Verres had dismissed the whole bench, he would not proceed with the trial of Sopater's case that day; but suddenly he was ordered to state the defense. He asked, "Where are the judges?"

Verres answered, "Here, if you think me competent to judge a mere Greek-Sicilian."

"You are competent," he said, "but I should like the presence of those other men who were acquainted with the case."

Verres replied, "State your defense, for they cannot be here."

At this, Quintus Minucius made a move to go and said, "I quite forgot; Petilius asked me too to join him in trying his case." Verres then lost his temper, insulted Minucius, and even threatened him for exposing him to suspicion.

Minucius did business in Syracuse, and was conscious of his social and legal position, and aware that he would better not earn a fee by means that would jeopardize his own freedom. Considering, therefore, all the circumstances involved, he refused to act as defense attorney now that the panel of judges had been dismissed, and left the courtroom, accompanied by all the other friends and supporters of Sopater, except the native Sicilians.

In spite of his incredible arrogance, Verres was thoroughly alarmed and bewildered when he found himself thus suddenly left alone. He realized that an adjournment then would result in Sopater's acquittal, once the absent judges had returned. But if on his own authority as praetor, he condemned this innocent man, and overruled the decision of Gaius Sacerdos, while depriving the accused of all legal aid, he thought that popular indignation would run too high. He was, therefore, quite upset, both mentally and physically, and everyone present could plainly see the fear and greed contending in his soul. A great crowd had gathered and was silently wondering how his avarice would vent itself. His attendant Timarchides kept whispering constantly into his ear.

At last he said to Sopater, "Come, state your case." Sopater implored him, by all that was sacred, to hear his case with a full panel of judges. But Verres abruptly ordered the witnesses to testify. When one or two of them had spoken briefly, without being questioned, the herald announced that the case was closed. Verres was afraid that Petilius might finish or adjourn his case, and return to the court with the other judges. He then got up hurriedly and declared Sopater condemned, on the verdict of a secretary, a physician, and a soothsayer, in spite of the fact that his case had not been properly tried, and that he had been acquitted by Gaius Sacerdos.

Verres should be kept in this city! He should be spared and preserved to go on functioning as a judge, and deciding questions of war or peace in the Senate, free from all personal prejudices as he is—although his possible activities in the Senate would matter little to us and to the people of Rome. For how much weight would his words carry there? When would he have either the courage or the power to express his views? A man accustomed to so much luxury and indolence would not even take the trouble to come to the Senate, except in February. Still, let him come; let him harangue for war against Crete, for granting independence to Byzantium, for giving Ptolemy the title of king! In short, let him say anything that Hortensius puts into his mouth! Such questions do not immediately affect our lives or endanger our personal possessions.

But there is a really serious possibility to be feared by every good citizen. If Verres should miraculously escape justice now, he would, by necessity, become one of those judges who decide the fate of Roman citizens; he would be a lieutenant of the man who wants to control our courts. The people of Rome reject this possibility; they will not sanction it. However, if you like his kind of company and want to make so splendid an addition to the Senate, the people do not mind your having him as a fellow senator, or even as a judge in your own cases. But those who do not belong to that august body, who by the Cornelian Law can challenge only three of their judges, prefer not to have this arch-criminal as their judge.

Actually, if it is a wicked thing (and it seems to me one of the wickedest) for a judge to accept a bribe and thus betray the trust placed in him, it is still more wicked and dishonorable of him to condemn a man from whom he has accepted a bribe. A praetor who does this is not even observing the honor common among thieves. It is a sin to take money from a defendant, worse yet to take it from a plaintiff, but still worse to take it from both parties. You, Verres, put your good name up for sale in Sicily, and sold it to the highest bidders. The thing may have been done before, I admit. But when you had already sold your decision to one party, and afterwards sold it to his opponent for a still higher price, did you not cheat both? Did you not after that decide as you pleased, without ever returning the loser's money to him? Do not mention the cases of Bulbus and Staienus!

Has anyone seen or heard of a creature so corrupt as this man who took a bribe from the defendant and afterwards decided in favor of the plaintiff? He dismissed from the bench the honest judges, acquainted with the case, and acting alone

condemned a man already acquitted, a man from whom he
had accepted money, which, of course, he never returned.
Shall we have this man as one of our judges? Shall his name
again be listed in the senatorial panel to preside over our
capital cases? Shall the court files be entrusted to him? If so,
they will be written not only in ink, but at times in blood.
Does he deny having committed any of these crimes? One
thing he must deny; that he took bribes; and naturally he
would deny that. But the Roman knight, Quintus Minucius,
who defended Sopater through the whole affair, declared
under oath that money was paid to him, and Timarchides admitted that the plaintiff had paid even more. All the Sicilians
confirm this statement; the citizens of Halicyae certainly will
agree, and also the young son of Sopater, who has been most
cruelly deprived of his poor innocent father and of his paternal
inheritance.

But even if I were unable to prove the bribery, could you,
Verres, deny that you got rid of the other judges who had
served with Gaius Sacerdos and were sitting on the bench
with you, and that you then pronounced sentence in a case
that had been already decided? Gaius Sacerdos and a full panel
of judges had acquitted Sopater after a thorough investigation
of the case. Did you not condemn him without any such
legal prerequisites? Now that you have confessed to committing these acts, which were witnessed by the whole province,
since they took place in the forum at Syracuse, deny, if you
like, that you took the money. Some people who saw what
you did openly, will be wondering what you did in secret, and
they will be inclined to believe my witnesses rather than those
who defend you.

I have said already that I will not recount all his acts of
this kind. I will, however, mention the more conspicuous of
his misdemeanors. Let me tell you about one notorious crime

of his, which includes elements of all his vices. Listen closely, and you will find that it sprang from avarice, grew by lust, and reached its climax in cruelty. Sthenius from Thermae,[14] here present, was formerly much admired for his honorable and noble character. He now is known everywhere for the injuries he has suffered at the hands of Verres. The latter has often enjoyed the hospitality of Sthenius in Thermae, and has practically lived there; yet he has taken out of Sthenius' house everything which could possibly delight the mind or the eye.

Now Sthenius had been from youth an ardent collector of Delian and Corinthian bronze furniture, of paintings, and of fine wrought silver, as much as a man from Thermae could afford. He had made this collection while in Asia Minor as a young man, not so much to please his own taste as that of some Roman visitors whom he counted among his friends. But Verres got hold of these treasures, by begging, demanding, or simply taking them, and Sthenius bore his loss as best he could. He was obviously annoyed to have his beautifully furnished house thus plundered. Still he told his indignation to no one, since he thought the abuses of a praetor must be suffered in silence, and those of a guest with calmness. Meanwhile Verres, with his well-known covetousness, set his heart on some exceedingly beautiful, ancient statues that stood in the public square of Thermae, and asked Sthenius to help him get them. This request Sthenius refused, and declared it out of the question to remove these ancient statues, memorials of Publius Scipio Africanus, so long as the city of Thermae, or for that matter the Roman Empire, stood firm.

At this point I think you should recall the just and noble character of Publius Scipio Africanus. Himera,[15] one of the most beautiful cities of Sicily, had been captured by the

---

[14] A north Sicilian town, now called Termini.
[15] A Greek town on the north coast of Sicily.

Carthaginians. Scipio considered it Rome's duty to see that, once the war was over,[16] our allies should, through our victory, recover what had once been their possessions. He took care, therefore, after Carthage was defeated, that all Sicilians should get back, as far as possible, whatever they had lost. Himera itself had been destroyed, but its surviving citizens had settled within their own territory at Thermae, not far from their former home. They now thought their former wealth and reputation would revive, if their old monuments were brought to their new city.

There were many bronze statues; among them a beautiful statue of Himera, personified as a woman, after whom the city and the river were called. There was also a statue of the poet Stesichorus,[17] showing him as an old man, stooped, with a book in his hand, a remarkable piece of sculpture. Stesichorus, incidentally, had been a citizen of Himera, and his fame was and is spread over all Greece. These were the statues which Verres yearned to possess. I almost forgot to add a statue of a goat, a masterpiece, even in the judgment of an amateur like myself. Scipio had not disposed of these statues needlessly, so that a sharp man like Verres might appropriate them, but had returned them to the people of Thermae. Scipio himself had gardens and villas where he might have placed them. But if he had taken them to his own home, they would not have been his for long, but would in time have been the property of his heirs. In their present position they will, I think, always be known as Scipio's statues.

When Verres made his demand and the matter was being discussed in the Senate, Sthenius voiced his violent opposition, and, being one of the ablest orators among the Sicilians, he spoke at great length. He said it would be more honorable to

---

[16] The reference is to the Second Punic War.

[17] Stesichorus (c.630–550 B.C.) was a renowned Greek lyric poet.

give up Thermae itself than to permit the removal from their city of the ancient monuments that had been returned to them from the enemy through Scipio's generosity and were thus visible symbols of their friendship with the Roman people. All were deeply moved, and ready to choose death rather than disgrace. So Verres found in Thermae almost the only city in the world where none of his tricks worked; for he failed to get what he wanted by open violence or by stealthy thievery, by official command or by private favor, or even by bribery.

But his other crimes of greed I shall discuss later; I must return to Sthenius. Verres was extremely annoyed at Sthenius, and in his anger repudiated his friendship and left his house —really moved out. Sthenius' furniture he had already taken. Sthenius' bitterest enemies immediately invited Verres to stay with them, that they might incite him further against Sthenius by telling damaging lies. These men were Agathinus, a nobleman, and Dorotheus, who had married Agathinus' daughter, Callidama. Verres had heard of Callidama, and chose to stay with Dorotheus. One night was enough to become so intimate that, one might say, they shared everything. Verres treated Agathinus, too, like one of his relatives. He even seemed to lose his fancy for the statue of Himera, so charmed was he by his beautiful hostess.

He now urged these two men to get Sthenius into trouble by inventing some accusation against him. They protested they had no evidence. He assured them that he would accept any fictitious accusation they might devise against him. Agathinus and Dorotheus thereupon accused Sthenius of having tampered with the public records. Since the charge was brought by his fellow citizens, Sthenius demanded that the case be tried by the local law. Any case of the kind came under the local law, for the Senate and people of Rome had restored to the citizens of Thermae not only their city and lands, but also their laws, because they had always remained faithful and loyal. And Publius Rupilius, we know, had later granted the Sicilians the right of settling their mutual difficulties by their own laws, basing his grant on the Senate's resolution on the report of the ten commissioners. Finally, Verres himself had confirmed the grant by an edict of his own.

Verres—now all justice, without one thought of personal gain!—said he would look into the case himself, and told Sthenius to appear in the morning ready to state his defense. It was not difficult to see what the scoundrel had in mind. He made no bones about it, nor could the woman hold her tongue. It was understood that he would condemn Sthenius, without admitting pleas or witnesses, and then would scourge the good old gentleman who had been his host. But the scheme became known, and on the advice of his friends Sthenius fled from Thermae to Rome, preferring to face the winter storms at sea rather than the ill wind then blowing over Sicily.

Verres, however, was on time in the morning, and ordered Sthenius to be summoned. When he found that Sthenius did not appear, he was furiously angry. He sent bailiffs to Sthenius' house, and dispatched mounted police in every direction to his farms and country villas. He waited at the court for information, and did not leave there till late at night. The next morning, he came down again early, summoned Agathinus, and asked him in Sthenius' absence to state his charge about the public documents. There was no one to oppose Agathinus and he spoke before a judge hostile to the defendant, but still he could not prove his point. He accordingly confined himself to a statement that Sthenius had tampered with public documents when Sacerdos was praetor. As soon as he had finished, Verres announced: "It is proved that Sthenius has tampered

55

with the public documents." And the servant of Venus added this unprecedented judgment: "For this crime, 500,000 sesterces [$25,000] shall be taken from the property of Sthenius and given to the sanctuary of Venus Erycina." He took steps at once to put the whole property of Sthenius on sale and would have sold it, had there been any delay in the payment of the 500,000 sesterces.

Even after that payment, he was not satisfied with the one illegal prosecution. He proclaimed publicly, as praetor: "If anyone wishes to bring a capital charge against Sthenius in his absence, I am ready to receive the indictment." At the same time, he urged Agathinus, his new relative and host, to take up the case and file an accusation. But Agathinus declined to do this and loudly protested, in front of everyone, that he was not Sthenius' enemy to the extent of accusing him of capital crimes. But at this point a man named Pacilius, a poor worthless creature, showed up and said that, if it was permitted to make an accusation *in absentia*, he would do so. Verres said it was permitted as a matter of course, and he would accept the accusation. So the accusation was made. Verres immediately issued a summons for Sthenius to appear at Syracuse on December first. Sthenius meanwhile had arrived in Rome after a voyage good for the time of year and had found people more just and humane than the praetor in Sicily, his former guest. When he told his friends what had happened, they recognized it for what it was, a wicked piece of cruelty.

The consuls Gnaeus Lentulus and Lucius Gellius promptly proposed to the Senate to issue an ordinance to the effect that no one in the provinces should be tried *in absentia* on a capital charge. They reported to the Senate in full the case of Sthenius, and the brutal injustice of Verres. Verres' father was present in the Senate, and tearfully begged the senators all to spare his son, but he made little impression. For they were determined to act. The Senate then decreed that since Sthenius had been accused in absentia, no verdict should be pronounced in his absence; and if one had already been pronounced, it should be void. Nothing more could be done that day, as the hour was late, for Verres' father had persuaded several senators to consume time with speeches.

Still later, the elder Verres approached the friends and defenders of Sthenius, begging them not to attack his son and not to be anxious about Sthenius. He assured them that Sthenius would suffer no more harm from his son, and promised to send trustworthy men to Sicily both by the land route and by sea, to ensure Sthenius' safety. There were still thirty days before the first of December, the date on which Verres had ordered Sthenius to appear in Syracuse. His friends were thereby persuaded to hope that the letters and messengers of the father would restrain the son in his mad career. Accordingly the Senate went no further with the case. The messengers with letters from his father reached Verres before the first of December, while the case of Sthenius was still pending. Verres also received many letters from friends and associates on the affair.

But never had Verres stopped to consider duty, his personal safety, or common decency when he saw a chance to gratify his own desires. Again in this instance, he disregarded his father's advice and the good will of his other counselors, for the sake of his private satisfaction. So, on the morning of December first, in accordance with his edict, he ordered Sthenius summoned. Such serious parental advice should have carried weight with any son, even if the father had given it at a friend's request, out of mere good nature, or in his own self-interest. But your father, Verres, had your safety at heart when he sent his trustworthy messengers to you. They reached you

57

in time, while the case was still pending. Could no consideration of your own safety, if not of decency, hold you within the bounds of duty and sanity?

What happened was this. Verres called for the defendant. The defendant did not appear. He then called for the accuser. Observe now, gentlemen of the jury, how Fortune herself turned against the blackguard, and, at the same time, helped Sthenius. When the accuser, Marcus Pacilius, was called, he did not answer, because—for some reason or other—he was not there. So even if Sthenius had been present, and palpably guilty of a crime, still, without an accuser, he could not have been condemned. Certainly, if it were possible to condemn a defendant in the absence of an accuser, it would not have been necessary for me to cross from Vibo to Velia in a small boat, and travel through territory thick with fugitive slaves, brigands, and your hirelings. I hurried for fear you might be acquitted if I did not arrive on the day fixed. It would have been most opportune for you in this trial, if I had not appeared when called upon. Why did you not let Sthenius take advantage of the fact that his accuser did not appear? You finished the case in the same style as you started it. The defendant was accused without being present. He was now condemned without being accused!

Besides the detailed letters sent him by his father, Verres immediately afterwards was informed that Sthenius' case had been brought up in the Senate, and also in the Assembly, where a complaint had been lodged by Marcus Palicanus, a tribune of the people. Verres also heard that I had pleaded for Sthenius before the board of tribunes, since, according to their edict, no one condemned on a capital charge was allowed to remain in Rome. I explained the facts to them as I have now done to you, and showed that the condemnation should not be considered valid. In fact, the tribunes voted unanimously that the edict of banishment from Rome did not apply to Sthenius.

When Verres heard this news, he was, at last, profoundly disturbed. He made changes in the record, and by so doing ruined his own case, for he thereby deprived himself of all means of defense. Otherwise he might have pleaded that a person could be accused in absentia, since there was no law forbidding it in the provinces. Though weak and dishonest, this still would have been some sort of defense. He might even have made the desperate claim that he acted in ignorance, supposing it lawful. Though this would have been a hopeless defense, still it would have been something to say. What he did, however, was to remove the only true statement from the record, and write: "The charge was brought against Sthenius in his presence."

With this, as you will see, he became so involved that he could never disentangle himself. In the first place, he had often declared in Sicily, both officially and in private conversation, that it was lawful to accept a charge against an absent man, and that he himself had done so, as in fact he had. At the first hearing several witnesses testified that Verres had frequently made this statement. These witnesses were Sextus Pompeius Chlorus, of whose integrity I have already spoken, Gnaeus Pompeius Theodorus, a man of high reputation and much respected by our noble Pompey, and Posides Macro of Solus, a gentleman of lofty rank and considerable renown. In the course of this present trial as many witnesses as you like will testify to the same effect, members of our own senatorial order, who have themselves heard him say that, and others who were present at Sthenius' trial. Finally, when the matter was brought up in the Roman Senate, Verres' friends, including his own father, defended him on the ground that his action was legal, that others had previously done the same, and that he had simply followed precedent, while the cities of Sicily in their common petition to the consuls, begged the Senate "for a clear statement that no trial *in absentia* should be permitted."

You have heard the testimony of Gnaeus Lentulus, the brilliant young champion of Sicily. He said that when the Sicilians asked him to speak for them in the Senate, they told him that the direct cause of their petition was the injury done to Sthenius. Under these circumstances, Verres, how could you be so foolish and rash as to tamper with the public record in a case already made quite clear by your own acts?

The way in which you did the trick can be proved by the record, even if we all are silent. Let us, please, have the document to show to the judges. You see that the passage which says that Sthenius was present is written over an erasure. What was written there before? What alleged error was corrected by this erasure? I do not have to prove my point now; I can keep silent. The document before us shows that it has been injured and altered. Do you, Verres, really think you can escape, now that we are after you on such a clear course, guided by your own tracks freshly and deeply printed in the public documents? The man who convicted Sthenius, without trial, of tampering with the public records, can hardly deny that he has committed the identical crime in dealing with that same Sthenius.

Behold another instance of his folly! Trying to free himself, he became all the more entangled! He appointed an attorney for Sthenius, but not a relative or an intimate friend, not even an honest citizen of Thermae, or any other Sicilian of prominence and high standing. The man Verres appointed to act as Sthenius' lawyer was a citizen of Rome. Who could approve of that choice? Sthenius, a leading man in his city, had many friends and relatives, and was influential and popular throughout Sicily. Surely he could have found a Sicilian to serve as his attorney. He himself could not have preferred a Roman citizen. Mention a single case in which a Roman citizen has acted as attorney for an accused Sicilian. Go through the records of all the praetors before you, Verres, and if you find a single example, I will believe every word of your statement.

It might be, however, that Sthenius thought it wise to take his defense attorney from the Roman citizens of his acquaintance. The man he took, whose name is down in the records, was Gaius Claudius, son of Gaius, of the Palatine tribe. I am not interested in the reputation, honesty, or skill of Claudius. It was possible for Sthenius to depart from the usual Sicilian custom and pick a Roman citizen for his attorney. I am not interested in all that. Sthenius might have been guided in his choice not by Claudius' high position, but by his own intimacy with him. Yet it so happens that this very Gaius Claudius was Sthenius' most dangerous opponent at just this time and on this very issue. He had appeared against Sthenius on the charge of tampering with public documents, and had fought him at every step. Shall we believe that it was in Sthenius' interests to have his enemy become his attorney, or that you, Verres, took advantage of this enemy in order to ruin Sthenius?

That no one may doubt the significance of this whole business—though I trust that Verres' malicious intentions have for some time been clear to you all—grant me, please, your attention a little longer. Do you see the dark fellow with curly hair, who is looking at us with what he considers a shrewd expression, taking down notes, and sitting next to Verres and whispering into his ear? That is Gaius Claudius! In Sicily, he functioned as Verres' agent, representative and business manager, a sort of colleague to Timarchides. Now he is second only to Apronius in his intimacy with Verres; indeed he considers himself an equal partner not of Timarchides but of Verres himself.

Doubt then, if you can, that Verres chose Claudius of all people as a spurious defense attorney for Sthenius, knowing that he was Sthenius' enemy and his own friend! Will you hesitate now to punish such incredible audacity, cruelty, and injustice, or to follow the example of the judges who, after Philodamus of Opus had been condemned by Gnaeus Dolabella, reversed the sentence against him? Philodamus, incidentally, was not convicted in absentia, the worst species of injustice, but after his city had appointed him ambassador to Rome. Those other judges acted fairly in a much less grievous case. So do not hesitate in this much more serious trial to follow the precedent which they established.

Tell us, Verres, who was this man you treated with such unparalleled injustice, whom you condemned in his absence for forgery and convicted without a crime, without a witness, and even without a plaintiff? He was a man, by heaven, bound to you not merely by friendship, a highly revered relationship everywhere, but by the even more sacred tie of hospitality. The worst fault of Sthenius, which I regret profoundly to mention, was that he, a modest and upright man, invited you, a lewd scoundrel, to his house. Thus he, unfortunately, added your name to the illustrious list, including Gaius Marius, Gnaeus Pompey, Gaius Marcellus, Lucius Sisenna, your defender, and other gentlemen, whose host he has been and still is. But I shall not lay emphasis on your breach of hospitality and abominable behavior there.

Nor are my observations addressed to persons who know Sthenius, that is, to anyone who has been in Sicily, for no such person can be ignorant of his high reputation both in his own city and all through the island. I am saying these things to enable those unfamiliar with the province to appreciate

Sthenius' character, and to realize how intolerable your treatment of him must seem to everyone, both because of its injustice and because of the eminence of the victim.

Sthenius is a man qualified to attain easily all the positions of honor in his city, and to fill them in the most satisfactory manner. At his own expense he has adorned his small city with numerous public buildings and monuments. His services to the community of Thermae and to all Sicilians is attested by a bronze tablet on the wall of the city hall of Thermae, officially recording his benefactions. At your command this tablet was removed, but I have brought it with me that you all may see the honors paid him by his fellow citizens.

Do you recall that the enemies of Sthenius once accused him to the illustrious Pompey of hostility to the republic because of his close friendship with Gaius Marius, a charge which, even if untrue, would stir up ill-will? But Pompey acquitted him, and made it clear that the evidence presented at the trial was such as to prove that Sthenius deserved being treated as his own friend. All the Sicilians then defended and praised him so warmly that Pompey felt the whole province was grateful for his acquittal, and not Sthenius alone. He is both a staunch supporter of the republic, and very influential with his fellow countrymen. During your praetorship he accomplished singlehanded what no individual Sicilian or even all Sicily could have done. He kept you from removing any statue or jewelry from any religious or secular building in Thermae, though there were many remarkably beautiful things, on all of which you cast your covetous eye.

In your name, Verres, the Sicilians celebrate days of festival and splendid games. To you gilded statues are erected at Rome, presented by the commonwealth of Sicily, as we read in the inscriptions. But what a difference there is between you, patron of Sicily, and this Sicilian whom you have condemned! He is praised by numberless cities of Sicily, who have sent public deputations here to speak in his favor. You, patron of all Sicilians, are praised openly only by the city of the Mamertines, your partners in robbery and crime.[18] And their praise, incidentally, is somewhat peculiar, for their individual deputies denounce you, even while as a deputation they eulogize you. Every other community publicly accuses you, blames you, convicts you by letters, deputations, and evidence. They are convinced that your acquittal would mean their complete ruination.

At the expense of Sthenius and his estate, you, Verres, have actually erected on Mt. Eryx a monument to your crimes and cruelty, inscribed with the name of Sthenius of Thermae. I have seen the silver Cupid with his torch. Why did you decide to spend your plunder from Sthenius on that particular object? Did you intend it as a symbol of your own cupidity, or as a memorial to his friendship and hospitality, or as a token of your love? It is the sort of thing men do who not only take pleasure in acts of wanton lewdness, but enjoy creating a reputation for wickedness, liking to leave behind marks and traces of their evil deeds in many places. He was madly infatuated with his hostess, to possess whom he violated the laws of hospitality, and he wished the fact to be known and recorded forever. It was only right, he thought, to reward the goddess of love out of the proceeds of the case he had won with the help of Agathinus, the woman's father, who acted as accuser. But to be truly grateful to the gods, you should, Verres, have offered this gift to Venus, not out of Sthenius' property, but

---

[18] At the end of the third century B.C., the city of Messina had been seized by a band of mercenary troups from central Italy, who had murdered many of the inhabitants and made themselves masters of the territory. They called themselves Mamertines, or sons of Mars, from Mamers, a dialect form of the name Mars.

out of your own, increased as it has been recently by the legacy from your mistress Chelidon.

On grounds like these I should have undertaken to plead this case, even if every Sicilian throughout the province had not begged this service of me. Even if my love for the republic and my distress at the damaged reputation of the Senate and the courts had not constrained me, I should have gone on with it, even if none of this had happened, and my only reason had been your brutal, wicked, and abominable treatment of my friend and host, Sthenius. For during my quaestorship I learned to love and respect him, and he, for his part, always acted for my best interests as long as I was in the province. I should think I had cause enough to incur the enmity of a scoundrel, if it were to defend the safety and fortunes of my friend.

In the days of our ancestors many a man acted as I have done. Just recently the eminent Gnaeus Domitius prosecuted similarly the ex-consul Marcus Silanus for having wronged his friend Egritomarus of Transalpine Gaul. It seems to me only right to follow their examples of friendship and devotion to duty, and I hope my friends and connections may have reason to expect to live more securely for my protection. But since the case of Sthenius signifies also peril to a whole province, and I am defending with him many other former hosts and friends, both citizens and private individuals, I am not afraid of anyone's imagining I am moved by any motive but that of strictest duty. However, there must be some limit to this accusation, and I will say no more of Verres' activities in the way of judicial investigations, proceedings, and decisions, for his misdeeds along that line are beyond counting. We will go on now to consider a few crimes of another sort.

You have heard Quintus Varius say that his agents paid Verres 130,000 sesterces [$6,500] for a favorable decision. You recall that his evidence was corroborated by the testimony of the illustrious Gaius Sacerdos. You know that Gnaeus Sertius and Marcus Modius, Roman knights, along with six hundred other Roman citizens and many Sicilians, declared that they too had purchased favorable decisions. Why expatiate on this charge, when all the evidence is furnished by first-hand witnesses? Why argue about indisputable facts? Will any man doubt that in Sicily Verres offered judicial decisions for sale, when at Rome he sold an entire edict and all his decrees? Did he not take money from the Sicilians for issuing provisional orders, and actually demand of Marcus Octavius Ligus the sentence he wanted? What method of extortion did he ever neglect or fail to devise, even though everyone else had overlooked it? Was there any position of honor, power, or authority in the Sicilian cities which he did not convert into a source of profit to himself?

At his first trial, evidence of these dealings was given by officials and private citizens. Deputies from Centuripa, Halesa, Catana, Palermo, and many other cities testified, together with many private individuals. Their testimony revealed that for the space of three years the office of senator in every city of Sicily was never filled except at a price. Senators were not elected as their laws prescribed but all were appointed on the oral or written orders of Verres. In the appointment of these senators not only was there no electing but none of the legal regulations for choosing senators was observed. No attention was paid to their incomes, their age, or any other Sicilian requirement. If anyone wished to become a senator, whatever his youth or lack of capacity or membership in a lower class, by bribing Verres sufficiently he could always gain his object and be made a senator. Not only the local Sicilian requirements were disregarded in these matters, but even the laws given them by the Senate and people of Rome. For the laws made by the official in whom the Senate and Roman people have invested supreme command and authority ought to be regarded as laws of the Senate and people of Rome.

The citizens of Halesa were granted independence because of the services rendered by them and their ancestors to our republic. Recently, however, in the consulship of Lucius Licinius and Quintus Mucius, they requested our Senate to legislate for them, since they were in disagreement among themselves over their own senatorial elections. The Senate honored them by voting that the praetor, Gaius Claudius Pulcher, son of Appius, should give them laws to regulate their senatorial elections. Gaius Claudius, with the help of all the Marcellus family then living, laid down the following regulations for the citizens of Halesa: that candidates for their senate should be over thirty years of age, and that no one engaged in trade should be elected. There were other stipulations about income and other matters. Until Verres became praetor, all these rules were enforced by the authority of our magistrates, and with the cordial good will of the men of Halesa. But from Verres even an auctioneer, if he so desired, bought the senatorship for a price, and boys sixteen and seventeen years old purchased the senatorial title. Verres made it easy for unqualified persons to obtain the office by bribery, although the citizens of Halesa, our ancient and faithful allies and friends, had been granted their petition at Rome, that men of that type should be debarred even from election by vote.

The people of Agrigentum have laws anciently given them by Scipio, governing elections to their senate. These contain the same regulations as those just mentioned, with an additional one, for here there are two classes of citizens, the old inhabitants and the newer settlers, whom the praetor, Titus Manlius, brought from other Sicilian towns to Agrigentum in accordance with a resolution of the senate. Accordingly the laws of Scipio prescribe that the senate of Agrigentum should comprise more of the original inhabitants than of the later colonists. But as Verres was the kind of man who annulled all laws for a bribe and leveled all types of distinction for a price, he not only violated all the regulations respecting age, rank, and occupation, but even confused the two classes of old and new inhabitants. For when at the death of a senator who was a descendant of the original inhabitants, the remaining number in each class was left equal, the law required that another of the old inhabitants should be elected in order to keep their group in the majority. But in spite of the law, some of the original inhabitants and some of the new settlers approached Verres for the purpose of buying the position of senator, and, as a result, an upstart won out by his bribes, and brought a letter of appointment from the praetor to Agrigentum. The citizens thereupon sent deputies to inform Verres of their law and point out their venerable tradition, that he might realize he had sold the senatorship to a man with whom he should have had nothing to do. He was not the least influenced by their pleas; he had already pocketed the money.

He did the same thing at Heraclea. For here too colonists had been brought in by Publius Rupilius, who had established similar rules about appointments to their senate and the relative numbers of original and later settlers. There Verres not only took money, as he did in other cities, but confused the classes and ignored the rule for relative numbers of original inhabitants and new settlers.

Do not think I intend to mention every city of Sicily in this speech! The following statement applies to the whole situation. As long as Verres was praetor no one could become a senator except by bribing him. I repeat the same charge with regard to all civil offices, administrative positions, and priesthoods. By his conduct Verres defied both the laws of men and those of the gods. At Syracuse the law for religious observances ordains that a priest of Jupiter be chosen by lot every year. The Syracusans consider this priesthood their most honorable office. Three men are first selected by vote out of the three classes of citizens, and the final choice is decided by lot. By means of his supreme authority Verres succeeded in having an intimate friend, Theomnastus, elected as one of the three. Since he could have no control over the lottery, everyone watched to see what he would do next.

He did the obvious, rascally thing; he forbade the lottery and ordered the appointment of Theomnastus without drawing lots. The Syracusans objected that they could not possibly do this for the reverence they owed their sacred laws; in brief, they said it would be impious. Verres ordered the law read to him. It was read. One clause provided that as many lots should be thrown in the urn as there were candidates nominated, and that the man whose name was drawn would become the priest. The astute Verres said, "Excellent! Is it not written, 'as many lots as there are candidates'? How many candidates are there?"

They answered, "Three."

"Then all that is necessary is to put in three lots and draw out one."

"Yes."

He then ordered three lots to be thrown in, on each of which was written the name of Theomnastus. There was a great outcry, for everyone considered it a scandalous and shocking proceeding. But by these means the honorable priesthood of Jupiter was bestowed on Theomnastus.

At Cephaloedium the high priest has to be selected in a certain month. The honor was sought by one Artemo, surnamed Climachias. He was, to be sure, both wealthy and a member of the nobility, but he could not possibly have been appointed if a certain Herodotus had been present. For it had been unanimously agreed that this high position should be given to Herodotus for that year, and not even Climachias had a word to say against it. The matter was referred to Verres, who decided it in his usual manner. Some famous and costly pieces of chased sliver were removed from Artemo's house. Herodotus meanwhile was away at Rome; he thought he would be in time for the meeting if he arrived the day before. But Verres contrived a scheme to avoid calling the meeting on an illegal day and yet at the same time avoid robbing Herodotus of the honor before his face. The latter deed would not have bothered Verres, but would have troubled Climachias exceedingly. (I have remarked before that no one is or ever was sharper than Verres!) He contrived, I say, a way by which the meeting might be held in the regular month, and yet Herodotus would find it impossible to be present.

In order to correct the discrepancy between their calendar and the solar and lunar year, it is customary for the Sicilians and other Greeks to eliminate occasionally a day, or at most two days, from the month, which they call lost days. Sometimes too they make a month longer by a day or two. When our new astronomer heard of this practice, his thoughts turned toward the heavenly silver instead of toward the heavenly planets, and instead of taking one day from the month, he ordered a month and a half taken from the year. Thus the day which ought to have been called the thirteenth of January was proclaimed the first of March. The step was taken in spite of universal protests and lamentations. Now March first was the legal day for calling the meeting, and on that day Climachias was designated high priest.

So when Herodotus returned from Rome fifteen days—as he

supposed—before the meeting, he arrived a month after it had been held. Then the people of Cephaloedium voted to insert an intercalary month of forty-five days, in order that the following months might fall again in their proper season. If such a thing could have been done at Rome, no doubt Verres would somehow or other have contrived to eliminate the thirty-five days between the two series of games, which is the only period during which this trial could have taken place.

We ought next to look into the appointment of censors in Sicily under Verres' praetorship. Now the Silicians take great pains in filling that office, because every citizen pays a yearly tax on the basis of his assessment, and for making the assessment the censor is authorized to appraise all his property and determine the amount due. So the people take care to select a man who can be trusted with their property. There is also strong competition for the position because of the power it carries with it. In this business Verres did not choose to do anything underhanded; he neither cheated in the drawing of lots, nor cut days out of the calendar; he countenanced no cunning or wicked tricks. But, in order to eliminate from each city the ambition and inordinate thirst for honors—weaknesses which frequently corrupt a state!—he would, he declared, himself appoint the censors in all cities.

When the praetor announced this open market, persons from everywhere flocked to him at Syracuse. His whole house was afire with the zeal of the aspirants. It was hardly strange when assemblies from so many cities were packed together in one house, and the hopes of an entire province were crowded into one chamber. Bribes were openly solicited and bids offered. At last, Timarchides appointed two censors for each city. His heavy labors, numerous visits in connection with the business, and painstaking methods, resulted in the conveyance of all the money to Verres without his having

71

to lift a finger. It is still impossible to know for a certainty how much Timarchides made, but at the first trial you heard many witnesses bear evidence to his constant, shameless depredations.

In case you should wonder how that freedman obtained so much influence over Verres, I will tell you briefly what kind of person he is. Then you may appreciate the low character of the man who employed him, especially in such an important position, and may realize also the disastrous consequences to the province. This Timarchides, as I have found out, had a wide experience in seducing women and similar kinds of dissipation and debauchery, and was hence wonderfully suited by nature to be of use to Verres in his profligate and infamous career. He investigated possibilities; he looked them up, made their acquaintance, bought them. Everything of this sort he put through with complete coolness, craft, and impudence. He devised some extraordinarily adept methods of thievery. Verres, on the contrary, has always been known for avid, unconcealed greediness, and utter lack of adroitness and foresight. His own personal misdeeds, some of which he committed, as you know, in Rome, seem more like plain banditry than intrigue.

Timarchides, however, was marvelously talented in spying out accurately the misfortunes and necessities of everyone in the province. He made a practice of tracking down and hunting out everyone's opponents and enemies, whom he then diligently cultivated, conversed with, made up to. He could thus find out the motives, aims, and resources of both sides. He knew when to inspire fear and when to hold out hope. He had in his power every accuser and every informer. If he wished to make trouble for anyone, he did it with no difficulty. All Verres' edicts, orders, and letters he sold for him in the most skillful and cunning manner. He both looked out for Verres' interests and did not forget his own. He amassed a big fortune by gathering up what slipped through his master's fingers, and even enjoyed the dregs of Verres' voluptuous pleasures. So do not imagine that Athenio [19] ever ruled Sicily, for he captured no city! Remember rather that the slave-king Timarchides reigned in every Silician town for three years. The children, the mothers, the property of the most ancient and devoted allies of the Roman people were all that time in his power. For it was Timarchides, I say, who sent censors into every city, after taking the bribes for their appointment. As long as Verres was praetor, elections for censor were never held, not even to make a pretense of legality.

Verres' most brazen piece of misconduct was open, for presumably it was permitted by law. Each censor was directed to pay three hundred denarii [$60] toward a statue of the praetor. One hundred and thirty censors had been appointed. They had bought their offices secretly, contrary to law; they now paid openly thirty-nine thousand denarii [$7,800] for the statue, as permitted by law. First, what was all that money for? Second, why did the censors pay it to you, Verres, for your statue? Is there a regular order or society of censors, as a distinct class of society? It is natural for cities to confer such an honor officially, or for groups of men to do so according to their occupations, acting as farmers, merchants, or shipowners. But why should censors do such a thing rather than aediles? Did they get some favor by it?

Will you agree then that they solicited their offices from you, since you dare not admit they bought them? Will you acknowledge that you conferred the positions on them as favors, and not for the best interests of the republic? And when you have admitted this, will anyone doubt that actually

[19] Athenio had been a leader of a slave insurrection that a generation earlier had terrified all Sicily.

you brought on yourself the hatred and loathing of everyone
in the province not for ambition's sake nor in order to confer
favors, but to get money? These censors acted just like our
own Roman magistrates who get their offices by bribery. They
used their power to reimburse themselves for their previous
expenditures. Under your praetorship they took the census in
such a way that no city administration could be run in accordance with it. For they made low returns on the incomes of
all the wealthiest men, and exaggerated those of all the poor
men. As a consequence, when taxes were levied, so heavy a
burden was laid on the common people that even without
saying anything, it needed only the figures to discredit the
whole census, as one can easily understand under the circumstances.

After my arrival in Sicily to conduct my inquiries, the sudden appearance of Lucius Letilius caused Lucius Metellus to
become not only a friend of Verres, but also his kinsman!
Now Metellus had realized that Verres' census was impossible,
and so had ordered the Sicilians to keep in force the previous
census, taken while the gallant and incorruptible Sextus
Peducaeus was praetor. For at that time there were legitimate
censors, elected by their cities, who could be punished by
law for anything unlawful which they did. When you were
praetor, what censor would either fear a law which meant
nothing to him, because it had not been enforced in connection with his own appointment, or dread your anger at his
selling what you had sold to him? Let Metellus then arrest
my witnesses and compel others to praise Verres, as he has
tried to do on many occasions, but let him also keep on with
what he is doing! For did anyone ever bring more disgrace
or dishonor on a fallen official? Every fifth year the census is
taken all over Sicily. A census was taken when Peducaeus was
praetor. The fifth year after that fell during your praetorship,

Verres, and the census was taken again. A year later Lucius
Metellus forbade any mention of your census, ordered new
censors appointed, and in the interim enforced the census of
Peducaeus. If an enemy had done this to you, the province
would probably have taken it calmly, but still would have
considered it a severe indictment. But it was the new friend,
the self-styled kinsman, who did it. He could do nothing else
if he wished to retain the allegiance of the province and live
in safety there.

Are you waiting now to see what your judges too will decide? If Metellus had deprived you of your office, it would
have been less insulting than his cancellation of your official
acts. Nor was Metellus' censure limited to this instance, but
before I arrived in Sicily he had acted the same on many other
important issues. He had ordered your friends of the gymnasium to restore the property of Heraclius the Syracusan, and
the people of Bidis to restore the property of Epicrates, and
Aulus Claudius to restore the property of his ward at Dre-
panum. And if Letilius had not arrived in Sicily with his
letters a little too soon, in less than another month Metellus
would have annulled the work of your whole three years'
praetorship.

As I have spoken of the money which the censors paid you
for your statue, I really ought to mention as well the sums
you requested from the cities on a pretext of erecting more
statues. The total, I see, was very large: two million sesterces
[$100,000]. It is proved by the evidence and by letters from
the cities. Verres admits this charge, which indeed cannot be
contested. Since then the actions to which he confesses are
so outrageous, imagine the wickedness of those which he
denies. And what does he expect us to think? That all this
money was spent for statues? Suppose it was! It is none the
less intolerable that our allies should be plundered in order

that statues of a malicious robber should be set up in every alley—which are hardly safe for human beings as it is.

But where are the statues on which that enormous sum of money was spent? It is still to be spent, you say. Are we then to wait until the end of the legal five-year limit? If within this interval he has not spent it, then, at last, may we indict him for extortion over these statues? Our culprit is being put on trial for many grave crimes. On just a single occasion, as we see, he collected two million sesterces. If you are now condemned, Verres, you will not, I presume, occupy yourself with spending that money for statues within the five years. If you are acquitted, who—after the five years have passed—will then be rash enough to raise the question of the statues, seeing you have escaped from so many graver investigations? If, therefore, this money is not yet spent, it seems clear that it will not be spent, and we may note that a system has been discovered by which one may, under merely one pretext, raise and acquire two million sesterces. If you, gentlemen, condone Verres' behavior, other officials may take what they please on similar grounds. Such an act on our part would encourage every man to enrich himself thus, and what is a base crime would be dignified by an honorable name through our apparent approval of one instance of it.

Suppose, for example, that Gaius Verres had simply demanded a hundred thousand sesterces [$5000] from the people of Centuripa, and collected that amount from them. No one, I imagine, would hesitate to condemn him, if the fact were proved. Suppose he demands two hundred thousand [$10,000] from the same people, collects that amount, carries it off. Shall we acquit him because the records state that the money was given him for statues? I think not, unless, indeed, we prefer to provide our allies with reasons for paying out money rather than prevent our magistrates from taking it.

Even though a man longs for the honor and glory of having statues erected to him, he should still abide by certain rules. First, he must not pocket for himself the money given for that purpose; second, there must be some limit to the number of his statues; and finally they must definitely not be extorted from an unwilling people.

Let us discuss the misappropriation of this money. I should like to ask whether the cities for the most part let out contracts for putting up the statues to the lowest bidder, or appointed an official to superintend their erection, or paid the money in to you or your agents? If the statues were erected under the supervision of the men who were honoring you, I am glad to know it. But if the money was paid in to Timarchides, I beg you to stop pretending that what you wanted was the glory of the monuments, now that you are caught in this flagrant robbery.

Should we fix no limit to the number of statues? But that would be an impossible arrangement. Just consider the situation this way. The city of Syracuse, to cite a specific instance, awards him a statue. It is an honor. They provide one too for his father, a fine display of filial devotion, and lucrative as well. They give one to his son, a plausible enough deed, for they do not hate the boy. Still, how often and on how many pretexts will you, Verres, go on taking statues from the Syracusans? You get them to put up one statue for you in the forum. You tell them to put another in the senate house. You order them to send contributions for statues to be erected in Rome. You bid the same men contribute again as farmers; they do that. You expect the same men to pay their share of the gift from all Sicily; they do even that. More than one city has paid in money on all these different scores. But still you feel no need to set bounds to your avarice!

No city did this willingly; they all paid the money, ostensibly for your statues, but only under the pressure of your authority, because they were terrified by threats of violence or punishment. Obviously, even if a man felt it was right to accept money for statues, he should make sure that under no circumstances was that money raised by extortion. But I am now calling all Sicily to testify on this point, and Sicily unanimously replies that immense sums were forcibly wrung from her under the pretext of setting up statues to you. Embassies from all the cities, in their general petition, instigated principally by your misconduct, have inserted the request, "that they may not be allowed to promise statues to anyone until he has left his province."

There have been many praetors in Sicily, Verres, and many Sicilians past and present have appealed to the Senate from them. Your praetorship, however, has brought about the introduction of a new kind of petition. The mere existence of this petition is peculiar, but still more so its form. There are points indeed in the petition, touching on your misbehavior, that are themselves novel, but that are not expressed in unusual language. The Sicilians, for instance, entreat the Senate to instruct our magistrates henceforth to follow the law of Hiero when selling the right to collect tithes. You, I hear, were the first to sell them by methods contrary to that law. The Sicilians ask also that they be not compelled to pay money in place of the grain ordered for the public granary. This too is a new request, made because you set a price on each measure of three denarii. But this kind of request is not unprecedented. Again the Sicilians ask that no criminal charge be preferred against a man in his absence, a request prompted by the misfortunes of Sthenius and your lawlessness. I will not enumerate their other points.

These requests of the Sicilians are of a serious nature and look like criminal charges, assembled against you personally; yet, though they all refer to new types of injustice, they preserve the customary forms of a petition. The request with regard to the statues, however, would appear ridiculous to a person who does not grasp both the facts and their implication. For here the petitioners do not ask not to be compelled to erect statues, but not to be allowed to do so. What does this mean? Are you asking me to forbid you to do something which you can do or not do as you choose? No, what you are really after is preventing anyone from forcing you to promise or do anything against your will. "But to say just that would be useless," you protest, "for they all would insist they used no compulsion on me. If you wish me well, please use some force on yourself, and make it illegal for me to promise anything." Your praetorship, Verres, was the first to call out such a petition! The framers of it imply and intimate plainly that they gave the money for your statues against their will and only for fear of your violence. Even though they have not said this in so many words, still must you not admit it is true? Then consider what defense you will put up; for you do, at last, understand that you must confess in full about those statues.

I hear that your lawyers have planned your defense with great ingenuity, and that you have instructed and trained them how to act. Whenever any influential or honorable Sicilian gives testimony at all damaging against you, as many of their leading citizens have already done at great length, you immediately say to your lawyers, "That man hates me because he is a farmer." Thereby, I presume, you mean to disparage the farmers as a class, suggesting that they have become your personal enemies because you were a little strict in collecting the tithes. The farmers then are all your enemies, all your adversaries? Not a man of them who does not wish you dead? Certainly you are doing well, when the finest and most honorable class of the population, the backbone of our republic in general, especially of that province, evince such unanimous hatred of you!

Be that as it may! Later we will consider the feelings of the farmers and the injuries they have suffered. For the moment I assume merely what you yourself have granted, that they are particularly hostile to you. To be sure, you give the tithes as the reason, but I grant that too. I am not now asking whether or not they have cause for their enmity. But what then is the meaning of those gilded equestrian statues near the temple of Vulcan, hideous and abhorrent to the Roman people? I see an inscription on one of them stating that the farmers presented it. But if they erected this statue in your honor, they are not your enemies! Let us, however, put our faith in the witnesses. Then they were thinking of your honor, now they are listening to their own consciences. But if they donated these statues under stress of fear, you must admit that you raised the money in the province for them by violence and terror. Choose whichever explanation you like.

Really, I would be willing now to abandon this charge about the statues, so that you might make the assertion that would do you most credit, namely, that the farmers of their own free will contributed the money for the statue in your honor. Yet if you do this, you will have at once destroyed the main part of your defense. For then you will not be able to plead the farmers' hatred and hostility. What an extraordinary situation! How miserable and ruinous a defense! The defendant, a former praetor of Sicily, cannot admit to his accuser that the farmers erected a statue to him of their own free will, or that they have a good opinion of him, are his friends or wish him well. He is afraid you might believe it, for he is ruined by the evidence of the farmers. I will take advantage of his dilemma. Surely you must see that the men who Verres wishes you to believe are his bitterest enemies did not willingly contribute money for monuments in his honor.

In order, Verres, to make this whole matter clear, will you question anyone you please of the witnesses I shall produce, men direct from Sicily, both Roman citizens and Sicilians? Ask even the man who seems most hostile to you, who says you robbed him, whether he personally contributed anything for a statue. You will find not one who says he did not. In fact they did all contribute. Do you then imagine anyone will believe that a man, naturally your enemy, because of the injuries you did him, paid out money for your statue of his own accord, out of friendship, and not under compulsion from your authority? I have not calculated, or been able to calculate, gentlemen, the total amount of the huge sum thus shamelessly extorted from unwilling men. I do not know how much was collected from the farmers, how much from the merchants trading at Syracuse, Agrigentum, Palermo, and Lilybaeum. By now, however, you know from his own admission that it was wrung from most reluctant contributors.

I come to the cities of Sicily. In their case it is exceedingly easy to find out how they felt about the matter. Did these Sicilians, as a group, contribute also against their will? Can that be likely? It is so generally agreed that Gaius Verres, during his term as praetor in Sicily, since he could not satisfy both Sicilians and Romans, set his duty to our allies above his desire for personal popularity among our citizens! For that reason, I saw him called, in an inscription at Syracuse, not only the patron of the island, but also its "Soter." [20] What does that word mean? It means more than can be translated by any single Latin word. "Soter" is actually one who brings deliverance. Under that name is now celebrated the splendid

[20] The Greek word "soter" is commonly translated savior.

festival of Verres, which does not imitate the festival of Marcellus, but supplants it, for it was abolished at Verres' command. In the forum at Syracuse stands a triumphal arch on which is a nude figure of his son, and Verres from horseback looks down on the province that he left stripped and bare. His statues indeed are everywhere in Syracuse, as if to prove that he erected almost as many statues as he took away. At Rome too we observe the inscription in his honor, carved in enormous letters at the base of his statues, "The gift of the whole people of Sicily." Can anyone be induced to believe that such exalted honors were conferred on a man by a people against their will?

But because that is the truth, Verres, you must plan your future line of argument more carefully than you did your story just now about the farmers. It is important whether you choose to call the Sicilians, both individually and collectively, your friends or your enemies. If you call them enemies, what will there be left for you? Where will you turn? On whom will you rely? You have just now declared a cleavage between yourself and the majority of the farmers, who are honorable and wealthy men and include both Sicilians and Roman citizens. What now will you do about the Sicilian cities? Will you say that these Sicilians are loyal to you? Yet how can you say that? Never before have they gone so far as to offer public testimony against anyone, even though many former praetors of Sicily have been condemned, and only two of those prosecuted have been acquitted.

And here they come with official letters, accusations, and evidence against you. If they were eulogizing you in the name of the province, it would probably be only a formal document, in keeping with the usual custom, not prompted by any merits of yours. But when these men bring a public complaint, does it not show that the enormity of your crimes has driven them to abandon their ancient habits and not keep silent about what you have done? You must, therefore, perforce admit that the Sicilians hate you, for they have made charges of exceeding gravity against you to the consuls, and have implored me to take their case to save them from destruction. Furthermore, though the praetor forbade them to come here and the four quaestors tried to prevent them, they have nonetheless considered their people's welfare more important than all threats of danger to themselves. At the first trial, they gave their evidence so vehemently and with such passion that Hortensius called Artemo, the deputy and official witness of Centuripa, a prosecutor, not a witness. But Artemo was chosen by his fellow citizens as their deputy, along with the honorable and trustworthy Andron, because of his integrity and his eloquence, so that he might explain in the clearest and most impressive manner the many different injuries they have suffered under Verres.

Men from Halesa, Catana, Tyndaris, Enna, Herbita, Agyrium, Netum, and Segesta also gave evidence. It is needless to rehearse them all. You know how many at the first trial gave evidence on numerous points. Now they and others too will speak. Everyone, in brief, will discover what the feelings of the Sicilians are on the subject, for if Verres is not punished, they actually are thinking of leaving their homes and dwellings, and moving, or, to be more exact, fleeing out of Sicily. Will you, Verres, persuade us that these men, of their own free will, contributed large sums of money to bestow honor and dignity upon you? Am I to suppose that men who did not want you left at liberty in your own city were anxious to keep reminders of your person and name in their cities? The facts show how they wished it!

But it seems to me now that I have been too elaborate, and have spent too much time assembling arguments about the

83

way the Sicilians feel towards you, whether they wanted to erect statues to you, or were compelled to do so. Has what happened to you ever happened to any other man, that statues of him, erected in public places, some even in the holy temples of his province, were forcibly thrown down by all the people? There have been guilty magistrates, many of them, in Asia, Africa, Spain, Gaul, Sardinia, even in Sicily, before now, but did we ever hear anything about them comparable to this? It was extraordinary behavior, gentlemen, and monstrously abnormal, certainly for Sicilians and all other Greeks. I should not have believed the report about the statues, if I had not seen them myself, wrenched from their bases and spread over the ground. All Greeks usually consider monuments set up in honor of men as to some extent consecrated, and under the protection of the gods.

Take, for example, the Rhodians, when, almost singlehanded, they were carrying on their first war against Mithridates, and withstanding the violent attacks of his hosts on their walls, shores, and fleets. At that time they, beyond all other nations, hated the king. Yet not even when their city was in dire peril did they touch his statue, located in the most crowded square of their city. There might, perhaps, appear to be some inconsistency in thus preserving the statue and likeness of a man they were struggling to overthrow. But when I was staying with the Rhodians, I saw that they still had certain scruples, inherited from their ancestors, and argued too in the same way. In the case of the statue, they recalled the time when it was erected; in the case of the man, they remembered how he had made war on them and been their enemy.

You see, however, that the habitual religious reverence of the Greeks, that normally protects monuments of enemies even in wartime, could not, in a time of profound peace, protect the statues of this praetor of the Roman people. The peaceable citizens of Taormina, a city allied to Rome, have long been secure from possible injury from our magistrates, because of the protection accorded them by their treaty. Yet they too did not hesitate to throw down that man's statue. After removing the figure, however, they decided to keep the pedestal in the forum, because they thought that the accusation implied would be more severe if it were plain that the Taorminians had had a statue and torn it down than if it appeared none had ever been erected. The men of Tyndaris pulled down the statue of Verres in their forum, and for the same reason left its horse without a rider. Even in the impoverished and forlorn city of Leontini, Verres' statue in the gymnasium was overthrown.

So why should I single out the Syracusans, when they acted not alone but in unison with their neighbors and well-nigh the entire province? A huge throng was on hand there, we were told, when his statues were pulled down and toppled over. And where was this done? In the most frequented and most sacred spot in the whole city, before Serapis himself, at the entrance to his temple. If Metellus had not then issued authoritative orders, sternly forbidding such acts, not a trace of Verres' statues would have been left in all Sicily.

I have no fear that any of these outbreaks will be attributed to my instigation, or be supposed to have any connection whatever with my arrival. For they all happened not only before my arrival in Sicily, but even before Verres reached Italy. During the time I was in Sicily, no statue was pulled down. But hear now what was done after I departed!

The senate of Centuripa issued a decree, confirmed by the people, that the quaestors should let contracts for the demolition of every statue of Gaius Verres, of his father, and of his son, and that no less than thirty senators should be present at the operation. Observe the sober dignity of that city. They did not wish to keep the community statues which they had been forced to set up against their will, especially as they were memorials of a man whom they were then publicly accusing of the gravest offenses, through an official delegation sent to Rome—an action they had never before taken. But they thought the step would seem more significant if taken on public authority, than if it were a matter of mob violence. After the people of Centuripa, in accordance with this plan, had publicly pulled down their statues of Verres, Metellus heard of it. He was very indignant and summoned the magistrates of Centuripa and ten leading citizens to appear before him. He then threatened them with severe punishment if they did not replace the statues. They reported the matter to their senate and the statues, which thenceforth could do no good to Verres' cause, were replaced. But the decrees of the people of Centuripa with regard to the statues were not rescinded.

Now a certain amount of concession should be made for some people, but I cannot pardon so foolish an act on the part of a wise man like Metellus. Did he think it would be a reflection on Verres if his statues were overthrown—a thing which often happens accidentally, in a wind storm, or under similar circumstances? In such an event there could be no reflection on or charge against the man. What then is it that implies a charge and a reflection? The deliberate intention of those who caused the statues to be pulled down.

If Metellus had not compelled the people of Centuripa to replace the statues, I should still be saying: "See, gentlemen, the exceedingly bitter indignation of our allies and friends at their unjust treatment by Verres! Although the friendly and faithful city of Centuripa is linked to the Roman people by so many mutual benefactions that it has always shown affection not only for our republic, but even for any private individual bearing the name of Roman, nevertheless, in an official public decree, it has declared that the statues of Gaius Verres ought not to remain in the city." I should then recite the decrees of Centuripa; I should extol that city as it truly deserves; I should say that those ten thousand citizens, our very brave and loyal allies, had all resolved that there should be no monument to that man in their city. I should be saying this, even if Metellus had not replaced the statues.

I should now like to ask Metellus if he has refuted any of the points of my speech by his display of authority? In my opinion, the very same language is still appropriate. For however the statues were knocked down, I could not have shown them to you on the ground. And I can still use the same argument, that so important a city did resolve that the statues of Gaius Verres should be demolished. Of this point Metellus has not deprived me. In fact, he has given me an additional advantage; he has enabled me to complain, if I see fit, that our friends and allies are being so arbitrarily governed that they are not allowed to use their unbiased judgment even in the conferment of awards. I might then ask you to guess how Lucius Metellus has hampered me wherever he could, since even in this matter, in which he could not hinder me at all, he has shown such obvious prejudice. But I am not angry with Metellus, nor do I wish to rob him of his claim, asserted on every occasion, that he has done nothing spitefully or with hostile intent.

But surely it is now clear, beyond denial, that no one wished to present you with a statue, and that any money for such a purpose was extorted by force. And included in this accusation I want it understood that you did collect two million sesterces [$100,000], and that the farmers and every other Sicilian hate you still, as they always have. This last point has come out clearly in the course of our trial. I cannot imagine what defense you can possibly put up. You may say, "The

Sicilians detest me because I have done so much for the Roman citizens." Yet the latter are your bitter enemies. On the contrary, you may say, "The Roman citizens hate me because I have defended the interests and rights of our allies." Yet our allies complain that you have treated them like enemies. Perhaps you will say, "The farmers are against me for the taxes." Yet the owners of tax-exempt property dislike you quite as much. Take the men of Halesa, of Centuripa, of Segesta, of Halicyae!

Is there, in short, any class or group of men, Roman citizens or Sicilians, who do not despise you? Even if I could find no reason for their hostility, I could say: "You too, gentlemen, must hate the man whom all men hate." Will you, Verres, dare to argue that the question whether the farmers and every other Sicilian love or hate you has no bearing on the case? You will not dare to claim this, nor would it be advantageous to you to do so. For your pretense of despising the Sicilians would be refuted by the equestrian statues, which you ordered them to erect just before you returned to Rome. The inscriptions on them were particularly intended to weaken the accusations of your enemies and accusers. For who could dare attack you, or bring action against you, when he saw the statues erected to you by the businessmen, by the farmers, by all Sicily? The scheme covers the whole province, does it not? It is thus proclaimed that the man Verres was loved and honored by the whole province, individually and collectively. Who would dare find fault with him?

Can you then really maintain that the evidence given against you by farmers, businessmen, and every Sicilian should not count, when you intended to gloss over your unpopularity and evil reputation by getting their names inscribed as donors on your statues? If you thought the statues would do you more honor when the names of these men were added, let me use the authority of their names to support my accusation.

You may have some hope left because of your popularity with the tax collectors, but I have seen to it that this popularity should be of little value to you. As a matter of fact, you have contrived to turn it against yourself. Let me briefly tell that story. The collector in charge of public lands in Sicily is Lucius Carpinatius, who was on intimate terms with Verres for his own profit, and also, perhaps, for that of his partners. Carpinatius accompanied the praetor wherever he went, and grew so used to taking in the bribes for selling Verres' decrees and verdicts, and doing similar business, that he became well-nigh a second Timarchides. In one respect he was even worse, for he lent out money at interest to persons attempting to bribe the praetor, and this moneylending was arranged so that Verres would make a profit. For the sums loaned to the men with whom Carpinatius was dealing were entered by him as derived from Verres' secretary, or from Timarchides, or even from himself. Besides this, he lent out at interest in his own name other large sums belonging to Verres, of which he made no entry at all.

Before Carpinatius became so intimate with Verres, he had often written letters to his associates describing Verres' iniquitous behavior. Canuleius, too, who worked at the harbor of Syracuse, had written accounts to his associates of many of Verres' misdemeanors, mentioning especially articles which he had exported from Syracuse without paying duty. It must be remembered that both the harbor and the public lands were in charge of the same tax-collecting firm. It is thus possible to gain much evidence against Verres from the files of this firm.

But once Carpinatius became intimate with Verres and shared in his profits, he sent numerous letters to his partners, praising Verres for his remarkable good nature and for his services to their common enterprises. And as Verres habitually granted more and more of Carpinatius' requests, the latter tried in his reports to efface all recollection of what he had previously written. Finally, when Verres was on the point of leaving Sicily, Carpinatius wrote to his friends asking them to demonstrate their gratitude to Verres, and to promise him to do anything he might ask of them. Accordingly the members of the firm followed the old custom, not because they thought Verres worthy of the honor, but because they thought it would be to their own interest to show themselves grateful.

They received Verres at their offices with great deference and told him that Carpinatius had often written them of the high favors he had received from him. He replied that it had been a pleasure to be of assistance to Carpinatius and that he had done a magnificent job. Then later on Verres asked one of his friends, who happened to be a director of the company, to see to it that nothing might be found in the company files that might be incriminating. The director accordingly dismissed the main body of the shareholders, and assembled the tax collectors, and referred the matter to them. They passed a resolution to have the incriminating letters removed, and care taken to prevent any harm coming to the reputation of Gaius Verres. I am able to prove that this was the response of the tax collectors, and, gentlemen, I am able to prove that the letters were removed from the files.

What more do you expect me to do? Is it possible to present more forcible proof of a man's guilt? He was in fact pronounced guilty there, by the judgment of these tax collectors —men who would sit as judges here in court, if the would-be reformers of our courts should have their way! (The proposal, incidentally, is said to be a demand of the populace, but actually is the plan not of men of my own social rank of knight, but of a member of the highest nobility.) It was these tax collectors—these princes, or, if you like, senators among state employees—who voted to remove the incriminating letters from the files. I shall call on some of them who were present at that meeting, men of good standing and wealth, top men of the equestrian order, the very men on whose excellent reputation the case for this newly proposed law rests. They will appear and tell their story. And indeed, if I know them, they will not lie. For though they might remove letters from the files, they cannot now disregard their own honor and consciences. These men of equestrian rank did themselves pronounce you guilty, but they were reluctant to have you condemned by a verdict of this higher court. You can now decide, gentlemen, whether you prefer to be guided by their judgment or by their feelings.

You can see now, Verres, how little aid to you have been the zeal of your friends, your own devices, the willing cooperation of your partners. I shall express myself still more plainly; for I am not afraid of being criticized for speaking with some heat instead of with cool objectivity. If these letters had not been removed, I could have used against you only what I could find in them; but since they have disappeared, I may say whatever I like, and the judge may suspect whatever he chooses. I say that you exported from Syracuse large amounts of gold, silver, ivory, and purple dye, many Maltese robes, carpets, pieces of Delian furniture, many Corinthian vases, a great quantity of grain and honey. You paid no export duty, but the information was sent by Lucius Canuleius, the harbor agent, to his company in Rome.

Does this seem a serious charge? I should say it was. And what will Hortensius say in defense? Will he demand that I produce the letters of Canuleius? Will he say that a charge of this sort is worthless unless supported by letters? I shall reply that the letters have been removed, and thus by a resolu-

91

tion of the participators, the proof and evidence of the crimes have been taken from me. He must either contend that this was not done, or he must bear the brunt of all my weapons. Do you deny that it was done? I shall be glad to hear your argument. I accept the challenge, and the contest will be fair. I will produce witnesses, and produce many of them at once. They were together when the removal of the letters was ordered, and they shall be together now. When examined they will be bound not only by the obligation of their oaths and the peril to their reputations, but also by their common knowledge of the facts. If it is proved that the removal took place, as I assert it did, you can hardly say, Hortensius, that there was nothing incriminating in those letters. You cannot say that, nor can you deny any of my accusations. So you see that the sole result of your careful planning was, as I have said before, to give me complete liberty for my accusation and to the judges permission to believe practically anything.

But, though I could do otherwise, I shall keep to the truth. I shall bear in mind that I have undertaken this case not for the sake of prosecuting anyone but simply to defend my clients. You have a right to hear the facts, as I learned them, not merely my story of the affair, and I shall be doing the Sicilians justice if I report exactly what I heard from them and what I myself saw in Sicily. I shall be doing the Roman people justice if I do not let myself be intimidated by anyone's force or influence. I shall be doing you justice if, by honesty and accuracy, I provide you with an opportunity to reach a fair and straightforward decision. I shall be doing myself justice if I refuse to swerve by a hair's breadth from the course of action I have set for myself. You, Verres, have no reason, therefore, to fear I shall invent anything to your disadvantage. On the contrary, you have good reason to rejoice, for I shall not mention many of the crimes I know you committed, because they are either too disgraceful or else too incredible.

But the business of this tax-collecting company I want to discuss further. In order to get to the bottom of the subject I shall ask first whether the decision I mentioned was actually taken. Once this is ascertained, I shall then ask whether the letters were actually removed. Once this is ascertained, you will yourselves be able to make the following deduction. If the Roman knights who voted to destroy the documents in order to protect Verres were to judge him now, unquestionably they would find him guilty, for they know that they themselves received the incriminating letters, which have been destroyed by their own orders. Since these Roman knights, who favor the defendant and have received benefits from him, would be forced to find him guilty, can there be any valid reason for acquitting him?

Nor need you believe that the documents in question were so carefully concealed that I, with all my pains, could acquire no knowledge of them. I have now, let me tell you, found out whatever could possibly be discovered about them. You are about to see Verres pinned down by unmistakable evidence. A great part of my life I have spent dealing with revenue cases, and so have acquired a good knowledge of the habits of our tax collectors. As soon, therefore, as I heard that the files had been tampered with, I established the exact period during which Verres was in Sicily. Next I found out— and this was very easy—who had been the officials of the company in charge of the records during those years. For I knew that it was a habit of the officials who kept the records to retain copies of the correspondence when they turned the files over to their successors. Accordingly I went first to the well-known Roman knight, Lucius Vibius, who had been in office during the year in which I was interested. Contrary to my expectation, I found him quite unsuspicious. I asked as much as I could and found out everything.

Only two small folders containing accounts were sent by Lucius Canuleius to the company while he was employed at the harbor of Syracuse. Among these accounts was recorded, under Verres' name, a list of goods exported over a period of several months, without payment of duty. These papers I sealed up immediately. It was not exactly the type of evidence which I had expected to find in the files of the company, yet I had found something, gentlemen, to submit to you as a specimen of first-hand proof. Whatever interest there is in these records, brief as they are, will at any rate come to light. The rest you must deduce from them. I shall now have read to you the contents of the two folders of Canuleius.

[Cicero pauses, while the records are read.]

I am not asking you, Verres, where you got those four hundred jars of honey, or all the Maltese cloth, the fifty couches, or so many candelabra. I am not asking at present where you got them, but I do ask for what purpose you needed them. Never mind the honey! But did you need so many dresses to give to the wives of your friends? Did you need so many couches to furnish all their villas?

And mind you, gentlemen, if this is the record of a few months, imagine the amount that was exported over the whole three years. I submit that on the basis of these few accounts, kept by one official of this company, you can reckon the amount of plunder Verres stole from all Sicily. From them you can judge the varied forms his cupidity took, and the enormity of the wealth he accumulated, not only in cash, but in goods and property. This will later be described to you in greater detail. But at the moment listen to this! Through these exports just enumerated the company lost sixty thousand sesterces [$3,000] in the five percent duty that should have been paid at Syracuse. So, in a few months, according to these insignificant records, the loot of the praetor, exported from a single city, amounted to twelve hundred thousand sesterces [$60,000]. Take likewise into account the fact that Sicily, as an island, has harbors on all its three sides. Imagine how much went through the other ports: Agrigentum, Lilybaeum, Palermo, Thermae, Halesa, Catana! Think especially of Messina, a port he considered particularly safe, where he always felt gay and lighthearted, because he had his arrangements with the Mamertines to take care of any shipments and export them secretly. After I unearthed these records, the others were removed and disposed of more carefully. But, as I am anxious to show, I had no ulterior motive, and am satisfied with the records I found.

Now let us return to the company's books which they could not very well destroy, and to your friend Carpinatius. In Syracuse I inspected the books of the company kept by Carpinatius, which revealed that most of the men who had given money to Verres had borrowed it from Carpinatius. You will see through this whole business when I produce the men who paid the money, and you will find that the dates on which the blackmail was paid to Verres agree exactly with those in the records of the company.

As I was examining these documents closely, I suddenly observed certain erasures which seemed to be of recent date. I instantly grew suspicious, and noted attentively the names involved. I read there that certain sums had been received for a Gaius Verrucius, son of Gaius. Up to the second r that name was untouched, but everything afterward was obliterated by the erasure. There were two, three, four—many other examples of the same thing. As it was obvious that the erasure indicated some significant error, I asked Carpinatius who was this Verrucius who kept such a large account. Carpinatius began to hesitate, tried to evade the question, and blushed. Since the law forbids taking the tax collector's records to Rome, I had Carpinatius and his books brought before Metellus to have the matter thoroughly investigated. A big crowd assembled, for everyone knew what had been going on between Carpinatius and Verres, and anticipated what the records would show.

I reported to Metellus that I had inspected the files of the company and had found there a large account, listed in many items, to the credit of a certain Gaius Verrucius. I said, too, that it was clear from the dates of the entries that this man Verrucius had had no account with Carpinatius either before the arrival or after the departure of Gaius Verres. I demanded to know who this Verrucius was, a merchant or a businessman, a farmer or a cattle-raiser. Was he still in Sicily or had he already left the island? The entire crowd shouted that there never had been anyone in Sicily by the name of Verrucius. I insisted on being told who he was, where he was, whence he came, and why the secretary of the company who kept the books regularly made the same mistake in writing his name. I made these demands, not because I thought I needed to compel Carpinatius to answer me against his will, but to lay bare to the public the fraudulence of one man, the dishonesty of the other, and the impudence of them both. I left him in the court, dumb from fear and realization of his crimes, more dead than alive. The records themselves I took to the forum, swarming then with a crowd of people. I engaged prominent citizens to copy the accounts accurately, making notes of all corrections that occurred in them. The work was done with utmost care, and checked and countersigned by absolutely reliable men.

Carpinatius refused to answer my questions. Will you, Verres, answer them now? Who was this Verrucius who, to judge from his name, may have been a relative of yours? It is quite impossible that you should not have known a man who, I see, was in Sicily while you were praetor there, and very wealthy, to judge from the records.

But enough of this! To solve the mystery, let us now examine a copy of the accounts, so that everyone can see the unmistakable evidence of Verres' criminality. Look at the name Verrucius. The first four letters are untouched, but the end of the name—shall we say the tail of Verres?—is blurred in an erasure, like a pig's tail in mud. You see what the writing is like, gentlemen. What then are you waiting for, Verres? Can there be any further doubt? Either show us who this Verrucius is, or admit that you and he are one and the same person.

The ancient orators, like Crassus and Antonius, are praised, because they were able, by their eloquence, to weaken strong evidence, and to plead their clients' defense in long, beautiful speeches. But no wonder they surpassed their successors among us, because they had not only genius but good luck. No one in those times committed crimes that left no room for defense; no one was so villainous as to be guilty on every count; no one's misdeeds were so flagrant that a denial of them would be more brazen than the acts themselves.

But look at the dilemma of Hortensius. Can he refute the indictment of avarice by praising his client's thrift? He has to defend a man who is thoroughly dissipated, thoroughly licentious, thoroughly vicious. Can he distract your attention from his client's bad qualities by mentioning any of his virtues? There is no man weaker, more cowardly, more effeminate. And as for personality, there is no man more obstinate, more impertinent, more arrogant. But these are the comparatively harmless aspects of his character. No man more implacable, more cunning, and more cruel has ever lived! Not even a Crassus or an Antonius could have successfully defended him. They, Hortensius, would have refused to take such a case, lest they lose their own good reputations by smearing themselves with another's vileness. For they were free and independent. They were not compelled to plead the case of an unworthy client in order not to appear ungrateful by refusing to defend him.

FIRST SPEECH AGAINST CATILINE

In the summer of 64 B.C. Cicero's highest ambition was realized. He was elected consul for the following year. Among the unsuccessful competitors for the office was one Lucius Sergius Catiline, a friend of the second consul elected at that time, Gaius Antonius, and the leader of a band of impatient young men set on some kind of social revolution. Cicero could hardly expect Antonius' cooperation in dealing with Catiline, but at least Antonius did not hinder his colleague, and the first months of the year 63 passed without disturbance. In the summer of that year, however, Catiline failed a second time to win the election and began soon after to plan an armed uprising, perhaps to seize the government, at any rate to take vengeance on Cicero. Just how far he intended to go it is impossible now to say, for the picture of events is blurred by the prejudices of the reporters. The four speeches delivered by Cicero at fever heat mark, of course, the high points of the crisis. But the account by the contemporary historian Sallust gives a more favorable interpretation of the motives of the conspirators, and Cicero himself, in a speech he made some years later at the trial of a young associate of Catiline's,[1] presents a much cooler analysis of Catiline's character.

We have not enough information to know whether the top men in the popular party, men like Caesar and Crassus, were involved in the plot with Catiline. Cicero himself denied it, but he may have thought it best to allow them to dissociate themselves from the fiasco which the conspiracy turned out to be. We know, however, that Cicero's main activity as con-

---

[1] See the speech in defense of Marcus Caelius below, p. 161.

sul up to the critical days in November and December had consisted of vigorous and successful opposition to certain measures supported by Caesar, which may have been parts of Catiline's program also.

The first oration against Catiline was originally extemporaneous; several years later it was edited by Cicero in its present form. He was forced into an impromptu speech by the unexpected daring of Catiline, who appeared suddenly in a session of the Senate called to consider his attempt on Cicero's life. Immediately thereafter he left Rome and Cicero's second oration was an explanatory address to the populace. In order to appreciate Cicero's position, one must realize that until then he had found it difficult to convince people of his belief that Catiline was in fact the head of a conspiracy against the state and not merely against his own person. All doubt, however, was soon dispelled by the revelation of certain foreign ambassadors that they had been approached by some of Catiline's friends to support him by arms. The Senate quickly declared him an enemy of the state, the ambassadors with the incriminating documents were seized by the police and Catiline's adherents still remaining in Rome were put under house arrest. At this point Cicero again addressed the popular assembly to inform it of the course of events.

The Senate then was reconvened to consider the fate of the prisoners. At first, when asked for their opinion, the leaders appeared to favor a death sentence, though they would not say so unequivocally. Julius Caesar, however, had the courage to plead not for clemency but for legality. By an old law, not always enforced, no Roman citizen could be punished by death until the popular assembly had confirmed his sentence. Caesar proposed, therefore, that the property of the imprisoned conspirators should be confiscated, that they should be banished and that the case should then be officially closed. At this point Cicero felt it imperative to speak again. In his fourth oration, he argued for an immediate and unambiguous decision, and indicated strongly his own preference for capital punishment. But Caesar's proposals appealed to the senators who were unwilling to see members of their aristocratic class put to death by the upstart Cicero. Votes in the Senate were taken in order of rank. Hence one of the youngest members, Marcus Porcius Cato, a recently elected tribune, was among the last to be called on for his judgment. His vehement protest against what he styled treasonable leniency, and his demand for execution of the enemies of the public safety, turned the scales again abruptly. By a majority vote Cicero was directed to proceed at once with the execution of Catiline's five lieutenants. A few months later Catiline himself was killed in battle.

Nevertheless, the case had not been officially closed, and Cicero realized with concern that he had seriously offended Caesar and his friends and had not himself gained the wholehearted support of the Senate and aristocracy. He had also failed to win the important friendship of Pompey, who was away conducting his spectacular campaigns in the East. He wrote a detailed letter to Pompey, describing, without too much modesty, what had been his achievements in the public service, but received merely a cool acknowledgment. On his last day as consul, he was escorted home by an applauding crowd, but a few years later he was tried and condemned to exile for having put Roman citizens to death without due process of law.

It is impossible to say how many of Catiline's plans were carried out later by Caesar. It seems clear that Catiline was interested primarily in economic rather than in political change, but that he stood ready to discard many of the established political institutions of the republic on the chance of solving thereby some of the social and economic problems that had grown ever more pressing since the days of the Gracchi. His revolutionary disregard of tradition certainly brought him into conflict with the conservative class to which he belonged, and it took a much greater man, with more popular following, to break that tradition. The man was to be Caesar.

FIRST SPEECH

AGAINST

CATILINE

[In Catilinam, I]

How LONG, Catiline, will you play upon our patience? How long will you continue your effort to deceive us? To what lengths will your unmitigated insolence carry you? Does not the night-long guard set on the Palatine and all through the city disturb you? Or the alarm of the populace and the assembling of all honorable men of rank, the forced meeting of the Senate in this fortified place,[1] and the looks upon our faces? Do you not see that your plots are detected and your conspiracy foiled already by our universal knowledge of it? Who, think you, is not aware of what you did last night, and the night before, where you were, with whom you talked, and what plans you made?

Oh, the depravity of these times! The Senate is informed of his conduct; the consul has his eyes upon it; yet the man still lives! Lives—why he even walks into the Senate. He participates in the public counsels; he notes down each man of us for the slaughter. And we, brave heroes, fancy we are fulfilling our duty to the state if we merely save ourselves from his furious clutches!

Long ago, Catiline, you should have been taken to execu-

---

[1] The temple of Jupiter Stator on the Capitoline Hill.

tion by the consul's order. You should have suffered the gruesome fate you have all this time been plotting for us all. The noble high priest, Publius Scipio, though he held no magisterial position, slew Tiberius Gracchus for tampering slightly with the constitution. Shall we, consuls, tolerate Catiline, whose aim is to destroy the entire world by fire and sword? I only mention Gaius Servilius Ahala, who killed with his own hand the revolutionist, Spurius Maelius, since that story belongs too far back. But long ago there was valor in this republic, when brave men punished a vicious citizen more sternly than a ferocious enemy. We have a serious resolution of the Senate that applies to you, Catiline! Rome does not lack the Senate's pertinent judgment. It is we, we only—I say it publicly—we, the consuls, who are failing her.

The Senate at one time decreed that the consul, Lucius Opimius, should take steps for the protection of the state. Not a night passed before Gaius Gracchus was dead, a scion of a noble family who was merely suspected of sedition. On the same occasion an ex-consul, Marcus Fulvius, with all his children was executed. By a similar decree of the Senate the republic's safety was entrusted to the consuls Gaius Marius and Lucius Valerius. Before the day closed, a tribune, Lucius Saturninus, and a praetor, Gaius Servilius, had felt the vengeance of the state in death. Yet we for twenty days have let the sharp sword, put into our hands by the authority of the Senate, grow blunt. For we possess just such a senatorial decree, but we keep it shut up in a book, like a sword concealed in its sheath. By the terms of this decree, Catiline, you should have been put to death at once. But still you live, and as long as you live your audacity grows instead of diminishing.

I should like, senators, to be lenient. But I would not appear indifferent to the dangers threatening the state, and I do now pronounce myself guilty of weakness and negligence. In the passes of Italian Etruria there is now an armed camp of men menacing Rome. The number of the enemy increases day by day. Yet the commander of this camp, the leader of the enemy, is to be seen in our city, actually in the Senate, plotting daily new destruction for the life center of the state. Even if, Catiline, I should this moment order your arrest and execution, I should, I believe, have still to fear that all loyal citizens would accuse me of sloth rather than of cruelty.

But though the step should have been taken long ago, I have had sound reason for postponing it. You will be put to death, but not until even a creature as base as yourself cannot deny that the punishment was merited. You will live as long as anyone dare to defend you. But you will continue to live as now, surrounded by my guards, who will keep you from any action against the republic. Without your knowledge, many eyes and ears will be observing and watching you, as they have been doing until now.

What, henceforth, can you expect, Catiline, if neither the darkness of night can hide your sinister assemblages, nor a private house hold secret within its walls your subversive conversations—if everything has broken out into the open? Repent of your purpose! Believe me! Forget your plots of murder and arson! On every side you are surrounded.

All your plans are clear to us as day. Let us here together recollect them. Do you remember my saying in the Senate, on October 21st, that your slavish imitator in recklessness, G. Manlius, would be up in arms by October 27th? Was I mistaken, Catiline, either in the event, shocking and unbelievable as it was, or, what is far more remarkable, in the day? I said also in the Senate that you had planned a massacre of the aristocracy on October 28th, and many leading citizens left Rome, not so much to protect themselves as to thwart your designs. Can you deny that on that day you were so closely encircled by my vigilant guards that you could carry out no attack on the state? That was the time you remarked that you would be satisfied with the flight of some senators and the slaughter of those who stayed behind. Again, you confidently expected to seize Praeneste by a night assault on November 1st, but you found that town by my orders heavily guarded and fortified. Whatever you do or devise or even contemplate doing I not only hear reported but actually behold for myself with my own eyes.

Let us, finally, recall last night's events and you will realize that the watch I keep over the safety of the republic is keener than any anxiety of yours for its destruction. You went last night, I say, into the scythedealers' street—more specifically to the house of Marcus Laeca, where many of your accomplices in this insane scheme had already assembled. Do you dare deny this? Why no word? If you should deny it, I can prove it, for I see here in the Senate some of the men who were there with you.

Immortal gods, what has happened to our people, our constitution, our city? Here in our very midst, senators, in this august and dignified assembly, are some who plot the death and the destruction not only of this city but of the whole world. I, the consul, see them; I request their opinions on questions of policy. Not even verbally do I attack those whom I should be exterminating by the sword. It is true, Catiline, that you were at Laeca's house last night and assigned a region of Italy to each of your band. You chose whom you would leave at Rome and whom you would take with you. You designated sections of the city for burning. You announced your intention to leave the city at once and said that only the fact that I was still alive was detaining you. Two Roman knights, eager to relieve you of this anxiety, promised to murder me in my bed before the next day. All this I had heard almost before your meeting broke up. I therefore posted an even stronger guard around my house. In the morning I refused to admit the visitors sent by you. I had, incidentally, foretold the time of their arrival and their names to a number of prominent men.

This being the situation, Catiline, depart! Now, at last, leave the city; the gates stand open; begone! Manlius and his camp await their leader's arrival only too anxiously. And take with you all your friends, or at least as many as you can! Cleanse the city of your presence! You will free me from a great dread when once the wall separates you and me. Your presence among us is no longer permissible; indeed I will not endure it. We owe our heartfelt thanks to the immortal gods, and to Jupiter Stator, the protector of this city from its earliest days, in that we have so many times been delivered from your insidious venom, so horrible, and so deadly to the republic. But the safety of the commonwealth must not be jeopardized too often by one man.

As long, Catiline, as I was still only a consul elect, I defended myself from your plots against me not by a public guard but by my own precautions. When I was actually consul and you tried to murder me and your competitors at the last election in the Campus Martius, I foiled your wicked efforts with my friends' assistance and resources, without creating any public disturbance. As often, in short, as you attacked me, I privately opposed you, and this I did even though convinced that my downfall would mean a grave disaster to the state. Now, however, you are openly aiming your assaults at the whole structure of the republic.

You propose to destroy the temples of the immortal gods, the city of Rome and its citizens, and all Italy. I do not yet dare to take the soundest course, the one dictated by my duty as a magistrate and by the traditions of our ancestors. I will, however, do what is more merciful, and also more expedient for the state. If I ordered your death, all the other conspirators would still be here, living in the republic; but if you leave us, as I have long been urging you to do, your companions, those worthless dregs of our society, will be drawn off from the city with you. What then detains you, Catiline? Why hesitate to do at my behest what you were about to do of your own accord? I, the consul, order the enemy to depart from the city. Do you ask whether you are to go into exile? I do not order that, but if you ask me, I advise it.

For what pleasure can it be to you, Catiline, to stay any longer in this city? Save for the low-lived members of your conspiracy, everyone fears and hates you. Is not your private life polluted with every conceivable stain? Are not your domestic affairs branded with disgraceful scandals? Is there any kind of crime which you have not witnessed or in which you have not participated? Is there a youth caught in your unsavory snares whom you have not encouraged in a career of violence and licentiousness?

Only recently, as soon as your first wife died, you got ready for a new wedding, thus adding another wrong to an old injury. But I pass over that episode and willingly consign it to oblivion, that no one may know that such a crime was ever committed and went unpunished. I pass over the financial ruin which will certainly overwhelm you by the middle of next month. I come to things that have nothing to do with your private vices, your personal difficulties, or your individual debasement, things that affect the life and welfare of the state and all of us.

How can you, Catiline, enjoy the light and the air of this city, when you know that every man here is aware of the fact that you came armed into the assembly, the last day of last year, while Lepidus and Tullus were consuls? We all know

that you had a gang collected to murder the consuls and lead
ing citizens, and that it was neither fear nor compassion on
your part, but only our own good fortune which prevented
that mad crime. Other incidents, to which I shall only allude,
are also, all of them, common knowledge. Many a time have
you tried to assassinate me, both as consul elect and as consul.
Many a time have I eluded your seemingly imminent attack,
one might say, by a mere hairbreadth. In your attempts you
never succeed, yet you do not stop trying! Many a time has
the dagger been wrenched from your hand, and many a time
has it slipped by an accident and dropped. Yet not for a single day can you go without it. By what sacred rites was that
dagger consecrated that you think you must bury it in a consul's body?

Look now at the life you lead! For I will speak to you not
with the loathing you deserve, but with the pity you do not
deserve. When you, a few moments ago, entered the Senate,
did anyone in all this vast assembly, did even your friends and
relatives greet you? Never has such a thing happened to anyone before; so why wait for the spoken insult, when already
you are condemned by the verdict of silence? How could you
bear seeing men leave their seats at your approach, seeing the
ex-consuls, whom you had often marked for death, rise from
their places when you sat down? If my slaves were as terrified
of me as all your fellow citizens are of you, I should quit my
house. Will you not quit this city? If I felt that my fellow
citizens suspected and hated me, even unjustly, I would rather
relieve them of my presence than subject myself to their hostile glances. Being conscious of your offenses, you must realize
that this animosity is justified, but you do not hesitate to come
face to face with men whose sensibilities are outraged if they
even think of you.

If your parents feared and detested you and you could not

possibly placate them, you would, I think, remove yourself from their sight. Now, your country, the common mother of us all, detests and fears you, since she believes you have long been plotting her death. Will you not respect her authority, accept her verdict, dread her power? Imagine, Catiline, that she pleads with you in words like these. For many years no crime or atrocity has been committed but by you. You alone have planned with impunity the murder of many citizens and the plunder of our allies. You alone have had the power not only to violate all laws and disregard all investigations, but to undermine their authority and annul them. Your earlier conduct, intolerable as it was, I bore as I could, but now I can no longer endure this constant dread of you alone, this terror that every sound may mean you are near. Whatever plots are devised against me I see originate with you. Depart, therefore, and rid me of this fear, so that, if it be justified, I shall not sink under your oppression, and if it be groundless, I shall at long last cease to fear.

If, as I say, your country should thus address you, ought she not to be heeded, even though unprepared to use force? It is true that you offered yourself for internment. You said that, to clear yourself of suspicion, you would live with Marcus Lepidus. And when he would not receive you, you dared to come to me, begging me to protect you in my house. I gave you the same answer, that under no circumstances could you and I live inside the walls of the same house, for I believed myself in peril as long as you were inside the walls of the same city. Then you went to the praetor, Quintus Metellus, and when he refused your petition, you turned to your own associate, the noble Marcus Marcellus, who, I presume you thought, would be a proper person to keep watch over you, handle you with suspicion, and report on your misconduct! But is any man who considers himself fit for internment very far from actual prison?

Since under these circumstances, Catiline, you cannot remain here in peace, why hesitate to go abroad, escaping thereby from deserved punishment, and finding safety in solitude as an exile? You ask me to put the question to formal vote in the Senate, and if this body approves your banishment, you say you will obey. I will not do this; it is against my principles. But I will make plain to you what these men think. Leave the city, Catiline! Deliver the republic from her fear! Go into exile—if that is the word you are waiting to hear! Now observe their silence! They acquiesce; they say nothing. Why wait for words, when their silence is proof of their attitude?

If I had spoken in this way, in this temple, to young Publius Sestius, or to brave Marcus Marcellus, the Senate would have violently disapproved my behavior as consul, and justly so. But with you, Catiline, their acquiescence means approval, their sufferance accusation; their silence a shout. And this is true not only of the senators, whose authority is so dear to you, cheap as you may hold their lives, but also of the honorable Roman knights, and other noble citizens now surrounding the senate house. A moment ago you could see their numbers, feel their wishes, hear the sound of their voices. For some time past I have with difficulty kept their hands and their swords away from you, but I can easily persuade them to accompany you to the gates, when you leave the city you have so long been working to destroy.

Yet, why trouble to say all this, when nothing will shake your purpose? Will you ever regain your senses or consider flight or exile? I wish the gods would grant you change of heart! And if my words should frighten you and you resolve on exile, I can imagine the storm of unpopularity that would threaten me, probably not immediately, while the memory of your crimes is still vivid, but some time in the future. But it is worth risking a personal misfortune, provided that through it the state is freed from danger. But we cannot expect you to feel remorse for your evil deeds, or fear of the law's penalties, or inclination to sacrifice yourself to the republic's necessities. For you are not the kind of man, Catiline, who is ashamed of infamy, or terrified of danger, or deterred by reason from lunacy.

So begone, as I have already said, and if, as you consider me your enemy, you wish to make me unpopular, go directly into exile. For scarcely shall I be able to endure the storm of criticism and disapproval I shall meet, if you go alone into exile at the consul's command. But if, on the contrary, you prefer to enhance my good reputation, go escorted by your vile crowd of scoundrels; go to Manlius. Call up your wicked citizens: separate them from the good. Wage a war against your country; exult in your lawless banditry. Then it will become obvious that I have not driven you away to strangers, but that you have gone on invitation to join your friends.

But why should I be exhorting you, when I know you have already despatched an armed guard to wait for you at the Forum Aurelium; when I know you and Manlius have already fixed on a day; when I know you have sent ahead the silver eagle standard which you worshiped sacrilegiously in your house, and which I trust will be a sign of disaster and death to you and your companions. How can you live any longer without the symbol you used to worship when setting out to murder, at whose altar you often wet your hand on your way to kill your fellow citizens?

In the end you will follow the course down which your unbridled, insane ambition has long been propelling you. And to you this is no cause for grief but for incredible satisfaction. You were born for folly like this, trained for it by lawless behavior, and preserved for it by sheer luck. You always abhorred peace: yet the only wars you desired were criminal ones. You have recruited a gang of rascals from men who had lost both fortune and hope.

Indeed you must be rejoicing, exultant and glad, for henceforth you will neither hear nor see one honest man in all your throng of friends. Your various activities have been preparing you for this kind of life. You have lain on the ground both to satisfy your licentious desires and to plot opportunities for crime. You have kept awake both to take advantage of sleeping husbands and to grab the goods of slumbering citizens. Now you will have occasion to display your heroic endurance of hunger, cold, and lack of all necessities, which will shortly put an end to you, as you will discover. I had this all in mind when I prevented your election as consul. Now you lead the attack on your country as an exile instead of as its consul, and your treasonous uprising can be called brigandage instead of civil war.

I wish next to answer an apparently justifiable accusation that our country may bring against me, and urge you, senators, to listen closely to what I am about to say, and take it well to heart. For our country, which is far dearer to me than life, all Italy, and the whole Roman state, may thus address me, "What do you now, Cicero? Are you permitting a known enemy to escape, one who intends to lead a war against me, whom the camp of my adversaries awaits as its general, the author and head of the conspiracy, who has summoned slaves and lowborn citizens to rebellion? This way you appear to be driving him not out of the city but against it. Why not give the order to throw him into prison, to administer the extreme penalty of death?

"What, pray, stands in your way? Is it tradition? Many a time in this republic has a private individual punished a dangerous fellow citizen with death. Are you by any chance in awe of the laws that govern the condemnation of Roman citizens? But in this city traitors have never enjoyed the prerogatives of Roman citizens. Do you dread the adverse judgment of posterity? You show little gratitude to the people of Rome, who have admitted you, a self-made man, to a public career, and raised you so early to the highest office, if for fear of unpopularity or any other unpleasantness you fail to ensure their safety. If you do fear unpopularity, fear the unpopularity that results from weakness and impotence more than that which follows on austerity and courage. When Italy has been laid waste by war, when its cities are besieged and its houses in flames, you will then be consumed in a perfect conflagration of hatred."

To this just appeal of the republic, and to men of the same opinion, I reply briefly: "Senators, if it had seemed to me wisest to have Catiline punished by death, I should not have granted that ruffian a single day of grace. If noble and illustrious citizens were not defiled, but rather glorified, by shedding the blood of Saturninus, of the Gracchi, of Flaccus, and of many before them, I, on my part, should not fear that the future would condemn me if I were responsible for the death of this butcher of his fellow countrymen. Even though I should meet with disapproval, I have always held that unpopularity earned by an act of courage is glory, not unpopularity.

"There are, however, some among us who either do not see our danger or pretend not to see it. By their soft-heartedness they have encouraged Catiline to hope, and have strengthened the rising conspiracy by not believing in it. The attitude of these men, if I should have Catiline executed, might influence the dishonest or the uninformed among our people to call my action brutal and tyrannical. But if he should appear as planned at the camp of Manlius, I know that no one, however stupid, can fail to recognize the existence of the conspiracy and no one, however dishonest, can refuse to admit it. I also know that if only Catiline were put to death, this disease of the state would be merely checked for the time being, not totally eradicated. But if he takes both himself and his friends away, gathering all these desperate characters, then their rampant poisonous growth will be exterminated entirely and with it the root and seed of all future evils.

"We have been living, senators, a long time in this atmosphere of danger and conspiracy, but in some way during my consulship what were merely old differences have turned into acts of criminal recklessness. If only Catiline is now removed and the gang left intact, we shall possibly enjoy a brief respite from fear and anxiety, but the peril will remain deep hidden in the veins and heart of the republic. As often happens with men who are miserably ill and shaken by fever, a drink of cold water seems at first to relieve them, but afterwards they suffer a sharp relapse. So this disease in the body of the republic may be alleviated by the punishment of a single man, but later it will recur in severer form, as long as the rest still live.

"So, let the scoundrels go, senators; let them join each other in their place of meeting and thus dissociate themselves from all good citizens; let the walls of our city, as I have said often, separate them and us! Let them cease plotting against a consul in his own house, surrounding the tribunal of the city praetor, invading the Senate with swords, preparing brands and torches to burn the city! Let every citizen's sentiments toward the republic be written briefly on his forehead! I promise you, senators, that we consuls will be so watchful, your authority so strong, the knights so loyal, the whole population so united in spirit, that when once Catiline has departed, you will see the whole conspiracy laid bare and defeated."

Go forth, then, Catiline, to your profane and wicked war! To the republic may it bring safety, to you and your comrades in evil, death and destruction! Thou, Jupiter, whose worship was founded by Romulus and the founding of the city and whom we rightly call the protector of our Rome and of her empire, protect from him and his followers thy sanctuaries, the houses and walls of the city, the lives and fortunes of all her citizens! Chastise with everlasting punishment both in this life and in the life to come all enemies of good men, traitors to the republic, plunderers of Italy, associates in their bonds of crime and villainy!

LETTERS ON HIS CONSULSHIP AND EXILE

While Cicero as consul was protecting the Roman republic from the revolutionary designs of the Catilinarians, Pompey was earning his title of the Great by reestablishing the power of Rome in the East and conquering new provinces. It was natural, therefore, that Cicero should anxiously seek the approval and commendation of so important a personage. The first of the letters translated below he wrote in the hope of eliciting from Pompey some expression of praise for his achievement.

At the end of the year 62 B.C. Pompey returned to Italy with his victorious army, having not yet committed himself to any attitude with regard to politics at home. However, he relieved much of the tension in Rome by discharging his troops at Brindisi. As a consequence, Cicero's friend, the staunch republican Cato, was emboldened to deliver a long speech in honor of Cicero at the first session of the Senate which Pompey attended after he reached Rome. The chief effect of this, however, on Pompey, who had expected to be celebrated himself, was to embitter him toward Cato, and not to increase his liking for Cicero. Nevertheless, he maintained outwardly amiable relations with Cicero during the following years. Cicero's letter to Atticus, written in 60 B.C.—Letter II below—shows the two making common cause in their opposition to Caesar.

Cicero's friend Atticus was away at the time, attending to his large business interests in Greece, and this letter was intended to bring him up to date on events at Rome. Cicero had become intimate with him during their student days in Athens, before he himself went on to study under other teachers in Asia Minor and Rhodes. Atticus had chosen to remain behind in Athens, where his long residence in the city had eventually procured him an honorary citizenship and the name by which he is still best known. The confidential nature of the letter is indicated both by the reference to Clodius Pulcher and by the frank discussion of the whole political situation at Rome. Clodius, brother of the notorious Clodia, had been the main figure in a social scandal two years earlier, in which no less a person than Caesar's wife had been involved.[1] Cicero had exploded Clodius' alibi of having been absent at Interamna by testifying that he had seen him in Rome on the very day in question, and had won thereby Clodius' undying enmity.

Cicero's exultation over his success in crushing Catiline's conspiracy and exposing Clodius was not long lived. When Clodius was elected tribune for the year 58, Cicero knew that his enemy might take advantage of his new position to attack him. He relied, however, on promises of support that he was able to secure from both Pompey and Caesar. But shortly after Clodius took office, he announced his intention of enforcing the old law that condemned to exile anyone responsible for the execution of a Roman citizen without the approval of the assembly. Five years before, when the sentence to be imposed on Catiline's partisans had been discussed in the Senate, Caesar, it may be remembered,[2] had called attention to the existence of this law, of which Cicero too was well aware.

Cicero's name was not now mentioned by Clodius, but everyone knew the target at which he aimed. Caesar, impatient to leave for his campaign in Gaul, professed himself in-

---

[1] On this affair, see the introduction to the speech in defense of Marcus Caelius, and passages in the speech itself. Below, pp. 157–197.
[2] See above, p. 100.

different in the matter. Pompey, with whom Cicero pleaded, replied that as a private citizen he could do nothing. Clodius, in a meeting of the assembly, called on the leading magistrates to express their views of Cicero's treatment of the Catilinarians. The consuls virtuously stated their strong disapproval of cruelty, especially of the illegal execution of Roman citizens, and Caesar once more evaded the issue by referring simply to his speech in the Senate, in December, 63. Clodius and his clique were in complete control and Cicero thought it wise to leave the city without more delay. After his departure, Clodius procured the passage of the edict pronouncing Cicero an exile and his property confiscated. A later provision extended the bounds of his exile beyond the five hundred mile zone, thus leaving him only the East as a place of residence.

The seventeen months of his banishment Cicero spent partly in the free city of Durazzo, on the east coast of the Adriatic, and partly in Salonika on the Aegean, under the protection of the Roman magistrate there (see Letter III, below). During the closing months of 58, attempts were made by his friends at home to have him recalled, but it took the better part of the following year and a new set of magistrates to get the question put to a vote. The majority then was overwhelmingly in favor of his return and the restoration of his property. It was, however, Pompey's influence and Caesar's tacit consent that actually secured his recall, even as Pompey's earlier indifference and Caesar's tacit acquiescence had permitted his exile.

The welcome that Cicero received on his return was not so extravagant as he had expected. In the opinion of many leading Romans he should never have been exiled, but they looked on his recall as simply the correction of an unfortunate error and not as an occasion for noisy fanfares. Cicero, on the other hand, saw himself both as the heroic savior of his country and a martyr for her sake, and was disappointed when neither he nor his views on all subjects were treated with any particular deference. It was therefore not surprising that his mind at this time tended to turn back and dwell on the period of his most redoubtable achievement, and that he even worked on an epic poem describing his own life. Letter IV was written to his friend Lucceius in the summer of 56, during a brief recess of the Senate which he was spending at his villa at Anzio. In reading it one should remember that Lucceius was an old and intimate friend, on whom Cicero felt he could count to sympathize with his opinions and to accede to his rather immodest request. There is evidence that Lucceius did agree to do what Cicero asked of him and that Cicero sent him his diaries, but so far as we know the promised history was never written.

Letter V, to Marius, gives a vivid and interesting account of the stage performances celebrating the opening of Pompey's theater in Rome. It likewise shows clearly that Cicero attended the costly show with little enthusiasm, and probably only to avoid offending Pompey, to whom he still apparently felt under some obligation.

It seems clear that Cicero never intended his letters for general circulation, for he took no pains to edit them, as he did many of his speeches. All the more authentic, therefore, is the picture they present of his thoughts and feelings and the intimate events of his life. The letters to his great friend Atticus were kept in the possession of Atticus' family until long after both Cicero and Atticus were dead and most of the other persons mentioned had passed from the scene. They were finally published during the lifetime of the philosopher Seneca, about the year 60, when a renewed interest in the last days of the republic made them seem peculiarly valuable as sources for the history of the period. The large collection of letters to relatives and acquaintances, known as the *Epistulae ad Famil-*

iares, owes its existence to the untiring efforts of Cicero's secretary and former slave, Tiro, who had access to Cicero's files, containing copies of many important letters, and was able to retrieve others from the recipients. All these Tiro must have assembled and published before the end of the century, when he died.

With the fall of the Roman Empire and the coming of an age indifferent to pagan history, the manuscripts of Cicero's letters and orations ceased to be copied or even preserved. When the Middle Ages revived the interest in antiquity, it was only Cicero's moral and philosophical essays, from which St. Augustine had quoted, that were read and admired by a few learned scholars. It took the men of the Renaissance, with their passion for literary form and style, to grow enthusiastic over Cicero and by hard search bring to light a handful of battered manuscripts of the letters and speeches. Petrarch's discovery, in 1345, of a copy of the letters to Atticus at Verona he heralded as the greatest triumph of his scholarly career. Besides these letters, he found also copies of the speeches against Verres and against Catiline, the defense of Archias, and the Philippics. A century later, practically the whole body of Cicero's writings in the form that we have them at present had been assembled from their obscure hiding places, scattered over Europe, ready for the new printing presses to turn into books that would not be forgotten or disappear again.

LETTERS ON HIS CONSULSHIP
AND EXILE

Letter One

To Pompey the Great In Asia

[Ad Familiares, V, 7]

Rome, 62 B.C.

IF YOU and the army are well, good! I too am well. I and everyone else have derived more satisfaction from your dispatch
than you would believe possible. For you held out hope of a
peace, such as I, in my complete reliance on you, had long
been promising them all. But you should realize that your former enemies, who now claim to be your friends, are badly
upset by that dispatch. They have lost their high hopes and
are at present much depressed.

Your private letter to me gave but slight indication of regard
for me; still, I assure you, it pleased me. For in general it
affords me the greatest pleasure to realize that I have been of
service to someone else. If the favor is not returned in like
degree, I am quite content to have the balance of friendliness
on my side. And even if my strenuous exertions on your behalf
have not yet quite won you over, I have not the slightest
doubt but that the interests of the state will forge a link between us. In case you may not understand what I missed in
your letter, I will tell you, with the frankness demanded by
my own disposition and by our association together.

Because of the ties between us, I did expect in your letter
some congratulations on my achievements, on the ground of
their importance to the republic. However, I assume you
omitted any such remarks for fear of offending somebody. But,
let me tell you, the world has judged and approved of what I

did to save our country. And after you come home, you too will recognize the wisdom and disinterestedness of my conduct. You are a far greater man than Africanus,[1] but you then will be glad to be my friend and join me in the framing of public policy, for I am not much inferior to Laelius! [2]

Letter Two
To Atticus [3] in Greece
[Ad Atticum, II, 1]

Rome, June, 60 B.C.

ON JUNE FIRST, while on my way to Anzio, happy to leave behind me Marcus Metellus' gladiatorial shows, I met your boy. He handed me a letter from you, together with your pamphlet on my consulship, written in Greek. I am glad that, shortly before, I had already given my own Greek version of the matter to Lucius Cossinius for you. If I had seen yours first, you might accuse me of plagiarism.

But I read your essay with pleasure. It seemed to me rather unpolished and simple; yet the deliberate avoidance of ornament was ornament in itself, just as the women who use no perfume seem the sweetest scented. My book, on the other hand, exhausted the whole perfume bottle of Isocrates [4] and all the rouge boxes of his pupils, to say nothing of Aristotle's colors. You say, in another letter, that you glanced at it briefly in Corcyra, after you had received it from Cossinius, I suppose.

---

[1] Scipio Africanus, the Younger.
[2] Gaius Laelius, the friend of the younger Scipio; both are speakers in Cicero's *Republic*.
[3] Titus Pomponius Atticus (109–32), Cicero's friend from youth, was a Roman scholar, chronologer, and bookseller, who spent much time in Greece. To him Cicero wrote many of his most confidential letters.
[4] Isocrates (436–338 B.C.) was an Athenian orator and teacher.

I should not have dared send it to you without revising it deliberately and carefully. One copy of my memoir I sent too to Posidonius,[5] hoping it would inspire him to write something more elegant on the subject. But he has just written from Rhodes that reading my work has not stirred him to write, but rather frightened him off. What do you think of that? I have embarrassed all the Greeks. Well, I am no longer bothered by people forever insisting that I give them something of mine to polish off. If you do approve of my book, please see that there are copies in Athens and other Greek towns, for possibly it may add some luster to my achievements.

I shall send you the little speeches for which you ask, and more besides, seeing that you like to show my writings to your youthful admirers. Your fellow citizen Demosthenes gained his reputation by the speeches called *Philippics*, in which he avoided the ambiguous type of oratory, common in law courts, in order to prove himself a determined politician. So it seems to me proper that I too should make some speeches that might be called truly consular. The first was delivered in the Senate, January first, the second, to the people on the agrarian law, the third, on Otho, the fourth, in defense of Rabirius, the fifth, on the sons of proscribed citizens, the sixth, in the Assembly, when I refused a province, the seventh, when I drove out Catiline, the eighth, to the people on the day after Catiline fled, the ninth, in the Assembly, on the day the Allobroges served as informers, the tenth, in the Senate, on December fifth. There are, in addition, two short ones on the agrarian law, mere fragments. I shall see that you have the whole collection, and inasmuch as you are pleased to approve both my writings and my achievements, you will learn from these just what I have done and what I have written.

---

5 Posidonius was the Stoic philosopher under whom Cicero had studied at Rhodes. Later he came to Rome and lived with Cicero.

Otherwise you should not have asked for them! I had no intention of inflicting myself on you.

You ask why I am telling you to come home; at the same time you imply that business is keeping you away. Yet you do not refuse to come, if it is necessary, or even if I wish it. Well, there is no absolute necessity, but it seems to me that you might plan your periods of wandering more agreeably. You are away too long, especially as you are in another country, where I cannot enjoy your company nor you mine.

Just now things are quiet, but if little Pulcher [Clodius] succeeds in behaving any wilder, I shall certainly send for you. However, for the present Metellus [6] is valiantly keeping him in bounds and will continue to do so. He is a patriotic consul, and, as I always thought, by nature a fine man. Clodius Pulcher, however, is not hiding his desire to be elected tribune of the people. When the subject was discussed in the Senate, I crashed down on him, accusing him of fickleness. Now in Rome, I said, he was trying for the tribuneship, whereas in Sicily he had always said he wanted only his inheritance. I added that we need not be too anxious, for a plebeian would not be allowed to ruin the country any more than patricians of his sort had been allowed to do so in my consulship. Then he bragged in the Assembly how he had come up from the straits [of Messina] in a week, and explained that no one could have gone to meet him, since he had entered the city at night. I replied that this was nothing new. "You came from Sicily to Rome in seven days? Once you went from Rome to Interamna in three hours. You came in at night? You did that before. No one went to meet you now? Nor did they before, when they should have done so." In short, I am dressing down that upstart both by serious speeches and in repartee of this kind.

---

[6] This is Quintus Metellus Celer, Cicero's friend, of whose death in the following year he speaks in his defense of Caelius, below, pp. 175, 188.

So now I jest and joke with Clodius quite familiarly. For instance, while we were escorting one of the candidates, he asked me if I used to get seats for Sicilians at the gladiatorial shows. I said, "No." "Well," he said, "as their new patron I intend to start the practice; but my sister, who as the consul's wife has so much space, will give me only standing room." "Don't complain about standing room at your sister's," I replied. "You can always lie with her." [7] You will say this was not a suitable remark for an ex-consul to make. I confess it was not, but I hate that woman, so unworthy of being a consul's wife. For she is quarrelsome, and fights with her husband, and not only with Metellus but with Fabius, because she is annoyed at their interference in her affairs.

You ask about the agrarian law. Interest in it seems to have cooled down. You reproach me, though gently, for my intimacy with Pompey. I should not want you to think I joined forces with him just to save myself, but things have reached such a pass that inevitably there would have been trouble in the state if we two had kept on disagreeing. And I took my precautions and made my plans, without changing my own thoroughly conservative policy, so as to influence him to become more conservative and less swayed by popular whims. He now speaks, let me tell you, more enthusiastically of my accomplishments than of his own, even though many have tried to set him against me. He says he glorified the state, but I saved it. What good this will ever do me, I do not know, but the state will certainly profit. Should I be hurting it if I could make a patriot out of Caesar, who now has everything his own way? Even when no one envied me and all were on my side, as they ought to have been, even then a treatment that healed

[7] The ill-famed Clodia, sister of Clodius, was at this time wife of the consul, Quintus Metellus Celer. Cicero's coarse jest refers to the relations rumored to exist between her and her brother. See below, p. 159.

with medicine the diseased portion of the state seemed preferable to amputation.

As it is, the Senate is now deserted by the equestrian order, which I once stationed on the Capitoline Hill, with you as its standard-bearer and leader. Our foremost citizens have abandoned all serious pursuits, and think they are on the edge of paradise if they have bearded mullet in their fish-ponds to eat from their hands. Do you not think I have accomplished something if I persuade those who have the power to make mischief not to make it?

I am quite as devoted to Cato [8] as you are, but, with the best intentions and in all good faith, he sometimes does the country harm, for he talks as if he were a character in Plato's *Republic*, and not just one among the rabble that followed Romulus. Unquestionably it is right to try a man who has accepted a bribe for a legal decision. So Cato voted for that, and the Senate agreed. Consequently the knightly order has declared war on the Senate, though not on me, for I voted against it. It is certainly effrontery for tax collectors not to carry out their contracts! Yet we ought to have stood the loss for the sake of keeping their good will. But Cato was adamant and won out. So now, with one consul in prison and riots occurring often, no help is coming from any of the men who used to assist me and the consuls who came after me to defend the state. "Must we then buy their loyalty?" you will ask. What else can we do? Shall we be slaves to freedmen, and even to slaves themselves? But, as you say, enough of serious business!

Favonius got more votes in my tribe than in his own; he lost out in Lucceius' tribe. His attack on Nasica did him no

---

[8] This is Cato the Younger mentioned in the introduction to this section. Cato's devotion to the republic was unquestioned; he committed suicide in 46 on hearing of Caesar's triumph.

credit, although he was moderate about it. But he spoke so badly that it sounded as if he had ground harder in the mills at Rhodes than in Molo's classroom.[9] He was inclined to be irritated with me because I appeared for the defense. However, he is now making up to me again for political reasons. I shall send you word how Lucceius is getting on as soon as I have seen Caesar, who will be here in a couple of days. You blame Cato and his imitator Servilius for your ill-treatment by the Sicyonians. But did not the same kind of blow fall on many other good citizens? Since such is the Senate's decision let us defer to it, and not stand out in a minority of one.

My Amalthea [10] is looking and longing for you. I enjoy my properties at Tusculum and at Pompeii very much, except that they overwhelm me, the prosecutor of debtors, not with Corinthian bronzes but with debts in the bronze coins of the Forum. We hope that all is peaceful in Gaul. Expect my *Prognostica* soon, along with some of my briefer speeches. And write me about your plans for coming. Pomponia has sent me word that you would be in Rome in July. That does not agree with your letter to me, in which you mentioned the census list.

As I wrote you before, Paetus has given me all the books his brother left him. The gift, however, will not reach me without your help. If you love me, see to it, please, that the books are preserved and brought over to me. Nothing could give me greater pleasure. I should like the Latin books kept as well as the Greek, and I shall consider them all as virtually a present from you.

---

[9] Molo was a surname of Apollonius of Rhodes, a Greek teacher of rhetoric, under whom Cicero had studied. There is a play on words here, for the Latin word for mill is *mola*.

[10] Atticus had a villa in Epirus named for the nymph Amalthea, and possibly Cicero also had given one of his retreats this name.

I wrote to Octavius. I had not spoken to him about the matter, for I did not suppose that your business included the provinces and I did not consider you a money lender. But as long as I had to, I wrote him with great care.

Letter Three
To Terentia, Tulliola, and young Marcus Cicero in Rome
[Ad Familiares, XIV, 4]

Brindisi, April 29, 58 B.C.

YES, I do write you less often than I might, because, though I am miserable all the time, when I write you or read your letters, such grief comes over me that I cannot bear it. If only I had been less fond of life! Then I should have felt little or no sorrow at these days. However, if fortune holds out some hope of my one day recovering my position, my mistakes have not been too serious. But if this wretched condition is to last forever, I wish I might see you, my dear love, as soon as possible, and die in your arms, since neither the gods, whom you have worshiped with such pure devotion, nor men, whom I have always served, have shown us any gratitude.

I have been in Brindisi for thirteen days, staying with Marcus Laenius Flaccus, a fine man, who has thought more of my welfare than of any possible risk to his fortunes and civil status. The penalty set by that abominable law has not prevented him from fulfilling his duties as a host and a friend. I hope I may some day be in a position to show him the gratitude I shall always feel. On April 29th, I shall leave Brindisi and go on to Cyzicus, through Macedonia.

Here then am I, a ruined man, bowed down by grief! Should I ask you to join me, while you are in poor health, physically and mentally exhausted? Or should I not ask you?

129

Must I live without you? To my mind, the wisest course of action would be this: if there is any hope of my return, to encourage it and help in whatever way you can; but if, as I fear, my case is closed, to try to join me by all possible means. Be sure of one thing; so long as I have you, I shall not think myself lost.

But what will become of my little Tullia? For her future you must make plans; I have none. Whatever happens, you must look out for the poor child's reputation and see to getting her married. As for my son Cicero, I wish I had him with me always. I cannot write any more; I am in tears. I do not know what has happened to you. Do you still own anything, or have you been stripped penniless, as I fear?

You write that Piso [11] is our friend; I hope he will stay so. You should not worry about giving the slaves their freedom. In the first place, your slaves have been promised it, as fast as each one deserves it. Orpheus has been diligent so far, but hardly anyone else. If we lose all our property, the rest of the slaves will be granted the status of freedmen, provided they establish their claims. If, however, we retain our property, they will remain our slaves, with a very few exceptions. But these are minor points.

You urge me to be in good spirits and keep on hoping to regain my position. I wish that circumstances warranted such optimism. At present I am miserable, not knowing when I shall have another letter from you. Who would bring it? I should have waited for it here if the sailors had been willing, but they did not want to lose the chance of a favorable wind. For what is to come, keep your courage up, dear Terentia, as well as you can. We have lived, and our life has been glorious.

---

[11] Lucius Piso, member of a distinguished family, was Caesar's father-in-law.

My downfall was caused not by my vices but by my virtues. I committed no crime, unless I should have laid down my life when I lost my civil status. But the children wanted me to live, and I will bear everything, even though I can hardly endure it. I try to give you strength, though I have none myself.

My faithful Clodius Philetaerus had to be sent home because his eyes were troubling him. Sallustius is the best of all my servants. Pescennius is very obliging with me, and I hope he will always treat you with courtesy. Sica said he would go with me, but he has left me here at Brindisi.

Take as good care of your health as you can, and remember that I am more distressed by your unhappiness than by my own. Farewell, dear Terentia, my good and faithful wife. Farewell, my dear little daughter, and you, Cicero, on whom my last hope rests.

Letter Four
To Lucius Lucceius
[Ad Familiares, V, 12]

Anzio, April or May, 54 B.C.

WHEN in your company I have often tried to bring up this subject, but a kind of stupid modesty has held me back. Now away from you, I shall speak out boldly, for a letter does not blush. I am fired by a great ambition, which I do not consider reprehensible, that you in your writings should make my name known and famous. You have often assured me of your willingness to do this; hence I trust you will forgive my impatience. The style of your writing has always led me to expect great things, but your work has surpassed even my expectation.

Now, I am so thrilled and delighted by it that I want you to record my deeds as soon as possible. Of course the hope of being remembered in future times impels me to snatch at this prospect of immortality. But I am even more eager to enjoy during my lifetime your authoritative judgment, the proof of your good will, the charm of your talent.

While writing this, I have not forgotten the weighty tasks you have already undertaken and accomplished in part. But I observe that your *History of the Italian and Civil Wars* is almost finished; you yourself have said you were beginning the last section. So I did not want to miss a chance to suggest that you might either weave my part in with the rest of your history, or else treat the civil conspiracy separately from the wars with foreign foes. The Greeks have, many of them, chosen the latter course—Callisthenes in his *Phocian War*, Timaeus in his *War Against Pyrrhus*, and Polybius in his *Numantine War*. All of them separated their accounts of the wars mentioned from their general narratives. For my part, I cannot see that it makes much difference to my reputation which you do, but it is the reason for my anxiety that you should not wait until you come to the precise point, but should immediately envisage the whole plot in its political setting. Also, if you should concentrate all your attention upon one event and one character, I can see in imagination how much fuller and more elaborate that treatment would be. I am conscious of my presumption in making so burdensome a request of you, which your previous commitments may cause you to refuse, and also, in asking you to eulogize me. What if my achievements, in your opinion, do not seem worth it?

But once a man has passed the bounds of modesty, he would better be completely shameless. So I frankly ask you, once and again, to recount my accomplishments with even more ardor than you, perhaps, feel, and to transgress the rules of historical writing to that extent. You have composed a charming introduction, showing clearly that personal partisanship has no more influence with you than sensual pleasure had with Xenophon's Heracles. But do not, please, despise partisanship, if it makes you think more favorably of me, but concede to our friendship a little more than truth alone might justify. If I can persuade you to undertake it, I am convinced you will have a subject worthy of your skill and your wealth of language.

You might, I think, write a fair-sized monograph, starting with the hatching of the conspiracy and ending with my return from exile. In such a work you might display your special understanding of civil disturbances, interpret the causes of revolutions, and propose remedies for their evils. You might criticize actions you consider blameworthy, and express your approval of others that you find commendable, explaining your reasons in each case. If you think it your duty to be outspoken, as you usually are, you will denounce the deceit, treachery, and machinations of many persons against me. My story will supply you with a wide range of topics, which, for an author, is an attractive feature, enabling you to take a strong hold on the reader's imagination. For nothing is more likely to fascinate him than the vicissitudes of circumstance and the caprices of fortune. Although I did not enjoy those events while they were taking place, I shall nonetheless enjoy reading about them; for the recollection in calm of a sorrow that is past is pleasure of a kind.

Furthermore, the rest of mankind, who have not themselves suffered from injustice, can regard the misfortunes of others with equanimity; indeed, the pity they feel is rather agreeable. Do we not enjoy recalling great Epaminondas' death at Mantinea,[12] even while we are moved by compassion? He told them finally to pull out the javelin, but only after he had heard that his shield was safe. Then, in spite of the agony of his wound, he died calmly and with glory. Whose interest is not kindled and held by reading of Themistocles' exile and return? [13] A mere chronological record of events of course has no more significance for us than an almanac; but the uncertain and fluctuating fortunes of one who is a leader of men stir in us emotions of wonder, expectation, joy, disappointment, hope, and fear. If his destiny is to succeed in the end, the reader's imagination glows with the greatest possible satisfaction.

I shall, therefore, be more pleased if you decide to separate from the main body of your narrative, which carries on the general history, this drama, so to speak, of my own activities and fortunes, the political and historical events which will furnish you with several acts and many scenes. Nor am I afraid of appearing to curry favor with you, when I say that I choose you in preference to any other writer to make my name known and famous. For undoubtedly you are conscious of your own worth; and surely you know that those who fail to admire you are only envious, and that your admirers are not insincere toadies. On the other hand, I am not so preoccupied as to wish the author of my everlasting fame to lose the renown that rightfully belongs to his genius, in the act of glorifying me.

Great Alexander did not choose Apelles to be his painter and Lysippus his sculptor in preference to all others as a favor

---

[12] Epaminondas was the valiant Greek general who for a few years made his city, Thebes, the mistress of Greece. He was killed at the battle of Mantinea, 362 B.C.

[13] Themistocles (c.525–c.460 B.C.) was the Greek statesman who made possible the victory of the Greek fleet at Salamis over the Persians. Later he was charged with treason, and went into exile. He made his way eventually into the court of his former enemies, and was received and honored by the Persian king.

to himself, but he thought their art would win as much glory for them as for him. The work of those artists, it is true, made strangers acquainted with the man's physical appearance, but even had those likenesses never existed, the man would have been no less illustrious. The Spartan Agesilaus [14] never had his portrait painted or his statue carved, but he is renowned quite as much as others who took particular pains to have these things done. For Xenophon's single pamphlet in praise of that king has accomplished more than all the portraits and statues of the rest. So your mention of me in your history will contribute more to my present peace of mind and my future glory than if other men wrote about me. I shall indeed profit by your genius, even as Timoleon [15] did by that of Timaeus, and Themistocles by that of Herodotus.[16] Of benefit to me too will be your established position as a person of high standing, recognized and respected for his own conduct of public affairs. Through you I shall acquire both the fame which Alexander, on his visit to Sigeum, declared that Homer had bestowed on Achilles, and also the weighty approval of a man of great personal distinction. I love the famous Hector of Naevius,[17] who was happy at being praised, especially by one who had been a receiver of praise himself.

---

[14] Agesilaus, king of Sparta from 399 to 361, carried on the intermittent war of Greeks against Persians, and defeated the combination of other jealous Greek cities against him. His life was written by the historian Xenophon.

[15] Timoleon (d.336), a Corinthian, went to Sicily to aid the Syracusans in their revolt against Dionysius the Younger. He did much to organize the government of the city and reestablish Greek power in the island. Timaeus (c.352–265), a Sicilian, wrote a history of the island covering these events.

[16] Herodotus (c.484–c.424), the celebrated Greek historian, recorded the events of the Persian Wars and the resistance of the Greeks.

[17] Naevius (d.204) was a Roman dramatic poet who wrote mostly on Greek themes.

Should my request be unanswered, that is, should anything prevent you from granting it—I cannot believe you would refuse me—I might be forced to write about myself. Many consider that reprehensible, yet there are numerous examples of illustrious men who have done it. But the weaknesses in this type of composition must be plain to you. In an autobiography the author is compelled to treat his own praiseworthy actions with comparative modesty and pass lightly over those that call for blame. Accordingly, his writing is less convincing and persuasive. In fact, the many who find fault with it say that the heralds at public games are more modest. For after they have crowned all the other victors and loudly shouted their names, when the time comes, before the games close, for them to receive their own garlands, they demand the help of other heralds to avoid proclaiming themselves victors.

All this I wish to avoid. If you accept my proposition, I shall avoid it; and I beg you to consent. Perhaps you will be puzzled that I now write so lengthy and labored an epistle to make this request, when you have already often intimated your intention of describing in full detail the policies and results of my consulship. But, as I said in the beginning of this letter, I am anxious for immediate action, because naturally I am impatient to have men know me through your books while I am still alive, that I, in my lifetime, may enjoy a little span of glory.

I wish—if it is not too troublesome—you would write me your plans. For if you do start on the subject, I shall collect some notes on what took place; but if you put me off to some future day, I shall talk the matter over with you first in person. Meanwhile, you will be keeping steadily at work, polishing scrupulously the writing you have already begun; with my lasting affection.

Letter Five
To Marcus Marius at Cumae
[Ad Familiares, VII, 1]

Rome, September or October, 55 B.C.

IF SOME physical pain or weakness kept you from the games, I credit that to your luck rather than to good sense. But if you were well and contemptuous of what others admire, I am happy on both counts—that you were free from pain and that you had the mental fortitude to scorn what others—inexcusably—find delightful. I only hope there was some fruit of your leisure. You should have thoroughly enjoyed it, left almost alone, as you were, in that lovely country. I am sure you were in your bedroom, with the window opened onto the Stabian bay, spending the morning hours of those days in cheerful reading, while the friends who left you there were half asleep, staring at vulgar farces. The rest of those days you passed in other congenial pleasures, while we had to put up with whatever Spurius Maecius had, I presume, approved.

If you ask me, the games were most magnificent, but not to your liking, I suspect, from my own reaction. In the first place, certain actors returned to the stage to grace the occasion, who, I thought, had left it to escape disgrace. Indeed, your favorite, my friend Aesop,[18] was so bad that everyone would thankfully have permitted him to retire. When he started to take the oath, his voice failed him at the words, "If, knowingly, I deceive."

Why describe other incidents? You know about the rest of the games. They had not even that slight touch of charm often seen in more modest performances. Merely to look at

---

[18] Clodius Aesop was a Roman tragic actor and friend of Cicero, whom Horace and others considered the equal of the great Roscius.

such gorgeousness depressed the high spirits of everybody, and I am sure you missed the show without a regret. How can anyone enjoy seeing six hundred mules in the *Clytemnestra* or three thousand craters in the *Trojan Horse*, or an infinite variety of infantry and cavalry equipment in any battle? All of this aroused the wonder of the populace, but would have given you no pleasure whatever.

If you spent those days listening to your reader Protogenes, provided he read you anything but my speeches, you were much happier than any one of us. For I do not think you regret missing the Greek and Oscan plays, especially since you can see Oscan farces in your own senate, and you dislike the Greeks to such an extent that you seldom take the Greek road, even in going to your villa. How then can I imagine you missed seeing the athletes, since you despise the gladiators? Why even Pompey himself admits that he wasted his trouble and his oil on them!

As for the rest, there were two wild beast hunts every day for five days. They were stupendous; no one denies that. But what pleasure can a cultivated man possibly derive from looking at a weak human being mangled by a powerful beast, or a splendid animal transfixed on a hunting spear? If such things are worth seeing, you have seen them often before, and I, who was a spectator, perceived nothing new in them. The last day was devoted to the elephants, which were a cause of great amazement to the crowd, but no pleasure. The result of the contests was to awaken our pity, and convince us of a definite kinship between the beast and the human species.

To keep you from thinking of me as entirely free and at ease, let me tell you that on the days of the stage performance I came near killing myself defending your friend, Gallus Caninius. But, by heaven, if my audience had been as inexpensive as Aesop's, I should positively retire from my profession to live with you and others like us. Even when my youthful ambition goaded me on, I was tired of it. But then I could refuse to take any case I did not want; and now life is hardly worth living, for I expect no reward for my labors, and I have to defend men who never did me a good turn, at the request of others to whom I am under some obligation.

So I am looking for all sorts of excuses for living eventually just as I like, and vociferously applaud and intensely approve of you and your scheme of leisure. I am not too distressed at our seeing so little of each other, because even if you were in Rome, my wearisome professional engagements would prevent us from enjoying each other's company. If I should get a respite—I do not ask for a complete release—I should teach you, who have been meditating for years on nothing else, what it means to live for culture. Only you must watch over and guard your delicate health—as you do now—so that you can visit my villas and take trips with me in my litter.

Though pressed for time, I have written you a longer letter than usual, out of my affection for you. You suggested, you may remember, in one letter that I should write you something to make you feel less sorry for having missed the games. If I have succeeded in that, I am glad. If I have failed, I console myself with the thought that henceforth you will come to the games and visit me, and will not rely on my letters as your only source of amusement.

IN DEFENSE OF ARCHIAS

From Cicero's speech in defense of Archias, one might gather that Archias was a great poet. As a matter of fact, he may have been famous in his time, but the few of his epigrams left to us seem uninspired and conventional. We do not know why his claim to Roman citizenship was challenged at this particular time (62 B.C.). We do, however, understand Cicero's interest in this Greek poet because as he himself tells us, he was expecting Archias to write a poem in honor of his victory over the Catilinarian conspirators. Archias had already written poems in praise of Marius' conquest of the Cimbri and Lucullus' defeat of King Mithridates.

Archias was born in Antioch in Asia Minor, and though at an early age he came to Rome, he continued to use the Greek language. Although by birth he was a citizen of Antioch, as marks of esteem he had received honorary citizenship from various south Italian communities, and finally, apparently at his own request, from the city of Heraclea. When, after the Social War of 90–89 B.C., all the inhabitants of Italy became eligible for Roman citizenship, as a citizen of Heraclea Archias availed himself of this right and was enrolled as a citizen of Rome as well. His Roman name, Aulus Licinius, he took in part from that of his friend and patron, Lucius Licinius Lucullus, with whose army he had spent some years in the East. Whatever may have been the reason, more than twenty years later, for challenging Archias' Roman citizenship, Cicero's defense seems to indicate clearly that the objection was ill-founded.

It is not easy to understand the exact significance of Roman citizenship for a Greek poet of Cicero's day, for the political and economic rights that went with it would ordinarily have meant little to a man of letters. It may have been that the plaintiff, Gratius, was scheming to prevent the poet either from becoming the beneficiary of a will or from legally disposing of his own property. Cicero undertook Archias' defense not only because he felt warmly toward the poet as one of his own teachers, but also because he had reasons for wishing to put him under an obligation. We do not know for certain the outcome of the trial, or whether Archias ever wrote a poem in Cicero's honor, but the indications are that he won his suit and did not pay his debt. Yet, apart from all personal motives, Cicero appears to have welcomed the opportunity to express publicly his views on poetry, not only as a literary connoisseur and enthusiastic admirer of the lyric art, but as a statesman who had but recently overcome a grave domestic crisis and whose words on all subjects, therefore, should carry special weight.

Cicero's speech for Archias is famous both for its style and its content. One cannot read the Latin without feeling that the poetry that Cicero was defending in the person of the Greek artist influenced his own choice of words and whole manner of expression, and that it is unfair to dismiss the piece as mere high-sounding declamation. The content is remarkable for its emphasis on the moral and patriotic value of serious poetry at a time when the poetry most in vogue at Rome was the frivolous and artificial Greek verse of the late Hellenistic society. The poet's inspiration, says Cicero, is divine, and poetry has its great uses in the state, both as noble entertainment for citizens and stimulating education for heroes. By recording the deeds of warriors and statesmen the poet preserves the memory of the nation's glory for the generations to come.

IN DEFENSE OF ARCHIAS

[Pro Archias]

IF, GENTLEMEN OF THE JURY, I have any talent, however slight, or any experience, as I believe I have, or if my method of oratory is based on a study of good literature—which at no period of my life have I ever neglected—certainly Aulus Licinius [1] here present should be among the first to claim the benefit of my abilities as his peculiar due. For as far as my mind can look back into the past and recall memories of my earliest youth, as far back as that, I see Archias as my chief inspirer to effort and my chief helper to a mastery of my studies. And if my voice, trained by his encouraging instruction, has ever been of service to anyone, then indeed I must, as far as lies in my power, endeavor to rescue him from whom I received the gift that has enabled me to aid and succor many others. Should anyone, perchance, be surprised at my saying this, since Archias' talents do not lie in the field of theory and practice of oratory, let me explain that I have never devoted myself exclusively to that one art. Besides, the liberal arts are all joined by a common bond, and in a manner related to one another, like members of a single family.

Some of you may think it strange that, in a formal public trial, conducted before an eminent Roman praetor and a most judicious jury, in the presence of a numerous assemblage of people, I employ this mode of speaking, unlike the ordinary usage in courts of justice, and unlike also the general style of forensic pleading. Yet in this case I beg you to permit me

---

[1] The Roman name which Archias had adopted on his admission to Roman citizenship.

to plead in a manner appropriate to the defendant, a manner which I trust you will not find disagreeable. And inasmuch as I am speaking on behalf of an eminent poet and exceedingly learned man, before this company of highly educated and cultured citizens and the praetor presiding over this trial, may I be allowed to discourse a little on the subject of good literature, and use a somewhat novel kind of oratory? For I represent a person, who, owing to his quiet and scholarly life, is hardly familiar with court procedure and its hazards. If, however, I may assume your indulgence as granted, I shall soon prevail upon you to think not only that my friend Aulus Licinius, now a citizen, should not be deprived of his citizenship, but that if he were not already a citizen, he ought immediately to be made one.

As soon as Archias outgrew childhood and advanced beyond the humanistic subjects by which young minds are usually shaped, he devoted himself to the practice of writing. Antioch, the city where he was born of a family of rank, was a famous and wealthy center of great scholars in the liberal arts. There first he rapidly outshone everyone else by the brilliancy of his talents. Later, throughout the rest of Asia [2] and all over Greece, a visit from him created so much excitement that anticipations of his personal appearance ran higher than the renown of his poetical gifts, and once he had arrived, the admiration he evoked was greater even than the eagerness with which he had been awaited.

Italy then was full of Greek art and philosophy. All over Latium at that time those subjects were cultivated with greater zeal than they are now in the same towns; and here at Rome, in the tranquil state of the republic, they were exceedingly popular. The people of Taranto, Reggio, and Naples con-

---

[2] By Asia is meant what is now known as Asia Minor.

ferred honorary citizenship and other distinctions upon him; and all men capable of appreciating his genius thought him well worth their acquaintance and hospitality.

When he came to Rome, in the consulship of Marius and Catulus, his fame had already preceded his personal appearance. At the outset he met with good fortune, for one of the consuls then in office could supply him with illustrious deeds to celebrate and the other could give him both deeds and the attention of an expert. Shortly afterward the Lucullus family, though Archias was still but a young man, received him into their household. His writing was so brilliant and his character so blameless that the house which was the first to be opened to him in his youth is also the house where he is most at home in his old age. At that time too he won the affection of Quintus Metellus,[3] the conqueror of Numidia, and of his son Pius; he frequently had Marcus Aemilius in his audience; he associated with Quintus Catulus, both father and son; he had the respect of Lucius Crassus. Ties of close friendship connected him with the families of Lucullus and Octavian, with Drusus and Cato, and the whole Hortensian clan. Everywhere he was held in great honor. His acquaintance was sought not only by those who seriously wished to learn, but also by all who pretended to feel such a desire.

Then, after a considerable interval, and after he had been to Sicily with Lucius Lucullus and returned from that province with him, he went on to Heraclea.[4] Since Heraclea was a confederate city, he wished to be enrolled as a citizen there. On his own account, he would have been thought deserving of the favor, but as it happened, he obtained it from the Heracleans through the influence and authority of Lucullus.

---

[3] Always impressed by the aristocracy, Cicero here enumerates Romans of the highest rank and achievement as sponsors for his client.
[4] Heraclea was an important seaport on the gulf of Taranto.

He later received his Roman citizenship through the law of Silvanus and Carbo, by which that citizenship was opened "to all citizens of confederate cities who had a residence in Italy at the time the law was passed, and had registered with the praetor within sixty days." By then Archias had had a residence in Rome for many years. He had registered also with the praetor, Quintus Metellus, an intimate friend of his. If we have nothing else to establish but his legal right to citizenship, I need say no more. The case is finished!

For which of these statements, Gratius,[5] can be disproved? Do you deny that Archias was, at that time, a citizen of Heraclea? A gentleman here of vast prestige, a most scrupulous and truthful person, Lucius Lucullus, declares not that he believes he was, but that he knows it; not that he heard of it, but that he saw it; not even that he was present when Archias was made citizen, but that he actually brought the event about himself. Deputies of the highest rank from Heraclea are here; they have come to this trial with a commission from their city to furnish official proof that Archias was enrolled as a Heraclean.

Do you ask now to see the public registers of the Heracleans, which we all know were destroyed in the Italian war, when the registry office was burnt? But it is preposterous to ignore the evidence we have, and call for proofs we cannot get; to disregard men's memories, and clamor for documentary evidence, when you have the solemn statement of a highly honorable man, and the oath and good faith of a respectable municipality; to reject assurances on which no one can cast a doubt and demand written statements, which, as you yourself admit, have often been falsified. Or did he not have a residence at Rome? For many years before receiving the citizenship he

---

[5] Gratius was the prosecutor of Archias.

had all his possessions assembled in Rome. Or did he not register? Indeed he registered, and in records which have the authority of a public document, being certified by the board of praetors.

To be sure the records of Appius were said to have been kept carelessly, and all confidence in them was destroyed by the irresponsible conduct of Gabinius [6] before his conviction and by his misfortune afterwards. But the scrupulously careful Metellus was so conscientious that he went to the court of the praetor Lucius Lentulus, and reported his own dismay at the erasure of one name. In these documents, however, you will find no erasure of the name of Aulus Licinius. Since this is so, what ground have you for questioning his citizenship, particularly as he was enrolled as a citizen in other cities as well?

We know that the Greeks used to confer citizenship on many ordinary individuals of little or no special talent. Then am I to believe that the peoples of Reggio, Locri, Naples, or Taranto would not have conferred on this famous genius what they were in the habit of bestowing on stage actors? Other men, after the grant of citizenship, and even after the passing of the Papian Law, wormed their way somehow or other into the registers of these municipalities. Why should he be ejected who never availed himself of those other registers in which he is enrolled, because he always wished to be known as a Heraclean?

You ask now to see our own censor's registers. No one knows, I suppose, that at the time of the last census Archias was with the army, accompanying the illustrious general, Lucius Lucullus; that when the preceding census took place he was with the same man who was then a quaestor in Asia; and

---

[6] Publius Gabinius was praetor in the year 88.

that in the census before that, when Julius and Crassus were censors, no regular count of the people was taken. Besides, the census does not establish a right to citizenship, but only indicates that whoever was counted in the census did at that time claim to be a citizen. I will add that during the time when, according to you, he never himself supposed he had any right to the privileges of a Roman citizen, he more than once made a will in accordance with our laws, and received bequests left to him by Roman citizens; he was recommended also for awards to the treasury by Lucius Lucullus in his capacity as proconsul. Search about then for other arguments, if you can; for he will never be convicted by either his own judgment of his case, or that of his friends.

You ask me, Gratius, why I am so deeply attached to my client. Because he supplies me with something to refresh my mind after the babel in the Forum, and to soothe my ears, wearied with wrangling. Do you imagine that persons like me could find material for daily speeches on so many different topics, if we did not cultivate the intellect by a study of letters? Do you suppose our spirits could endure this contention and strife, if we did not relax them by that same study? I for one confess I am devoted to these pursuits. Others may be ashamed of their occupation, if they bury themselves so deep in their books that they cannot produce anything out of them for the common good or show any tangible results. But why should I be ashamed, gentlemen, I, who for so many years have conducted my life that whenever the necessity or the welfare of a fellow man was involved I was never too engrossed in my leisure, nor too absorbed in my pleasures, nor too dulled by sleep to come to his aid? Why, then, should anyone reproach me, or who has a right to be vexed that I allow myself so much time to spend on my studies? Some spend quite as much time on their business or on holiday games, or other amusements, or on repose of their minds and bodies. Others waste time on long banquets, games of dice, and ball-playing.

I ought all the more to be permitted to follow my interests because out of them grows my skill as orator, which, small as it may be, has never yet failed my friends in time of peril. And poor as it may seem, I myself know the source from which I derive the foundation principles of it. For in early youth I was taught by my numerous teachers and my books that there was nothing in life greatly to be desired but fame and a good name, and that in quest of them all bodily pain and all perils of death and exile were to be reckoned things of slight importance. Otherwise I should never have exposed myself in defense of your safety to so many arduous struggles and day-by-day assaults of unprincipled men.

But from time immemorial, all the books and teachings of the philosophers, which are filled with this wisdom, would have lain buried in darkness, if the light of poetry had not fallen upon them. How many a picture of splendid heroes have the writers of Greece and Rome left to us to admire and imitate! They were always my models in my conduct of public affairs. The mere contemplation of the lives of these eminent men did much to form my character.

Someone will ask, "Were these great men whose virtues are recorded in books proficient in the same learning that you praise so highly?" One can hardly assert that they all were, but I can find some answer to the question. I admit that many who have become great were also humble men, without learning, but with an almost divine instinct of nature. I will even add this, that often their innate valor, without learning, contributed more to the glory of their characters than learning would have done without their natural qualities. I maintain, however, that when to an already remarkable nature a thorough formal education is added, there arises from that combination an extraordinary perfection of personality. Examples of this are the god-like Africanus,[7] whom our fathers knew in their lifetime, and Caius Laelius and Lucius Furius, both modest and unassuming men, and that doughty character, Marcus Cato the Elder, the finest scholar of his day. If these men had gained no real help from literature in their pursuit and cultivation of goodness, they would never have spent their time in the cultivation of it.

Even if the manifest fruits of this labor were not so great, and mere pleasure were the end of these studies, still I believe you would call them a worthy pastime for an educated and liberal mind. No other pleasure suits every occasion, every age, or every place. But the study of letters is the food of youth, the delight of old age, the ornament of prosperity, the refuge and comfort of adversity, a delight at home and no burden abroad; it stays with us at night, and goes with us on our travels, near and far.

And even though we ourselves should be unable to rise to these pleasures, and are insensible to the savor of them, still we ought to respect them when we see the joy of others in them. Who of us was so ignorant and so callous as not to grieve at the recent death of Roscius?[8] The man was old when he died, yet one might say he should never have died, because of the excellence and beauty of his art. He had won a great place in our affection simply by his bodily dexterity. Shall we

---

7 Scipio Africanus the Younger was both an able general and a man of unusual culture. Lucius Furius, consul in the year 135 B.C., was one of the famous circle of the Scipios. Marcus Cato the Elder, known as the Censor, was great-grandfather of the Cato who figured in the struggle against Catiline, and was renowned as a statesman and writer.
8 Quintus Roscius was the greatest Roman actor of the day. Cicero had once defended him in a lawsuit.

count as nothing the amazing dexterity of a mind, the agility of a genius?

Let me trespass again on your kindness, gentlemen, since you listen so attentively to my extraordinary plea. Many a time have I seen my friend Archias, never writing down a word, recite extempore a long series of excellent verses on events at that moment taking place. Many a time have I watched him go back and describe the same incident again, with an entire change of language and ideas. The poems he has composed with more care and thought receive, I observe, as much recognition and praise as the writings of the ancients. Why, then, should I not love and admire him? Why should I not think it my duty to defend him in every possible way?

Wise men tell us that, whereas the practice of all other arts is based on systematic instruction and acquired skills, the true poet is born a poet, supported by forces within his own soul, and inspired by a vision that is divine. So our own great poet Ennius [9] says rightly that poets are holy, being sent to us as a gift or reward from the gods. Let the name of poet be sacred to you, gentlemen, civilized as you all are, since not even barbarians have ever desecrated it! Rocks and deserts echo the human voice; savage beasts are often moved and tamed by a song. Shall we, so nobly nurtured, stop our ears to a poet's words?

The Colophonians declare that Homer was of their country; the Chians claim him as theirs; so also do the people of Salamis. The men of Smyrna protest he was a citizen of Smyrna and have dedicated a sanctuary to him in their city. Many other regions contend for the honor of being his birth-

---

[9] Quintus Ennius (239–169 B.C.), an epic and dramatic poet, and translator of Greek plays, was one of the founders of Latin literature. Only fragments of his work survive.

place.[10] These cities lay claim to a stranger, even after his death, because he was a poet. Shall we reject in his lifetime one who, by his own choice and by our laws, is our fellow citizen, especially one who has employed all his genius with utmost enthusiasm in proclaiming the glory and renown of the Roman people? While still a youth he tried his hand on a poem on our wars with the Cimbri,[11] and thereby gained the favor of Caius Marius, a man somewhat obtuse to that type of art. But even the grimmest enemy of the Muses will readily consent to have his own deeds made immortal in poetry. Themistocles, the great man of Athens, when asked what music or whose voice he liked best to hear, is said to have replied: "The voice of him who best celebrates my exploits."

Hence the great Marius was also much attached to Lucius Plotius, whose genius, he thought, would record his achievements. Plotius did indeed describe at length the Mithridatic war, great and difficult as it was, waged on land and on sea through many vicissitudes of fortune. His book celebrates also the gallant and noble Lucius Lucullus, and the Roman people as well. For the Roman people, under Lucullus as general, opened up Pontus,[12] in spite of its strong defense by the forces of the king and by the character of the country itself. A small troup of Romans under the same general routed count-

---

[10] Seven cities are said to have vied for the honor of being Homer's birthplace; in addition to those mentioned here, Rhodes, Argos, and Athens.

[11] The Cimbri, a tribe of central Europe, pushed southward in 113 B.C. into Roman territory, and with the Teutons and Gauls drove back the Roman armies until the general Marius routed and practically exterminated them in northern Italy.

[12] The kingdom of Pontus (now northern Turkey) was enlarged and made more powerful under Mithridates. At its peak it included the Crimea, parts of southern Russia, and most of the Roman possessions in Asia Minor. Although both Sulla and Lucullus won victories over Mithridates, he was not finally conquered until Pompey's defeat of him in 66.

less hosts of Armenians.[13] To the glory of the Roman people
and by the skill of the same general, the city of our friends,
the Cyzicenes,[14] was delivered and defended from all assaults
of the king, from the very jaws, as it were, of the ferocious
battle. Our amazing naval victory off Tenedos,[15] won under
Lucullus' valiant leadership, when the fleet of the enemy was
sunk and its admirals slain, will always be remembered and
praised. To us belong those trophies, to us the memorials, to
us the triumphs. And the men whose genius commemorates
these deeds make illustrious at the same time the glory of the
Roman people.

The elder Scipio Africanus loved our countryman, Ennius.
It is even thought that Ennius was carved in marble on Scipio's
family tomb. But surely his eulogies make famous not only
him for whom they were written but also the name of the
people of Rome. Cato, the ancestor of this Cato, has been
extolled to the skies. Therewith, too, high honor has been
paid to the achievements of the Roman people. Whenever
the famous names of Maximus,[16] Marcellus, and Fulvius, are
celebrated, they share their renown with all of us. For this
reason, the native of Rudiae [17] who composed those eulogies
was made a citizen by our forefathers. Shall we deprive of
citizenship this poet from Heraclea, sought after by many
cities, and already a citizen here?

Should anyone fancy that less glory will be derived from
Greek poetry than from Latin he is mistaken. For the Greek

---

[13] The king of Armenia was Mithridates' son-in-law and ally.

[14] The city of Cyzicus stood on the Asiatic side of the Sea of Marmora.

[15] Tenedos was a small island off the coast near the site of Troy.

[16] Quintus Fabius Maximus was the general to whom was given the
temporary power of dictator after Hannibal's invasion of Italy in 217.
By his delaying tactics, he is thought to have saved Rome. On Marcellus,
see above, pp. 38–39.

[17] Ennius was a native of Rudiae, in the district of Calabria.

tongue is spoken by well-nigh every nation, while Latin is confined to its own small territory. If our deeds take place all over the world, we should want our glory and our fame to penetrate as far as our armies reach. To have accomplished a task may be reward enough for the nation whose deeds are thus celebrated; but the thought of glory is a strong inducement to undergo dangers and hardships, especially for those who risk their lives in battle.

Alexander the Great, so it is reported, had many historians of his own with him; yet, when he stood on Cape Sigeum, before the tomb of Achilles, he said, "O happy youth, who had Homer as the herald of your deeds!" And he was right; for, if it were not for the *Iliad*, the same tomb would hide both Achilles' body and his fame. Our own Pompey, as fortunate as he is brave, before an assembly of his troops, conferred citizenship on Theophanes, a native of Mytilene, for his record of the general's accomplishments. And our brave soldiers, peasants though they were, loudly acclaimed the act, because they too were moved somehow by the sweet thought of glory, as if they shared in the honor.

Am I to assume, then, that if Archias were not now legally a Roman citizen, he could not contrive to obtain the citizenship from some victorious general? Am I to assume that Sulla, when bestowing it on Spaniards and Gauls, would have refused Archias, if he had asked for it? A mediocre poet in the crowd once offered Sulla a flattering epigram, with every other line a little too long; and we saw Sulla instantly present him with a gift out of the spoils he was then selling off, on condition that he would write no more. A man who thought the labors of a poet deserved some reward would certainly have done more for Archias' prolific genius and excellence. Or Archias might, at his own request or through the Luculli, have obtained the freedom of the city from his intimate friend, Quintus Metellus Pius, who conferred it on many others. Metellus was so eager to have his own deeds commemorated in literature that he gladly gave hearings even to the native poets of Cordova, who write most awkward, foreign verses.

It is a fact that cannot be concealed and should not be denied but candidly admitted, that we all are moved by a love of praise, and the best men are the most attracted by the idea of glory. The same philosophers who write books in which they urge a contempt for fame set their own names on the title page. In the very act of recording their scorn of eulogies and renown, they show their longing for such distinctions. The eminent citizen and general, Decimus Brutus, inscribed the verses of his friend Accius [18] on the gateways of the temples and monuments which he erected. And Fulvius, who took Ennius with him on his war against the Aetolians, was keen to devote the spoils of Mars to the Muses. So in this city, where generals still in armor have paid their honor to poets and the shrines of the Muses, judges in the garb of peace should not fail to do reverence to both the Muses and the poets.

To give you more heart to do this I shall now cite myself as an example, and confess my own love of glory, which is too covetous, perhaps, though quite sincere. This Archias has undertaken to compose a poem about the events in which you and I had a part during my consulship, and the steps we took to preserve this city and empire and defend the lives of its citizens and the liberty of the whole republic.[19] I have heard this poem and encouraged him to complete it, for the

---

[18] Accius followed Ennius as a Latin writer of poetry and prose, including many adaptations from the Greek. Various fragments of his works have been preserved.

[19] Cicero is referring of course to the suppression of Catiline's revolt.

subject seems to me one of high importance and interest. Brave deeds ask for no other reward than praise and renown for the hardships and perils endured, but if that be denied, what is there in this short span of life worth our exertion? Certainly, if our minds took no thought of the future but concerned themselves solely with things of this present life, they would be less distressed by failure, less tormented by sleepless anxiety, and would less often struggle to save that life. There is, however, in every brave man a spirit that night and day inspires him to strive for glory, and reminds him that all memory of his name may not cease with death, but that it may live on to posterity forever.

Are all of us who experience danger and toil in the public service in truth so dull as to believe that everything will perish with us, even while we never draw an easy breath until the end? Many an illustrious man has been careful to leave behind him statues and images, portraits not of his mind but of his body. Shall we not rather choose to leave behind us a record of our plans and deeds, composed with skill and genius? In the midst of my performance of my duties I have thought that my achievements were being spread like seeds over the wide earth to be always remembered. And if, after my death, I am not conscious of that reward, or if some part of my soul is aware of it, as all wise men have believed, in any event, the expectation of it now fills me with joy.

Do you, therefore, gentlemen, protect for us one whose sincerity is proved by the lasting and deep affection of his friends, and whose talent you may estimate by the fact that men of high rank and superior talent themselves seek out his company. His case rests on the support of the law, the authority of his municipality, the testimony of Lucullus, and the documentary evidence supplied by Metellus. Under these circumstances, gentlemen, if even this august body has need of both human and divine assistance, I beg you to grant a favorable hearing to one who has at all times celebrated your victorious generals and the exploits of the Roman people, and who now promises to immortalize with his plaudits the recent domestic conflicts in which we all shared. He is one of those mortals whose name is revered always, among all nations. By your liberality, you may relieve him, and not crush him by harshness.

What I have here said, with my customary brevity and simplicity, has, I trust, met with your approval. That part of my speech which was unlike the usual argument in the Forum and had to do with my client's genius and field of interest has also, I hope, been favorably received. I am sure that your presiding judge listened not unkindly.

IN DEFENSE OF MARCUS CAELIUS

Cicero's speech in defense of Marcus Caelius was delivered on April 4, 56 B.C., the year after his return from exile. Caelius was being tried under a law especially aimed at violent provokers of sedition. His leading accuser was L. Sempronius Atratinus, a youth only seventeen years old, whose father, L. Calpurnius Bestia, had, two months earlier, been charged by Caelius with bribery, but successfully defended by Cicero. Atratinus was supported by L. Herennius Balbus and P. Clodius, a distant relative of the lady Clodia; both were rather obscure persons. It was normal procedure in this period to have one chief and two assistant prosecutors. Five formal charges were laid against Caelius, alleging his complicity in a sedition at Naples, an attack on the Alexandrian embassy at Puteoli, another on the property of one Palla, the murder of the head of the Alexandrian embassy, Dio, and the attempted poisoning of Clodia. In reply Caelius spoke first in his own defense, then his advocate, Crassus, handled more freely the first three of the five charges and Cicero the last two. In the first part of his speech, Cicero addressed Atratinus; later he concentrated on Herennius, who had made the more serious accusation of murder.

The political setting should be kept in mind. The first triumvirate had recently been formed, a coalition of three men, Caesar, Pompey, and Crassus, representing the military and financial powers that then dominated the republic. While it lasted, it kept peace at Rome, but already there were rumors of trouble between the triumvirs. One of the three, Caesar, was then in Gaul, Pompey and Crassus at Rome. High policy was in the background, as indicated by the affair of the Egyp-

tian embassy. Some years before, Ptolemy Auletes had usurped
the throne of Egypt, a country bequeathed to Rome by the
preceding king. But for some time thereafter, Auletes was in
an awkward position, inasmuch as his rule was tolerated, but
not formally acknowledged by Rome. With Caesar's aid, however, and at the cost of 6,000 talents, he had finally succeeded
in having himself recognized, only to be deposed by his own
subjects during the next year, 58 B.C. The deputation sent by
the people of Alexandria to represent their stand in the affair
was waylaid and murdered at Puteoli. An attack was also made
on the head of the Alexandrian embassy, Dio, an Academic
philosopher, who was at that time living with L. Lucceius,
an old friend of Cicero. Lucceius at the time was engaged in
writing a history of Rome, which Cicero hoped would include
a detailed account of his own consulship.[1] Ill-fated Dio later
moved on to the home of Coponius, where he was eventually
murdered by one P. Asicius, at the instigation of Ptolemy and
probably abetted by Pompey. The persistent charges against
Caelius of complicity in the murder of Dio may have been
an attempt of Pompey's enemies to bring out his part in the
crime and thus injure him through Caelius.

The trial also brought together a surprisingly large number
of the well-known personalities in Roman society, in peculiar
combinations and alignments. Local party politics played a
part, as was inevitable in a case which saw Cicero on one side
and his arch-enemy Publius Clodius [2] on the other. Yet Caelius,
whom Cicero defended, had been one of Catiline's followers,
while Clodius had been one of Cicero's supporters during the
Catilinarian trials.

Finally, the whole scene was overshadowed by a cloud of
secret personal intrigue. In the past, there had been a mys-

[1] See Cicero's letter to Lucceius, above, pp. 131–136.
[2] On Clodius, the enemy of Cicero, see above p. 118.

terious relationship between Clodius and Caesar's wife; when this had become public in 62 B.C., Clodius' alibi, by which he was defended, had been discredited through Cicero. Cicero's testimony, if we may trust gossip, he had been forced to give by his own wife, who was jealous of Clodius' sister, Clodia, whom she suspected of being too friendly with her husband. Clodia herself, once accused of immoral conduct with her own brother, had a sinister reputation. Her husband and cousin, Quintus Metellus Celer, had died suddenly under suspicious circumstances in 59 B.C. This illustrious gentleman had been Pompey's legate in Asia in 66, praetor in 63, when he vigorously supported the consul Cicero against Catiline, and consul himself in 60. In the trial of Caelius, or at any rate in Cicero's speech, Clodia is the central figure. She, incidentally, was probably the woman to whom the poet Catullus addressed some of his most caressing verses. In time he too became disillusioned, as some of his later poems indicate.

In addition to all these malodorous intrigues of a dissipated, fashionable set in a great city, there was a generous and touching aspect to Cicero's defense of Caelius which should not be overlooked. Caelius, more than twenty-five years younger than Cicero, had, in his boyhood been Cicero's pupil and friend. As he himself tells us, Cicero guided his education in oratory and encouraged him to enter public life. By a strange misfortune, however, young Caelius had been attracted to Catiline; and it is characteristic of the personalities of both Cicero and Caelius that the former should have tolerated this intimacy and that the latter should have insisted upon it. Even after the collapse of Catiline's conspiracy, Caelius did not return to the circle of Cicero's friends or support his policies. Nonetheless, when his old pupil got into trouble, Cicero was ready to defend him in a trial the outcome of which was certainly dubious. It has been said that his hatred for Clodia and her brother incited him to undertake the task, but it may also be that he felt in some degree responsible for young Caelius. Although he says little in this oration about himself, the reader feels as if he might almost be Socrates talking in defense of Alcibiades.

As a result of Cicero's efforts, Clodia vanished from the Roman scene and Caelius was acquitted. That he was grateful to Cicero, several of his later letters show.[3] His subsequent career, however, could have given his defender little pleasure. For Caelius became an ardent supporter of Caesar and went to Spain with him. Later, growing dissatisfied, he left Caesar to join Milo in raising southern Italy in revolt against his former leader, and met his death at Thurii in 48 B.C., at the hands of Caesar's troops.

---

[3] See letters below, pp. 258–261.

IN DEFENSE

O F

MARCUS CAELIUS

[Pro Marco Caelio]

IF THERE were anyone here unfamiliar with our laws, judicial procedure, and customs, he might wonder what enormous crime is involved in this case, that the trial is taking place on a national holiday, when all other public business is suspended. He would be sure that some criminal was under prosecution for a crime which, if overlooked, would imperil the very existence of the state. If the same man were to hear that we had a law which ordered a daily investigation of seditious and dangerous citizens, suspected of armed attacks on the Senate or the magistrates, or of undermining the constitution, he would not object to that. He would only inquire what was the crime now before the court. He would then learn that there was no enormous crime at all, and no question of any violent disturbance, but that a suit had been brought against a young man of great talent, industry, and charm by the son of a person whom the young man had prosecuted in the past and might prosecute again in the future. On hearing, however, that the suit had been instigated by an influential prostitute, our good visitor would not blame the filial affection of Atratinus, but would recommend putting a curb on the woman's ambition. He also would consider you jurymen overworked, since you cannot rest even on national holidays.

So, gentlemen, if you will listen attentively and form a correct impression of the case, you too will realize that no one who was a free agent would have ever brought this accusation into court, or would have had the slightest hope of a favorable verdict, if he had not been urged on to it by some other person's insatiable passion and unappeasable hate. For Atratinus, a decent and honorable young fellow, and a great friend of my own, I am willing to make allowances; filial affection, external pressure, and youth are his excuse. If this suit against my client was his idea, I attribute it to his loyalty to his father; if he was told to bring it, he acted under pressure; if he had any hope of success, I impute that to his youthful inexperience. But for those who are behind him I have no pity, and with them I shall do battle to the limits of my strength.

I think, gentlemen, that the youth of my client, Marcus Caelius, is the best starting point for my reply to the slanders spread about him by the plaintiff. On various occasions he has been reproached for his father, once because he was not noble enough, another time because he exacted too little respect from his son. The older men among us and those who know Caelius' father do not have to be assured of his excellent reputation. As for those who do not know him so well, since his advanced age has been keeping him from many public appearances, they may be told that he represents all the best qualities of Roman knighthood, a class that now and always has been distinguished by high standards. To be the son of a Roman knight is no sin, and should not be considered as such by the prosecutor, the jury, or by me, the counsel for the defense. Of Caelius' affection for his father, or lack of it, his parents can judge better than we. My statements will be supported by witnesses under oath, but the tears of his mother and the grievous distress of his father testify visibly to their feelings in the matter.

It is charged also against him that the people in his native city did not approve of him. Yet never have they paid to anyone living in their midst the honor they paid to Marcus Caelius after he moved away. In his absence, they elected him a member of their local senate, conferring the office on him without his request, although they have often denied it to persons who asked for it. His former fellow citizens have now sent a delegation of Roman knights to attend this trial and to bear witness to his high character.

These facts will, I think, be the cornerstone of my defense, a stone well laid, since it rests upon the opinion of his neighbors and family. For how could one find his life admirable, if his own father and his fellow citizens disapproved of it? I myself, if I may be allowed to mention it, have a background similar to his, and owe my reputation as lawyer largely to the support given me by my relatives and fellow countrymen.

My client is attacked on moral grounds, a common, slanderous charge made by all accusers. Yet I dare say they will not drive him to the point of regretting he is handsome. This kind of abuse is heaped on all young and attractive persons. But it is one thing to spread slander, and another to bring suit. In the latter case, there must be a well-defined crime, proved by evidence and testimony, whereas slander has no settled aim except to disparage. If the remark is spiteful, we call it scurrilous, but if it is made with wit and humor, we call it banter.

I was surprised and indignant to find this particular section of the accusation assigned to Atratinus, for, as you can well see, his youth and modesty make him ill at ease with this kind of topic. I should have preferred to see one of the older, more experienced men undertake it. Then it would have been possible for me to retort to these scandalous charges with more force and less restraint. With you, Atratinus, I will deal more gently, because your own innocence binds my tongue, and because I owe it to my friendship with you and your father.

And I must warn you not to give people a wrong impression of your own character. Avoid bad language as scrupulously as you do improper conduct. Use no words denouncing your neighbor that would make you blush if they were used, however falsely, against you. Anyone can try this line of attack. Anyone can speak ill of a young man of such prominence, even though there is no ground for suspicion, nor sound evidence to present. The real blame, however, attaches to those who stand behind you. You are to be commended for the obvious reluctance with which you spoke, and for the talent revealed in your polished and brilliant effort.

As it is, my answer to your speech can be brief. The youth of my client encouraged this type of accusation, but from it he is protected by his own good character, and the careful training and strict discipline of his father. As soon as he received the toga of manhood, his father—and this I say without intention of praising myself—at once brought him to me. Since then Marcus Caelius has been either at his father's or in my company, or else a member of the aristocratic household of Marcus Crassus,[1] where he has obtained excellent education.

It has been said against Caelius that he was on intimate terms with Catiline,[2] but this should not be a cause for suspicion. You all know that he was very young when Catiline and I ran for the consulship. If he had then joined Catiline's party and deserted me—and many fine young fellows did support that charlatan—then it might be thought that he went too far in his liking for Catiline. We all know that he was

---

[1] Marcus Crassus, general and politician, served under Sulla and in the East, where he amassed a fortune. Later he joined with Pompey and Caesar to form the first triumvirate.

[2] On Catiline and his conspiracy, see above, pp. 99–102.

one of Catiline's friends; there is no doubt about that. But I am now defending his conduct at a period of life when young men are particularly weak and prone to be influenced by others. During my praetorship he had been continually with me; he then knew nothing of Catiline. After that, Catiline went as praetor to Africa. The next year he was prosecuted for extortion and peculation. Caelius was then on my side and did not even defend Catiline's position. The next year was the one when both Catiline and I were candidates for the consulship. Caelius did not go over to him; he did not desert me.

But after thus spending several years in public life without a blemish on his character, Caelius did support Catiline when he tried for the consulship a second time. How long, then, do you think Caelius should have been kept under surveillance like a child? In the old days, young men used to dress modestly for one year, and wear a tunic even at exercise and games on the Campus Martius. The same rule applied to military life, if young men entered the service early. During that first year, only those who of their own accord, without parental supervision, showed themselves serious, chaste, and well disciplined won the name of well-behaved. Once they had proved themselves irreproachable during that year and had been accepted as adults, their character and morals were never again questioned.

As a matter of fact, Caelius had already been active in public life for several years when he decided to support Catiline. Many others from all classes and age-groups were doing the same. For this man Catiline, as I trust you will remember, had many good qualities, although they were never fully developed. He made use of scoundrels, but he carefully cultivated the noblest of our citizens. He had the power to excite men's passions, but he could also drive them to hard work.

He was consumed by the flame of a perverted ambition, yet conspicuous for vital energy and military skill. Never has there existed on earth such a hybrid creature, compounded of such diverse and contradictory ambitions and desires.

He was, at the same time, companionable with the finest men, and linked close to the underworld. One moment he had the state's best interests at heart, the next he was its worst enemy. He was indiscriminate in his pleasures, and a patient and tireless worker. He was penurious to the point of avarice, and exceptionally generous. Those were his amazing qualities. He counted many as his friends, protected them solicitously, shared with them whatever he had, helped them in time of need with his money, his influence, and his own physical efforts, even to the point of crime. He could adapt his disposition to his environment; he was serious in the company of sober men, joyous with merry folk, dignified before the old, at ease with the young, daring in crime and extravagant in his emotions. By means of his two-faced personality he was able to assemble around himself dishonest adventurers from everywhere, while at the same time, by a specious display of virtue, he retained the friendship of many men of honor. His infamous attempt to destroy the Roman state was made possible only because underneath all his vices lay his fundamental powers of skill and endurance.

I beg of you, then, not to hold against Caelius his intimacy with Catiline. For he shared his error with many others, some of them very good men. I myself once came near being deceived by Catiline, for I thought him an earnest patriot, working for the good of the country, and a faithful and reliable friend. In fact, I had actually to see his crimes with my eyes before I could believe in them. I caught him red-handed before I even suspected him. If Caelius was really one of Catiline's circle, he should be vexed at his mistake, just as I myself regret my poor judgment in that instance, but he should not have to fear that the association would be charged against him as a crime.

It appears, however, that the charge has progressed from a mere denunciation on the score of immortality to a sinister attempt to connect Caelius with Catiline's conspiracy. For you made out, though by implication, that Caelius must have been an accomplice in the conspiracy, because he was Catiline's friend. The evidence has not substantiated that charge, and our young friend, with all his eloquence, could not present a convincing case. Why should Caelius have taken part in such a piece of madness, when he had never been injured in either reputation or fortune? Furthermore, the name of Caelius was never mentioned in that connection. I have enlarged too much already on an obvious point, but I must add this. Caelius employed his youthful talents in prosecuting members of the conspiracy. He thereby proved that he was no partner in the crime, but a determined opponent of it.

I wonder, since I have touched on that incident, whether I should also answer here the charges of corruption and bribery. Caelius would never have been so insane as to accuse someone else of bribery, if he had committed the same crime himself; nor would he have dared to appear publicly to suspect another man of it, if he had wished to practice it himself without hindrance. Nor, if he had thought he might ever have to face a similar charge, would he have twice prosecuted a man on such grounds. True, his act then was unwise, and I did not approve of it, yet it clearly shows him as one who neither hesitated to attack an innocent person nor feared to be attacked himself.

A few words will suffice to dispose of the charges against my client of debts and luxurious living, and to answer the demand for an examination of his accounts. He has no accounts, since he is still under his father's authority. He never had any debts. He is criticized for extravagance because of his expensive residence, for which he is paying, so it is said, 30,000 sesterces [$1500]. As a matter of fact, the whole block belongs to Publius Clodius [3] and is for sale for 10,000 sesterces [$500], and Caelius lives in one small house in this block. In its anxiety to please Clodius, the prosecution has seen fit to manufacture a falsehood appropriate to the occasion.

Caelius is criticized for having left his father's house. Yet at his age he should not be blamed for that. As it happens, his father not only permitted but even suggested the separation, after Caelius had won a remarkable victory in his political career (though a hard one on me), and had reached the age for holding public office. As his father's house is a long way from the Forum, he hired a place at a low rent on the Palatine Hill, in order to pay and receive calls more easily.

At this point I should like to repeat what noble Marcus Crassus said not long ago. He was speaking with some irritation of the visit of King Ptolemy, and quoted the lines of Ennius: [4]

"Would that in Pelion's grove—"

There is another good allusion in that play:

"For never does my lady stray—,"

and give us all such trouble.

"Medea, sick at heart, pierced by cruel love."

You will understand the allusions when I explain later on how the Medea of the Palatine Hill, together with Caelius' change

---

[3] Clodia's brother.

[4] The following lines are from *Medea*, one of the lost tragedies by Ennius.

of residence, became the cause of all this young man's misfortunes, or rather of all the rumor and gossip.

Gentlemen, I have full confidence in your sagacity, and so I am not alarmed by other stories of the accusation, which I long ago recognized as pure fiction. They said that a senator would come forward to testify that Caelius had struck him at the pontifical election. I will ask this man, if he dares to appear, first of all, why he did not retaliate immediately, and secondly, if he preferred to file a complaint rather than to act, why he had to be urged by you to do so instead of bringing his charge at once. If he is able to find a satisfactory answer, I shall then inquire the source from which he drew his inspiration. If he thought of the answer himself, I shall be impressed, but if he got his cleverness from the author of the accusation and is following a line laid down for him, I shall then be glad that not more than one senator was willing to gratify you by supporting a prosecution which enjoys such influential patronage.

I am not afraid of the witnesses to the nocturnal adventures. We are told that certain men will appear and say that their wives, when returning from supper parties, were molested by Caelius. They will be men of rank, and they will speak under oath. Nevertheless they will have to admit that they took no steps to avenge the insults and have never even communicated directly with Caelius.

By now, gentlemen, you have gathered the whole nature of this accusation against my client, and will be able to dismiss it when it is brought before you. These accusers of Marcus Caelius are not his real enemies. Their shots are fired openly, but the ammunition is supplied secretly. I do not say this to insult those who have a right to be proud of their conduct. They are simply doing their duty in defending their friends, and are acting courageously. They feel injured; they are excited and angry; they fight back when attacked. You, however, as intelligent judges, must decide the case according to your own judgment and not allow yourselves to be influenced by someone else's grievances, even if there are brave men who have reason for resentment against Marcus Caelius.

You see the great crowd assembled in the Forum, made up of all kinds of people, from different classes and with different aims. How many of this throng do you think are likely to offer their help and testimony gratis to powerful and influential men looking for support? If persons of this type should appear in this trial, you must be sage enough to discount their selfish contributions. In this way you will assist my client, discharge your sacred duty, and, at the same time, protect the nation from the influence of dangerous elements.

However, I shall call your attention away from these witnesses. I shall not permit the unquestionable truth in this case to rest on the discretion of persons whose testimony can easily be manipulated, twisted, and distorted. My weapons will be evidence. I shall base my defense on proofs clearer than daylight. Fact will stand over against fact, reason against reason.

I shall not dwell on the topics that Marcus Crassus has already sufficiently discussed in his dignified and skillful oration —the riot at Naples, the violence to the Alexandrians at Puteoli, the property of Palla. I wish he had also discussed the case of Dio. For what can I be expected to say about that? The man who committed that deed is not afraid to acknowledge it, for he is a crowned head. The man who is said to have been his helper and accomplice, Publius Asicius, has been acquitted in court. Where does the guilt lie, then, if the one who committed the crime does not deny it and the one who denied it has been acquitted? Should a man be afraid of being charged with it who was far from the scene, and was not even suspected of having known about it? Asicius was assisted by the merits of his case more than he was harmed by the odium of the crime. But my client cannot be the offender, for neither suspicion nor malice has connected him with the deed.

It is said that Asicius was acquitted through collusion. I can easily dispose of that charge, since I was his defending attorney. Caelius believes that Asicius had a good case; but however that may be, his own trial has no connection with it. Caelius' view is shared by two well-bred young gentlemen, devoted to serious studies and the finer pursuits. I speak of the brothers Titus and Caius Coponius, who were especially grieved at Dio's death, since they had been his classmates and intimate friends. You have probably heard that Dio stayed with Titus, whom he knew from Alexandria. You will hear for yourselves what Titus and his noble brother think of Marcus Caelius, when they appear before you. Now that these minor details have been dismissed, we may at last proceed to the charges on which the case really rests.[5]

I noticed, gentlemen, that you gave your undivided attention to my friend Lucius Herennius.[6] It was mainly his brilliant and skillful oratory that held you spellbound. Yet I fear that his subtly incriminating remarks may have penetrated your minds and influenced your judgments. Inevitably he discoursed at length on luxury, passion, the sins of youth, and moral standards. All his life our friend Herennius has been known for moderation and courtesy, but he acted in this case like a cross uncle, a moral censor, and a schoolmaster. He scolded Marcus Caelius as no father ever did. He delivered a lengthy harangue on incontinence and intemperance. What shall I say to it, gentlemen? I understand your absorbed atten-

---

[5] At this point the reply to Atratinus is ended.
[6] Lucius Herennius, an able and popular lawyer, was at this time Cicero's rival. They later became good friends.

171

tion because I myself was startled by the sternness and harshness of his language.

His first point, however, did not impress me much. I mean his assertion that Caelius had been on intimate terms with my friend Bestia, had been his dinner guest, had stayed at his house, and had aided Bestia when he ran for the praetorship. I am not moved by these statements because they are palpably false. He says that two people dined together, when they were in different places, and he admits the fact.

I am also not impressed by Herennius' statement that both Caelius and he were members of the Wolves' Club, which is a rough and crude organization, harking back in its uncivilized habits to a time before culture and law were developed. At any rate, members of the club do not, apparently, hesitate to go to law with one another, or to mention their common membership; so they do not object to having others know about it. But enough of this! I wish now to reply to those parts of Herennius' speech that seem to me of more importance.

The charge of pleasure-seeking he presented calmly and reasonably but at great length, and since there was something to that, it received considerable attention. My friend Publius Clodius made quite a spectacle of his tempestuous emotions and ranted violently in his excitement, at the top of his voice. I admired his eloquence, but was not intimidated by it. I had seen him fail in other trials. But I address myself to you, Balbus—if your scrupulous feelings are not wounded by my defense of a man who accepted every proffered invitation to dinner, spent his time in flower gardens, used perfumes, and took the baths at Baiae.

I have seen and heard of many men of our nation who not merely tasted pleasure and luxury but devoted their entire youth to them, and yet eventually proved their mettle, and became solid citizens and excellent members of society. We all agree that some allowance should be made for persons of that age, since nature itself plants these desires in the hearts of the young. If their escapades stop short of endangering the lives and property of their neighbors, we can tolerate and pardon them.

You, however, appear to be trying to put the blame on Caelius for the universal naughty reputation of youth. Your speech, therefore, was greeted by silence because, as we heard of this particular culprit, we were reminded of the faults of many, many others. It is easy to attack luxury in general. One would talk forever if he were to say everything possible on that subject, including seduction of women, adultery, wantonness, and extravagance. It would be a very long speech indeed! Even though you specified no individual criminal, the vices themselves provide ample material for lengthy and solemn harangues. But it is your duty, as intelligent judges, not to be distracted from the particular case. You must not be severe with one individual, especially one on trial, because his prosecutor has stirred you up against the sins and immoralities of his age. You must not charge the faults of the crowd against a single youth, who is being unfairly held up as an example.

I do not propose to reply to your severe tirade, as I might have done. I might have implored clemency and indulgence for my client's youth, but under the circumstances I shall not do this. I shall not take advantage of that excuse, granted as it is to all other young men. I ask only that in spite of the general disapproval of the prodigality, impertinence, and recklessness of our young men, you should not be prejudiced against my client because of others' sins and the depravity of our times. To all the charges which Caelius has brought upon himself through his own conduct I am ready and eager to reply in detail.

Two instruments of evil are mentioned in the case, gold

and poison. And one and the same person is involved in both connections. From Clodia the gold was received; for Clodia the poison was destined. All the other charges are mere personal slander that should not have been brought before a criminal court. To call a man an adulterer and a shameless pimp is a libel, but not a legal accusation. There is no evidence or foundation for those charges; they are simply insulting expressions poured forth by an excited and irresponsible accuser.

But as to the two last charges, I can see plainly who was their author. Caelius, we are told, needed money; he got it from Clodia, without witnesses, and kept it as long as he wanted it. That is manifestly a sign of extraordinary intimacy. But Caelius wanted to kill her; he obtained poison, got hold of slaves, prepared a drink, arranged an opportunity, and brought the poison secretly. Next, a violent quarrel sprang up between the two and led to serious estrangement. All this part of the case has to do with the noble and notorious lady Clodia.

I shall say no more about her than is necessary to refute the charge against my client. But you must realize, Gnaeus Domitius, as knowing a man as you are, that the whole case hinges on her. If she herself did not say she gave the money to Caelius, and that he prepared poison for her, then I should have no right to mention so disrespectfully the name of an honorable matron. But if we took her name out of the case, the plaintiff would be left without a charge or a weapon with which to attack Marcus Caelius. I as his defense attorney am compelled to do battle with those who bring charges against him. I should do it more energetically if I were not the enemy of the woman's husband—brother, I meant to say; I am always making that mistake. For the present I shall proceed with moderation, and go no further than I am compelled by my duty to my client and the nature of his case. I have never yet felt it necessary to fight with a woman, especially with one who has always been considered a friend to everybody rather than anybody's enemy.

I should now like to ask her whether she would choose to have me interrogate her in the severe old-fashioned style, or more informally, in a milder vein. If I took the former course, then I should have to summon from the shades one of those old men with a beard—not like the goatees she seems to fancy —and with a face that inspires awe, such as we have seen on the ancient statues of our ancestors. A man like that might reprove her, speaking in my stead, so that she would not be angry with me. I should wish to call on some member of her own family, preferably old, blind Appius Claudius [7] himself. He, certainly, could speak without offense, since he would not see her.

If, then, Appius could rise from the dead, he would say this to her. "Woman, what is this young lad Caelius to you, this stranger? Why were you on such good terms with him as to lend him money, or on such bad terms as to fear he would poison you? Do you not remember that your ancestors for five generations were consuls of Rome? Have you forgotten that you were married to noble Quintus Metellus, one of our greatest patriots, who, from boyhood, surpassed most of his fellow citizens in uprightness, dignity, and renown? You came from the aristocracy, and married into the aristocracy. How then did it happen that you were so intimate with Caelius? Was he a relative, by blood or marriage, or a friend of your husband? Not at all! What reason then had you but lust or passion?

---

[7] Appius Claudius, Roman statesman, consul and censor of the third century B.C., who had much to do with the formulation of the laws of the early republic.

"Even though your male ancestors meant nothing to you, did the example of my daughter Quinta Claudia, fair flower of feminine virtue, make no impression on you? Did no recollection come to you of the vestal virgin Claudia, who threw herself upon her father during the celebration of his triumph, and thus saved him from being dragged from his chariot by an enemy tribune? Why did your brother's vices influence you more than the virtues of all your ancestors, male and female? Did I break the peace sworn with Pyrrhus that you might daily form new alliances of love and shame? Was it for this I brought water into the city,[8] that you might use it for your profane purposes? Was it for this I built the Appian Way, that you might travel along it escorted by men other than your husband?"

You may say, gentlemen, that I should hesitate to introduce the awe-inspiring figure of Appius Claudius lest he turn toward Caelius and begin attacking my client with his well-known censorious vigor. I shall take up this subject later, and trust I shall then vindicate the life of Marcus Caelius against the disapprobation of even the most severe jurors. But to you, Clodia, I shall speak now in my own words. I too must say that you will have to explain your intimate friendship with my client, if you wish us to believe in your acts, your words, your insinuations, your motives, and your accusations. The present accusation makes mention of passionate love, adultery, banquets, drinking parties, singing feasts, musical entertainments and boating parties at Baiae. All this, with your consent, is to be discussed. You must have been quite out of your mind when you decided to make this case public by bringing

---

[8] The Appian aqueduct, which brought water down from the hills to Rome, was finished by Appius Claudius, and the Appian Way, the first of the great Roman public roads, which ran from Rome to Brindisi, was begun by him.

it into court. You must, in fact, either repudiate these charges and prove them false, or else admit that no credence should be given to any charges or testimony from you.

Perhaps you would prefer to have me pick my words more carefully. Here then is what I would say. I shall not use the harsh, almost rude language of old Appius, but rather that of one of his descendants, preferably that of your young brother, who is such a polite and skillful orator. He loves you dearly. Ever since he was small, because of some childish timidity, I suppose, or fear of the dark, he has slept with you, his eldest sister. Imagine him then talking to you.

"What has upset you, sister? Why are you so enraged? Why do you raise your voice and by your talking make so much of a small matter? There was, to be sure, a young man living next door; he was fair, tall, and handsome, so you wished to see more of him. You were sometimes found in the same garden with him. You, a noble lady, tried with your riches to captivate him, a son of a thrifty and parsimonious father; but you did not succeed. He was willful and stubborn; he did not think much of what you had to offer. Well then, try someone else! You have gardens on the Tiber, which you laid out carefully at the very place where all the youth of the city come to bathe. From that situation you may every day pick out others to suit you. Why pursue the one lad who disdains you?"

I turn now back to you, Caelius, and take on myself the role of a strict father. I wonder, however, what type of father to choose. Shall I act the part of the stern and violent parent in one of the plays of Caecilius? [9]

"Now, at last, my soul is on fire, and my heart stormy with

_____

[9] Caecilius Statius was brought to Rome from northern Italy as a prisoner about 200 B.C. He became a writer of comedies, fragments of which survive.

177

wrath!" Or the part of the other father who says, "Oh, thou unhappy sinful son!" Fathers like these are hard as flint. Or, "What can I say or wish, when all I wish for is ruined by your villainy?"

Fathers like these are not easy to bear. Such a man would say now, "Why did you move into the neighborhood of a loose woman? Why did you not stay away from her notorious blandishments? Why did you get entangled with her? Squander your money then; throw it away; I do not care! If you come to want, it is you who will suffer, not I! For myself, I intend to spend what is left of my life in peace and contentment."

To this gruff and disheartening reproof Caelius could reply that he had never left the path of virtue, nor been a slave of passion. What proof is there of that? Well, actually he has incurred no great expense or losses, and has borrowed no money. But what about the gossip? How can anyone escape that, especially in such a scandal-loving city? Clodia's brother could not keep free of it. No wonder then that the young man living next door was the subject of talk. In the eyes of a gentle and lenient father, such as his own, Caelius' case could easily be condoned. "A door is broken open? Well, call the carpenter. A suit is torn? Send it to the tailor." Indeed, Caelius could be cleared of every charge against him.

I shall not say more now about Clodia, but let us imagine some other woman, quite different from her! Let us imagine a woman indiscriminate in the company she keeps, always seen with some favorite or other. In her gardens, her house, and her villa on the shore she collects reckless and excitable people. She supports young men and makes up for the stinginess of their fathers out of her own wealth. Imagine, I say, such a woman, a widow, utterly depraved, immensely rich, and

lecherous as a prostitute. Would you call a man an adulterer
who gets on rather intimate terms with her?

Someone may reproach me, "Is this then the discipline you
maintain? Do you teach young men this way of life? Was this
why a father entrusted you with his son, that you might plant
in his tender heart a thirst for amorous pleasures, and, worst
of all, might defend such a way of life and such adventures?"

I myself should consider a man godlike who possessed such
strength of soul and such aspirations for virtue and self-control
that he refused all pleasure and devoted his whole life to
physical toil and purely intellectual pursuits, a man, I say, who
took no delight in recreation, relaxation, the sports of people
of his own age, and entertainments. A man like that, who
asked nothing of life but glory and honor, would certainly be
gifted with superhuman strength. To such a group belonged
Camillus, Fabricius, Curius,[10] and all those others who
achieved their mighty ends with totally inadequate means.
But such paragons of virtue are not found among us today,
and occur rarely even in our books, and the books that describe that old-fashioned austerity are no longer read. This is
true not only of those of us who aim to follow that way of life
in deeds, if not in words, but of the learned Greeks, who still
continue to write in the old, high-minded style, though they
have ceased to live by that code. For even they have been
influenced by the changing times, and have set up new ideals.

Some say that all the practices of the philosophers were in
fact intended to be pleasurable; even learned men do not
hesitate to utter such nonsense. Others have the idea of com-
bining pleasure and honor, and thus joining, verbally, at least,
things that are entirely incompatible. The few who insist that
hard work is the only straight road to glory find their schools

---

[10] These were victorious generals and heroes of the Roman wars of earlier
days with their neighbors in Italy or across the Adriatic in Epirus.

entirely deserted. Nature herself, it must be admitted, offers many allurements that lull our virtue to sleep. To young people she presents many hazardous paths, which they cannot follow without slipping or falling. Both for youths and for adults she provides an infinite variety of exquisite delights that are hard to resist. A man who closes his eyes to beauty, whose senses are not stirred by fragrance, touch, or flavor, whose ears are shut to all sweet sounds, may be considered a favorite of the gods in the judgment of a few, including myself. Most persons, however, will think him a victim of God's wrath.

Let us, accordingly, pass by that austerer way of life, and allow the already deserted path to be overgrown with weeds. Let youth have its gaiety; let it be free! Do not deny it every pleasure! A strict and unrelenting discipline is not always best. Let it make room occasionally for love and pleasure, as long as moderation remains the rule. Young men should take care of their chastity and that of others. They should not squander their fortunes or impair them by debts. They should not trespass on the property of others or bring shame on honorable persons, disgrace on the upright, or scandal on the good. They should abstain from violence, conspiracies, and crimes. And after a period of pleasure, youthful sports, and frivolous enjoyment, they should turn to their duties at home, in civic life, and politics. Then their abundant experience will help them to despise and abandon the pleasures which in youth they could not rate at their true worth.

Many great and illustrious citizens of days gone by, as well as of the present, have risen to magnificence in maturity after their youthful passions had cooled. I need mention no names; you can recall them yourselves. For I refuse to connect even the faintest flaw in the character of a great man with his later fame. Otherwise, I could name many men of eminence and distinction, some of them notorious for wild dissipation in their early days, for prodigal luxury, enormous debts, extravagance, and debauchery. But as their early errors were afterwards overshadowed by numerous virtues, everyone has been ready to condone and even justify their youth.

In the case of Marcus Caelius, I can speak with complete confidence of the seriousness of his career, and relying on your wisdom, gentlemen, I feel free to be quite frank. In his character you will find no tendencies to luxury, extravagance and debts, nor any excessive craving for food or women. A weakness for food and drink, indeed, increases rather than decreases with age. And even the love-affairs and their attendant pleasures, which are fleeting and normally harmless for a strong character, never absorbed his mind or interfered with his conduct. You have heard him speaking in his own defense, and on an earlier occasion as a prosecutor. Without flattering him, I may say that you, with your experience, must have observed his superb qualities as an orator, the wealth of his ideas and vocabulary. You undoubtedly noticed not only his talents, which are probably his without effort, but also his logic, which, unless I mistake, is the fruit of his broad education and studious preparation.

It should be clear to you, gentlemen, that one person cannot have the moral weaknesses attributed to Caelius, and yet follow the career of which I am now speaking. It is impossible for any man consumed by sensuality, a prey to love, desire, and passion, who is one moment rich and the next penniless, to carry on the laborious profession of a lawyer. For his arduous duties include not merely the actual pleading, but also the intellectual task of preparing his cases. That is the reason why, in spite of all the recognition, pleasure, fame, and honor which their eloquence earns, so few men, now and in the past, have ever devoted themselves to the profession. All pleasures are banned; all amusements, sports, and festivities forbidden; even the joys of friendly conversation must be seldom indulged in. That is why men do not choose this kind of work, not because they lack the talent or the training. If Caelius really had been addicted to a life of pleasure, he would never, as a young man, have undertaken to prosecute an ex-consul. If he had been anxious to escape effort and had preferred erotic intrigue, he would not be making daily appearances in the Forum, thus courting hostilities. Neither would he endanger his life by acting as prosecutor, nor in the sight of all Rome would he struggle for months for the welfare and greater glory of his country.

You may ask at this point whether I make nothing of his intimacy with this lady, and all the gossip and the stories which the shores of Baiae could tell. By no means; but they all go only to show that she has sunk so low in her depravity that she makes no attempt to hide her excesses in privacy and darkness, but enjoys conducting her affairs in public and broad daylight. If some martinet believes that young men can be kept entirely away from loose women, I fully agree that they should be. But he certainly is not taking into account the laxity of our age, or the habits tolerated by our ancestors. For when was such conduct unusual or treated as reprehensible and forbidden? When, in short, was there a law against such thoroughly natural behavior?

I should like at this point to describe a general case, mentioning no lady by name, and leaving it to you to draw your own conclusions. Imagine then an unmarried woman, who opens her house to anyone who cares to visit her, and leads the life of a prostitute. She attends banquets with men who are no relatives of her family, here in the city, in the country, and in public resorts like Baiae. Imagine that she displays herself as a prostitute, and a low-grade prostitute at that, not only by her bearing, her dress, and her choice of friends, by the play of her eyes and the freedom of her tongue, but also by her fondling and caressing of men at sailing-parties and banquets. I ask you, Lucius Herennius, if a young man should happen to be seen in her company, is he to be called an adulterer or a seducer? Can he be said to have brought disgrace on a virtuous lady, or merely to have attempted to satisfy his desires?

I am disregarding, for the present, all the harm you have done me, Clodia. I am putting aside all recollection of my own unhappiness. I am overlooking your cruelty to my family in my absence, so that this description does not apply to you. Let me ask you one thing, however, since the prosecution claims that you furnished them with this charge, and you are their chief witness. If there is any such woman as I have just described, a professional prostitute—quite different from you, of course—does it seem to you extraordinarily wicked or immoral for a young man to have an affair with her? And if you are not such a woman—as I should prefer to believe—just what is it that Caelius is supposed to have done? If the prosecution makes you out such a woman, why should my client and I fear a charge which means but a trifle to you? Tell me now on what lines shall I conduct this defense? For either your purity will clear Marcus Caelius from the charge of debauchery, or your impurity will ensure his acquittal and that of everyone else.

My speech and I have now passed through the preliminary difficulties, and the rest of the road will be easy to travel. There are the two capital charges, both connected with this woman. Caelius is said to have received gold from Clodia, and to have prepared poison to kill her. He took the money, so the prosecution claims, to give to some slaves of Lucius Lucceius. They, in turn were to kill Dio of Alexandria, who at that time was staying in Lucceius' house. It is indeed a grave crime to intrigue against an ambassador, or to secure the help of slaves in killing their master's guest. It is a horrible and audacious plot.

Let me first ask, however, whether or not my client told Clodia for what purpose he was taking her gold. If he did not tell her, why did she give it to him? If he told her, she then shared in the responsibility for the crime. I wonder whether Clodia would have dared to draw money from her strong-box and take jewels off her statue of Venus, goddess of plunder, if she had known for what a heinous crime it was to be used, if she had known it was wanted for the murder of an ambassador, and would bring down everlasting disgrace on noble, honest Lucius Lucceius. A woman of your respectability, Clodia, would never have known of anything so shocking; her house would never have been open to assist in so sinister a plan, and her goddess Venus would never have helped to carry it out.

Balbus, seeing this point, has declared that Clodia was kept in the dark, and that Caelius pretended to need the money to pay the expenses of some public games. But if he was really so intimate with Clodia as your stories about their connection imply, he surely told her the true reason. If he was not on such terms with her, then, indubitably, she never did give him the money. So, if Caelius told you the truth, unscrupulous woman, you knowingly gave him money to commit a murder; if he did not dare tell you the truth, you never gave him the money at all.

Is it really necessary to produce the evidence, of which we have a plenty, in order to refute this charge? I might say that such an atrocious act of violence is completely foreign to the character of Marcus Caelius, and it is quite incredible that an intelligent, clever man should have entrusted the execution of so serious a crime to a pack of strange slaves. I might follow the custom of other defense attorneys, which I myself sometimes employ, and question the prosecutor, asking him where Caelius met Lucceius' slaves and how he found access to them. If he personally negotiated with them, what a risky business! If he employed a go-between, who was he? I might, in the course of this speech, make a point of dwelling on every shady and suspicious aspect. But there is absolutely no evidence that Caelius was connected with that murder; he had neither cause nor opportunity for it; he had no accomplice and no idea of either perpetrating the deed or of hiding it, no means whatever of executing it.

These are all points for oratory, of which, with my experience if not my talent, I might make good use, but for the sake of brevity I shall refrain from elaboration. But I am in a position now to present to you, gentlemen, one whom you will easily recognize as your peer, Lucius Lucceius. This deeply religious gentleman and reliable witness must know whether Caelius was responsible for the injury to his good name and fortune; if so, he would not have ignored or tolerated it. A man as kind as Lucius Lucceius, and as devoted to the study of arts and literature, would not have overlooked a danger threatening his friend Dio, with whom he shared his studies. A man who would have been indignant at an affront shown to a stranger would not have been careless about protecting his own guest. A man who would have grieved at hearing of such an enormity committed by strangers, would certainly have been aroused if his own slaves had been involved in it. If the crime had been perpetrated in the open country or a public place, Lucceius would have taken some action. Shall we suppose he took it lightly when it was committed in his own city and in his own house? If a peasant had been endangered, he would have moved to protect him. Shall we suppose

185

he feigned indifference to an attack on a scholar like himself?

But why, gentlemen, am I detaining you so long? You will hear now the sworn statement of someone trustworthy; listen carefully to every word of his evidence. Read the evidence of Lucius Lucceius.

(The testimony of Lucceius is read.)

What more do you expect? The truth of our case could not be more explicit. Innocence in person defends my client, and the case speaks for him with the voice of truth.

There are no certainties about this charge, nor any facts that can be disputed. Nothing is known of any conversations preceding the affair, nor of any details of time or place. No eye-witness or accomplice is mentioned All the evidence for the charge comes from a hostile, disreputable, cruel, wicked, and salacious source, from one household, that is, the members of one family. On the other hand, the house in which the crime is said to have taken place is famous for the integrity, dignity, kindliness, and nobility of its inhabitants. A member of the latter household has given you a solemn statement of fact, which removes all doubt from the subject under consideration. For the question is simply whether a rash and wanton woman, in a fit of rage, invented this charge, or whether an honorable, wise, and upright gentleman has made a false statement under oath.

There still remains the question of the poison. The origin of that charge or its objective I am unable to detect. Why should Caelius want to poison Clodia? Might it be to avoid repaying the loan? Did she ask him for it? Or was it to prevent a lawsuit? Did anyone threaten him? Undoubtedly, his name would never have been mentioned, had he not previously started a prosecution against someone else. In fact, you heard Lucius Herennius say that he would never have accused Caelius, if Caelius had not prosecuted his intimate friend a second time on the same charge, after he had once been acquitted. Is it credible that so shocking an accusation was filed without any reason? You should realize that this outrageous charge was invented in order to make the other appear more plausible.

Let me put these questions with regard to the alleged poisoning. Who was Caelius' confidant, who his assistant, companion, or accomplice? To whom did he entrust the deed, and with it himself and his own safety? The accusation states that he conspired with Clodia's slaves. Was this man whom you call shrewd, even if you grant him no other good qualities, so foolish as to commit his whole fate to another person's slaves? And to what kind of slaves—for that makes a considerable difference? He must have noticed that these were not kept in a normal position of servitude, but were treated freely by their mistress as her companions. Gentlemen, you all must know that in the house of a prostitute, where secrecy veils every act, where unusual and extravagant dissipation and luxury are the custom, and crime and orgies nothing new, in such a house, slaves are not really slaves, for they receive all kinds of confidences, act as go-betweens, share in the orgies, keep the secrets, and enjoy much of the daily festivity and voluptuousness. Was Caelius ignorant of this fact? If he was an intimate with Clodia as you say, he certainly knew the status of the slaves in her house. But if the intimacy you claim did not exist, then how could he have been on such familiar terms with her slaves?

What do we know of the poison? Where was it acquired? How was it prepared? To whom was it delivered, and how and where? The prosecution claims that Caelius had it at his house and tried its strength on a slave he bought for that purpose. The fellow's speedy death, they say, proved to him the poison's strength. O ye immortal gods! Why do you sometimes overlook men's greatest sins, and postpone for days the punishment of their crimes?

The most bitter grief of my life I felt when our country was bereft of Quintus Metellus! Only three days after he had appeared well and sound in the Senate, on the speaker's platform, and in public, he, who rightly had thought himself born to lead his country, was undeservedly taken away from the enjoyment of his estates, and from his service to the state, though still at the prime of life and the peak of his strength. At the time he lay dying his mind was partly confused, but in his thoughts on politics he retained complete clarity to the last. Looking at me, whose eyes were filled with tears, in the broken voice of a dying man, he predicted a dangerous storm that threatened both me and the republic. He struck his hand again and again on the wall that separated his house from that of Catulus,[11] and again and again spoke my name and that of Catulus, but he talked most of our country. It was clear that he felt less sorrow for his own death than for the fate of our country and, in particular, for my fate when I should lose his protection.

If a sudden plague had not carried off this great man, would he, as an ex-consul, have tolerated the iniquitous behavior of his cousin, when as a consul, he had declared to the Senate that he would with his own hands kill the fellow, then just beginning his rabble-rousing? How can Clodia, a member of the same family, dare mention fast-working poison? Is she not afraid that the walls of the house that witnessed the crime might speak? Does she not dread the memory of that night of sorrow and death?

Let me, however, return to the accusation against my client. The recollection of the great Metellus' glorious career has

---

[11] Quintus Catulus had been with Metellus and Cicero in the crushing of Catiline's conspiracy.

drowned my voice in tears and clouded my mind with grief. We are not told, mind you, the origin of the poison, nor the way it was prepared. But the prosecution claims that it was given to Publius Licinius, here present, a fine young man and Caelius' intimate friend. Clodia's slaves, it is said, were to go to the Senian baths and Licinius would meet them there and give them the box of poison. Let me first ask why all this business of the pre-arranged meeting? Why could the slaves not come to Caelius' house? If that friendship and intimacy between Caelius and Clodia still existed, it certainly would not have appeared suspicious if her slaves were seen at his house. But if that friendship had come to an end, and enmity and hatred had taken its place, there undoubtedly was a very good reason, which was the origin of all these alleged crimes. Yet it is said that the slaves, telling their mistress everything beforehand, reported Caelius' wicked plot, and that she, astute woman, ordered them to agree to his every suggestion. Then to have witnesses to Licinius' handing over the poison, she had them select the Senian baths as the meeting place and sent friends of hers there to attack and hold Licinius when he came with the poison.

All these details, on the other hand, show me an easy way to dispute the charge. Why, for instance, did Clodia select the public baths as a meeting place? Such a spot offers no concealment for men fully dressed. The vestibule of the baths cannot be called a proper site for an ambush. If her friends decided to enter the bath proper, they could not very well do so while wearing their shoes and garments. Indeed, they probably would not be admitted, unless, perhaps, this forceful lady had made a personal deal with the bath-attendant to let them in.

At all events, I should certainly expect these honorable gentlemen to be summoned now as witnesses to the transfer of the poison. As you know, none of them has yet been named. I have no doubt, however, that they are gentlemen since, on the one hand, they are intimate friends of Lady Clodia, and, on the other, they consented to assume the role that had to be played in the baths. Whatever power Clodia might have, she could never have persuaded anyone to do that except brave, well-grown men.

But why talk about their character? Look at their courage and competence! These marvelous witnesses lay then hidden in a public bath. These dignified gentlemen jumped then suddenly out into the open. You must picture Licinius appearing with a box of poison in his hand and just at the point of handing it over, when these splendid yet anonymous witnesses sprang out of their ambush. Licinius, who was stretching out his hand with the box of poison, immediately drew it back, and, terrified at their onslaught, turned and fled. Great, indeed, is the power of Truth, strong to defend herself against the cunning machinations and wisdom of men, and against all their treacherous plots!

This is Clodia's purely imaginary story, lacking all proof and entirely unconvincing! This is what she tells! But why, I say, did this considerable body of men let Licinius escape? For there must have been more than a few to ensure his prompt capture and provide witnesses enough of the transaction. And why was it more difficult to seize Licinius before he turned over the box than it would have been afterwards? The men were set to catch Licinius in the very act of delivering the poison, or else while he still held it in his hand. This was the whole of Clodia's scheme and that was the role assigned them.

I am unable, therefore, to discover why, as the prosecution now claims, their sudden appearance was premature. The entire plan was based on the assumption that they would intercept the poison and expose the whole plot. Could they have sprung forward at a better time than when Licinius had just arrived with the box of poison in his hand? If they had not emerged from their hiding and seized Licinius until after he had already delivered the poison to the slaves, he could have implored them to believe his denial that he had given them any box. Could they then have said they had seen him? The delay would have meant losing a most crucial piece of evidence. Then too they would have had to claim to have seen something they could not possibly have seen from where they were in hiding. Apparently they appeared at the exact instant when Licinius had arrived with the box and had stretched out his hand to give the poison to the slaves. It all sounds like the end of a farce rather than of a real play. In a farce, when no solution can be found, someone escapes miraculously, the bell rings, and the curtain falls.

I should like also to know why Clodia's private regiment permitted Licinius to escape, at the moment when he was startled, hesitant, backing off, and turning to flee. Why did they not catch hold of him, and prove the charge beyond doubt by the culprit's own clear confession, their own testimony as eye-witnesses, and, finally, the evidence of the deed itself? Was this band of strong, vigorous men afraid that they could not overpower a weak Licinius, scared to death?

Obviously, in this whole story there is not the slightest evidence to support the charge. This is why the case here rests solely on witnesses' testimony, and not on any factual or reasoned proofs, nor on any of those deductions through which truth can be approached. And, as for the witnesses, gentlemen, I am looking forward to seeing them, not with anxiety, but with expectation of great enjoyment. I eagerly anticipate this performance by well-groomed young men, intimate friends of a rich and high-born lady, stalwart knights, ordered by their mistress to lie in ambush in a public bath as if it were a castle. I shall ask them how and where they hid, if in the belly of a second Trojan horse, that held and protected so many heroes, waging war for a woman's sake. I shall compel them to tell me why such a multitude of warriors failed to seize this weak man here, when he stood alone, or, at least, why they did not chase him when he fled.

If, actually, they ever appear here, they will never be able to explain that. They may be good at dinner conversation; they may even be eloquent over their wine. But a forum is no dining hall, and what may be appropriate for an easy couch is not suitable for the judges' bench. Judges are not, after all, drinking companions; the difference is as wide as that between clear daylight and the dim glow of candles. We shall, therefore, be able to dispose of the pleasantries and jests of those gentlemen, if they should appear. I expect, however, that they will follow my advice, and occupy themselves with other business. Let them win someone else's good opinion, and try their hand at some other enterprise! Let them amuse themselves agreeably with their mistress, and take over the management of her wealth! Let them cling fast to her, eat with her, serve her in every possible way, but leave the lives and fortunes of innocent men alone!

The slaves involved in this affair have been freed on the advice of Clodia's noble and distinguished relatives. Here, at least, is one instance when the lady followed the advice of her eminent family. I should like, however, to know the special significance of the act of emancipation. Was it intended to incriminate Caelius, or to prevent the examination of the slaves under torture, or to reward slaves who knew too many secrets? One might call it a family decision. But how could they fail to advise it, after you, Clodia, had told them the whole story, saying that you had your information not from hearsay but first hand? I wonder whether any other sordid story accompanied her tale of the poison box, for, in such a situation, the lady does not stop at anything. Everyone has heard about this and talked about it.

I am sure, gentlemen, that you long ago perceived what I wish to say, or rather what I wish not to say. Even if the crime was committed, it certainly was not committed by Caelius; for what interest did he have in it? Perhaps there was a bold and crazy young man guilty of it. But if the whole thing was an invention, it was a clever, though a gross, piece of fiction. No one would ever have thought of believing it, if every disgraceful and ugly detail had not seemed to fit the lady concerned.

I have come now to the end of my pleading. I trust that you realize, gentlemen, how important is your decision, and how grave the case entrusted to you. The trial turns on a charge of violence, which comes under a law for the protection of our government, our sovereignty, the well-being of our country and of us all. This law, proposed by Quintus Catulus, was passed at an almost desperate moment in the history of our country, a time of civil war. As a result, the revolt that disturbed my consulship was suppressed, and the last remnants of the conspiracy destroyed. The same law is now being applied to young Marcus Caelius, to satisfy not a public grievance, but the desires and caprices of a woman.

On this occasion too the convictions of Marcus Camurtius and Caius Caesernius are being recalled to our minds. What nonsense, or shall I say, what extraordinary insolence! Do you prosecutors, coming straight from Clodia's house, dare even to mention those men? Do you dare to remind us of that outrage, the memory of which time has dulled but not effaced? Do you remember the kind of crime for which those men died? They were bent apparently on avenging the cha-

grin suffered by this same woman at Vettius' abominable deed?
Can it be that the case of Camurtius and Caesernius is being
revived solely in order to bring the name of Vettius into this
trial, and call up again that old story? Although the law on
violence did not apply in their case, their guilt was so flagrant
that any law could have applied to them.

Why, I now ask, has Marcus Caelius been brought before
this court? No charge under that law has been made against
him, nor do any acts of his, not violating the law, deserve your
condemnation. His early youth was spent in study of subjects
required for a political career, in order to speak in the Forum
and win honor, success, and an excellent reputation. He cultivated the friendship of older men, whose industry and
sobriety he was anxious to emulate. He joined in the activities
of his contemporaries, and altogether seems to have pursued as
commendable a course as any of our best and finest citizens.

When somewhat older, he went with the proconsul Quintus
Pompeius to Africa, and thus became associated with an
honorable and strictly conscientious man. Caelius' family, as
it happened, owned property in that province, and a post in
the provincial administration there was rightly considered appropriate for a man of his age. When he left Africa, he had
served to the complete satisfaction of Pompeius, whose testimony will confirm my statement.

Thereafter Caelius was bent on following the tradition and
example of other eminent citizens by serving as a prosecuting
attorney and thus proving his zeal before the public. I wish,
indeed, that his thirst for distinction had led him in some
other direction, but it is too late now to complain. He attacked my colleague as consul, Caius Antonius. That unfortunate man had gained little profit from his real services to
the country, while he was made to suffer for errors he had
only contemplated. From that point on, Caelius outdid his

contemporaries in activities in the Forum and in business, supporting his friends' causes, and endearing himself to his family. No one but an alert, serious, and hardworking man could have achieved by steady labor as much as Caelius did. Yet at this time in his career (for I rely on your sympathy and wisdom and shall speak candidly), the reputation of our young man hung in the balance, for he met Clodia, who was unfortunately his neighbor. Moreover, he had not then much control over his passions, for, as often happens, desires too long repressed and restrained in early youth suddenly broke out and ran away with him. However, that kind of life, or rather, what it was said to be—for there was less to it than gossip made out—came to an end. Caelius freed himself so completely from his discreditable relationship with the lady that he is now having to defend himself from her venomous attack.

To put an end to the gossip about his erotic excesses, he then set about prosecuting a friend of mine for bribery. He did it, I must say, greatly against my will, but still he did it. The defendant was acquitted, but Caelius persisted with his accusation. He did not follow my advice, and behaved more vehemently than I thought becoming. Yet I do not ask for the moderation of wisdom, for that virtue cannot be expected in one of Caelius' age. But I wish to call your attention to his ardor of spirit, his will to succeed, and his passion for glory. In men of my age desires of that kind must be more temperate, but in a young man, just as in any growing young thing, they indicate the virtues that may be expected as fruits of his maturity.

Young men of promise indeed have always had to be held back from the pursuit of glory, rather than urged on to it. Men of that age, if they are good at all, need restraint more than stimulation. If anyone therefore objects to my client's

195

apparent desire to start and keep up a quarrel, and the vigor and fierce tenacity with which he pursues his enemies, if some trifling details of his conduct seem obnoxious, his elaborate dress, his retinue of friends, his elegance and splendor, let him be assured that these extravagances will run their course, and time and circumstance will exert their mitigating influences.

So, gentlemen, I ask you to preserve for our country one who by his education and political views belongs among the group of good citizens. If my own views are considered satisfactory, I can promise you and our country that, in the future, my friend Caelius will follow the same policy as I do. I can make this promise in reliance on our mutual friendship, and because Caelius has already pledged himself by the most binding commitments. It is obviously incredible that one who has prosecuted an ex-consul for violation of the constitution, should himself turn out to be a subversive character. Nor can one who was not satisfied to have an opponent acquitted on a charge of bribery ever be liable himself to the same charge.

In both of his suits as prosecutor, gentlemen, Marcus Caelius gave us guarantees and pledges of honest intention. I accordingly beg and entreat you not to let the influence of one loose woman in our city cause the acquittal of one man and the conviction of another. You remember that only a few days ago Sextus Clodius was let go scot-free. That man has been involved in every incendiary action, when he was not its leader. Look at his record! No property, no loyalty, no hope, no settled residence, no money, degraded in appearance and expression, in action, in his whole life! It was he who pulled down the statue erected to Catulus, who wrecked my house and set my brother's on fire, who tried to burn the temples and the public records of our past history, who, finally, called publicly on the slaves to murder and revolt. Let not this one woman and her husband-brother have the power to bring about on one day the release of a notorious criminal, and on another the conviction of a young man of honor!

Now that you have taken into account the youth of my client, look, I beseech you, at the aged figure of his wretched father. This is his only son, on whom he leans, and whose hopes and fears he shares. He begs for your mercy and bows to your power. Appealing to your sense of right dealing, he kneels, so to speak, at your feet. Come to his aid, calling to mind your reverence for your own parents, and the pleasure you derive from your own children, for in relieving his grief you will be demonstrating your piety and clemency! Let no act of yours hasten the death of this old man, whose life is already drawing near its natural close! Take not on yourselves to bring sudden disaster on his young son, whose character is but now beginning to set firm in its mold! Preserve them for each other, father and son; do not become agents of destruction for a helpless old man or of ruin for a promising young life, which it is your duty to cherish! Save him instead for yourselves, for his family, and for our country; and you will put him under an everlasting obligation to you and to your children, and will reap, gentlemen, to the full the abundant and lasting harvest of the toils and labors of Marcus Caelius.

LETTER ON THE COMPOSITION
OF THE REPUBLIC

During the eleven years that elapsed between Cicero's two terms in high public office, his tumultuous consulship in 63 B.C., and his governorship in Cilicia, 51 B.C., he achieved some of his most important writing. He had an urge to express himself which was not satisfied by his everyday speeches in the Senate or his arguments in the courts, as attorney for this or that individual in difficulties. His first book was a treatise on oratory, laying down the requirements for success in the art of public speaking, through which he had won his own way to fame and honor. The *Orator* was widely read and praised by other Romans of literary taste, who urged him to continue writing.

Encouraged by their applause, he turned to expounding and defending the object for which he had pled with all his eloquence in the past, and would plead again in the future— the constitution of the Roman republic. His first and finest book on politics was *The Republic*, on which he worked between the early summer of 54 B.C. and the end of 52. On no other of his books does he seem to have spent so much time and pains.

The form he chose for it, and used again for many of his other works, was the philosophical dialogue, or imaginary conversation between a group of friends. It was the form that had been used by Plato, Cicero's model in the literary expression of ideas, as well as by other disciples of Socrates. It made possible a livelier and freer presentation of all sides to an argument than could be given by a plain exposition, and was therefore more likely to interest the reader. Cicero's introduction of this dialogue form into Latin, as a medium for the discussion of theories and ideas, set an example that was followed in course of time by writers in many other languages down to the author of the latest of the *Republics*, the discourse on American political principles by our contemporary Charles Beard.

Cicero's dependence on Plato for even the minor details of his form and on Aristotle for suggestions as to certain of his ideas is shown in Letter VI below, and in many surviving fragments of his *Republic*. In Plato's *Republic*, the chief speaker is the Athenian Socrates, Plato's own beloved teacher, who at the time of Plato's writing had been dead for some years. Cicero went back for his speakers nearly a century to what seemed to him the heroic age of Rome, the period of her earlier victorious wars, when her citizens still lived simply, served their country bravely and honorably and revered their gods, the period that came abruptly to an end in the time of the social disturbances led by the Gracchi, around 130–120 B.C. Thereon had followed an era of expanding imperial rule, growing wealth, unrest, civil strife, misgovernment, and occasional dictatorial seizure of power, which Cicero was resisting with all his strength, but which was to lead directly to the empire of Augustus.

The chief speaker in Cicero's dialogue was not, like Socrates, a philosopher but a general and man of action, the younger Scipio Africanus (c.185–129 B.C.), who had finally defeated and destroyed Carthage in 146, a famous year, when the Roman legions took possession also of Greece. This Scipio had been by adoption the grandson of the elder Scipio Africanus (c.234–c.183), the conqueror of Spain and victor over Hannibal in the Second Punic War. Neither Scipio had been merely a soldier. Both were men of exceptional intelligence, who had used their great influence at Rome to promote an interest in the newly discovered Greek culture and literature, so superior to anything the Romans had of their own.

199

It was therefore not inappropriate to have them both figure in a literary debate on political ideals. The revolutionary Gracchi had been, as it happened, members of the same family, but they had been leaders of the new popular party that had risen to oppose the old, aristocratic republicanism of the Scipios, which Cicero was defending. So Tiberius Gracchus is said to have deserved to be murdered for his "impious machinations."

Though a debtor to the Athenians in the matter of form and in certain of his ideas, in the general substance of his political theory Cicero was thoroughly Roman, basing his views on Roman observation and experience. Plato had distinguished the three fundamental types of government, monarchy, aristocracy, and democracy, and had described the virtues and weaknesses of each. Aristotle in his *Politics* had shown that the lines between these types were not always easy to draw, that democracy, for example, might have features of an aristocracy. A Greek historian of Scipio's time, Polybius, had come to Italy as a hostage and had studied the Roman institutions; he had pointed out that the Roman constitution combined in itself the best features of all three types, with its monarchical, powerful consuls, its aristocratic, sagacious senate, and its popular, patriotic assembly. Each department of this government, he observed, had its duties well defined, and each could act as a check on the usurpation of power by another. It was, in short, a mixed type of government, so designed as to create a juster, better balanced, and more stable political community than any other. Cicero followed Polybius' lead and glorified the handiwork of his ancestors, the ideal Rome of the still uncorrupted republic. He knew that the days of the Scipios were gone, but he still cherished a hope that by dint of hard, patriotic effort their virtues might yet be regained, and freedom need not go down before the rough tyranny of an ignorant mob or the stern despotism of a military dictator.

Cicero's ideal republic was never more than a vain dream, but to his book and to his second political work, the Laws, later generations were to owe many principles that would prove fruitful in the thought of after times. In the realm of moral philosophy, Cicero was always a Stoic. The principles, therefore, that he laid down as the essential foundations of a true commonwealth were the broad Stoic rules of universal justice for all mankind, without distinction of race or class. "All men are bound together by a natural feeling of kindliness and good-will, and by a fellowship in justice. The state is an association of the people to ensure justice, and a partnership for the common good." Man merely as man has a right to receive justice. And wise men look on themselves, not as the Greeks had been prone to do, as citizens of one city or state only, but as members of the vast community of the human race.

Unfortunately, no legible copy of the entire Republic has come down to our day. It was, evidently, well known and highly esteemed for some five hundred years after Cicero's death. St. Augustine, writing in the early fifth century his great Christian treatise on the state, the City of God, made much use of it. Through his quotations and those of other authors of his or an earlier time, fragments of varying length were saved for the future. But to the Middle Ages, the Republic was already a lost book. In 1822, a fourth-century manuscript of the whole or a large part of it was discovered in the Vatican Library, but the text had been erased and the parchment covered by a later scribe with something he considered more valuable. Only a few short, disconnected passages of the palimpsest could be deciphered. One of the first copies of these passages was sent to Thomas Jefferson.

201

LETTER

ON THE

COMPOSITION

O F

THE REPUBLIC

To Atticus
[Ad Atticum, IV, 16]

Rome, June 24, 54 B.C.

YOU CAN see how busy I am from the fact that this letter is
written by a secretary. I make no complaint about the number
of letters I get from you, but most of them merely tell me
where you are. Since they are written by your own hand, they
also show that you are well. I was particularly pleased by the
two letters written about the same time from Buthrotum, for
I was anxious to learn whether you had had a good crossing.
On the whole, it is the number of your letters rather than
their contents which is satisfactory. But the one your guest,
Marcus Paccius, brought was really important and full of information, and I am now, therefore, answering that.

First of all, I have made a special point of showing Paccius
by word and deed how much weight your recommendation
carries with me. I did not know him before, but I now count
him among my friends.

For the rest, I shall follow your suggestions and include
Varro,[1] if possible, somewhere in my book. Yet you know the
plan of my dialogues. In the *Orator*, which you praise so
highly, no individual was mentioned by any of the interlocutors who was not in some way known to him in real life.

---

[1] Varro (116–27 B.C.) was a prolific Roman writer whose works covered
a great variety of topics.

Similarly, the discussion in the *Republic*, on which I am now working, is carried on by Africanus, Philus, Laelius, and Manlius. I have added besides several young men: Quintus Tubero, Publius Rutilius, and the two sons-in-law of Laelius, Scaevola and Fannius. However, I am planning to add introductions to the individual books, just as Aristotle did in his popular works, and in one of those I may easily mention Varro, which is apparently what you want. I only hope I shall be able to finish the job. I have tackled an ambitious subject, as you are well aware. It is extremely important and requires peace of mind, which I need more than anything else.

You criticize my omission of Scaevola in the book you otherwise approve. I omitted him purposely, following the example of our divine Plato in his *Republic*.[2] There, Socrates goes to the Piraeus to call on Cephalus, a rich old man who enjoys life. At the opening of the conversation the old man is present and participates, but after some gracious remarks, he excuses himself to attend some religious functions and does not come back. I believe that Plato thought it inappropriate to keep a man of his age in such lengthy conversation. I thought I should take even more precaution with Scaevola, whose age, state of health, and official position, you will remember, would hardly have permitted him to spend several days on Crassus' estate at Tusculum. And though the topic of the first book has some connection with Scaevola's interests, the rest, you must admit, is very technical. In that part there is no place for the old man's facetiousness, which you will remember.

In the matter of Pilia, I shall do as you say, for the case is clarified by Aurelianus' testimony, as you describe it. At the same time I shall be pleasing Tullia. I am backing Vestorius.

---

[2] See Plato, *Republic*, I, Classics Club edition, pp. 223–4.

I know you like this and I shall see that he realizes it. It is a very difficult situation, though he has two such easy-going people to deal with.

As to your questions about Gaius Cato, he was acquitted, as you know, on the basis of the Junian and Licinian laws. He will also be cleared, I can tell you, by the Fufian Law, to the relief of his accusers even more than of his supporters. At any rate, Cato has made up with Milo and with me. Drusus has been accused by Lucretius. The date on which the jury can be challenged is set for July 3rd. The common talk about Procilius is not promising, but you know how the law courts are. Hirrus is on good terms with Domitius. The Senate's decision about the provinces, which the two consuls suggested —"Whosoever from now on . . ." [3]—will, in my opinion, prove ineffectual.

So much in answer to the letter Paccius brought! Now, please, let me expostulate with you—if I am right. You say in your letter from Buthrotum which Gaius Decimus brought me that you think you will have to go to Asia. I cannot possibly imagine that it would make the slightest difference whether you did your business by agents or in person, while it means you are far from your friends so often and so long. But I wish I had brought this matter up when you were still undecided; then I might have had some success. As it is, I cut short my complaint. May it at any rate hasten your return!

I am writing you less often, because I do not know where you are or where you are going to be. I expect to give this letter to someone who may be seeing you. Please, since you are planning on going to Asia, let me know when we may expect you back. Let me know too what you have done about Eutychides.

---

[3] In future an interval of five years was to elapse between a magistracy and a provincial command. This law came into force in 52 B.C.

SCIPIO'S DREAM

The best preserved portion of Cicero's *Republic* is a section from the sixth book, known commonly as *Scipio's Dream*. We owe our possession of it to a fourth-century grammarian and philosopher named Macrobius, who wrote a lengthy commentary on it. In this setting, plucked out of its original context, it was much admired and often recopied during the Middle Ages, and thus has been preserved to modern times.

It is clear that Cicero wished to close his *Republic* as Plato had closed his, with an inspiring revelation of the reward awaiting a good citizen after his death. Plato had employed the device of a miraculous vision, that had transported the soul of the reporter into the next world, and from which he had later awaked to tell what he had seen. Critics coming after Plato, however, had found fault with the nature of the vision, as too unnatural to be convincing. Cicero, accordingly, substituted for the vision a dream, such as anyone might claim to have had. In his dream the younger Scipio sees his dead grandfather among the stars, is shown by him the splendors of the celestial universe and given hints of the divine life that lies before him. For through his immortal mind, he is told, man himself is a god.

The content of Scipio's dream is different from that of Plato's clearly delineated vision. It is more mysteriously prophetic, more comprehensive and grandiose. The astronomical details and the majestic language used to describe them were borrowed probably from Posidonius, the Stoic teacher under whom Cicero had studied at Rhodes. The thought of Scipio looking down from heaven past the huge, luminous stars to the sorry little earth he had momentarily left behind may have

205

been in Dante's mind, thirteen hundred years later, when he portrayed his Beatrice pausing to show him the same sight as they mounted upward into the empyrean.

Unhappily, the English language does not allow accurate translation of some of the terms used by Cicero, and even more unfortunately, many terms which Cicero found in his Greek sources had no equivalents at all in the Latin tongue. There may have been some earlier Latin writing on politics, but how inadequate the language still was to express anything in the way of abstract or philosophic ideas is shown by the difficulties which Cicero's contemporary, the poet Lucretius (c.96–55), encountered in his effort to translate the theories of Epicurus into his native speech. For this reason Cicero's accomplishment in helping to create a philosophic vocabulary in Latin deserves much credit.

SCIPIO'S DREAM

[De Republica, VI, Somnium Scipionis]

ON MY ARRIVAL in Africa, where I was, as you know, military tribune of the fourth legion under the consul Manlius, there was nothing I wanted more than to see King Masinissa, who, for good reasons, had always been a special friend of our family. When I went to him, the old man, weeping, embraced me, and then, looking up to heaven, exclaimed: "I thank thee, supreme Sun, and ye other celestial beings, that before I depart this life I behold in my kingdom and my palace a Publius Cornelius Scipio. The mere mention of his name gives me new strength, for I shall never forget his grandfather, that noble and invincible hero."

Afterwards I inquired of him concerning the state of his kingdom. He, on the other hand, questioned me about the condition of my country, and the whole day passed in this kind of conversation. Later I was royally entertained, and we continued talking late into the night. During all this time the old man spoke of no one but Africanus, recalling not only his deeds but his every word. Finally, we retired and I fell into a deeper sleep than usual, partly because I was weary from my journey, and partly because we had sat up extremely late.

I then had the following dream, caused I truly believe by our preceding conversation. For it frequently happens that our thoughts and words by day influence our dreams, even as Ennius dreamed of Homer, who was so often on his mind during his waking hours.

In this dream Africanus appeared to me as I know him from his portraits rather than from my own experience. When

I recognized him, I was frightened, but he said, "Have courage, Scipio; do not be afraid, and remember carefully what I am about to say.

"Do you see this city, which I once made vassal to Rome, but which now revives its old wars and cannot live in peace?" And from his high seat, surrounded by brilliant and glittering stars, he pointed to Carthage. "You have now come as a simple soldier to conquer this city. Within two years you will accomplish the task as consul, and, by your own merit, will win the title Africanus, which you already wear as my heir. After destroying Carthage, you will celebrate a triumph in Rome. You will then hold the office of censor, and will visit as ambassador Egypt, Syria, Asia, and Greece. Then, while still absent from Rome, you will be elected consul for a second time, and will conquer Numantia, thus putting an end to a serious war. But when in triumphal procession you return to Rome, you will find the republic disturbed by the intrigues of a grandson of mine. Then, my dear Africanus, you will show your country your true character, skill, and ability. The outcome of that crisis is, as I see it, uncertain. The number of your years will then be seven times eight, and the union of these two numbers, each perfect in itself, though for different reasons, will produce your hour of destiny. Our whole country will turn to you, the bearer of the proud name of Africanus. The Senate, all patriots, the allies, and the Latins will appeal to you; you are to be the savior of the state. In brief, you will have the power to restore order in the republic, if only you escape the murderous hands of your relatives."

At this point, Laelius called out, and the rest of the company groaned loudly, but Scipio smiled and said, "Hush, I beg you. Do not wake me! Kindly listen to the rest.

"Now for your encouragement, my dear Africanus, that you may be the readier to assume our country's defense, you must

208

know that there is a sure place in heaven for all who have preserved, defended, and enlarged their country; here they will enjoy eternal happiness. For nothing finds greater favor in the eyes of the supreme God who rules the universe than the orderly associations of men, founded on law, which are called states. The rulers and preservers of states descend from this heavenly place and return hither."

At this point I asked him whether he and my father Paulus were still alive, and other friends who I thought were dead. Yet it was not so much the fear of death that gravely disturbed me as the threatened perfidy of my own relatives.

"Indeed, Africanus," he replied, "we are all alive, freed, so to speak, from the chains of the body as from a prison. What you call life on earth is only a kind of death. Look, here comes your father Paulus to you."

When I saw him I burst out weeping, but he took me in his arms, kissed me, and begged me not to cry. As soon as I could stop my tears and speak, I said, "Tell me, dearest father, if this here is the real life, as Africanus says, why must I stay on earth? Can I not immediately come up where you are?"

"That cannot be," he replied. "You cannot come here until God, whose sanctuary includes all that vast expanse you see, sets you free from the fetters of the body. For men were created to inhabit the globe called earth, which you see there in the center of the universe. The soul given to man is part of those eternal fires which you call stars, the round balls endowed with reason that roll through their orbits at astounding speed. So you, Publius, and all other religious men must keep your souls imprisoned in your bodies, and not leave your life without the permission of Him who gave you your soul, lest you desert the post assigned you by God himself.

"Rather, my Scipio, ought you to follow the example of your grandfather and of me, your father, and cherish the justice and piety which you owe your parents and relatives, and especially your country. Such a life leads to heaven and to the company of those who, having finished their life, are released from their bodies, and now inhabit this place you see."

I was looking on a brightly shining region which excelled even the burning stars in luster. Following the Greek custom, you call it the Milky Way. I found myself there, and as I looked around, beheld everything wonderful beyond description. For I saw stars which we can never see from the earth, and the size of these heavenly bodies surpassed anything we might have imagined. The smallest of them, and the farthest removed from heaven but nearest to the earth, was the moon, which shines with a borrowed light. The stars themselves, however, were all far bigger than the earth. Indeed our mother earth appeared so small to me that I felt sorry, seeing our empire a mere point on it.

As I stayed still gazing down on the earth, Africanus interrupted me. "How long, pray, will you keep your attention earth-bound? Look up and see the heavenly space to which you have come. Nine circles, or rather spheres, compose the universe, the outermost of which is heaven, that surrounds all the rest. This heavenly sphere is itself the supreme God, who rules and controls all the others. Within it the fixed stars revolve in their unchanging course. Beneath it seven spheres rotate in a contrary direction. One of them contains the planet which on earth they call Saturn. Next comes Jupiter, whose brilliant ray is auspicious to mankind. Then follows Mars with his red gleam boding ill for the earth. The middle sphere is that of the Sun, the chief of the stars and their leader. On it depend the system and order of the universe; its size is so tremendous that it fills everything with its light. After the Sun come the spheres of Venus and of Mercury. The eighth and lowest sphere is that of the Moon, which reflects the rays of the Sun. Below it is the region of mortality and decay, except for the human soul, which the gods gave as their gift to man; whereas above the moon's sphere eternity reigns. Last of all the Earth, the ninth sphere, lies in the center, immovable. Since it is at the bottom of the universe, all things gravitate toward it."

When I had recovered from my astonishment at the sight, I asked, "What is this loud and pleasant music that strikes on my ears?"

"This music," he said, "is made by the motions of the spheres, which sound in different but regular intervals, and by their combinations of high and low notes produce a variety of harmonious melodies. It is natural that this tremendous motion should be accompanied by sound, and that the outermost sphere should emit a high note, the innermost, a low one. The heavenly sphere of the fixed stars revolves most rapidly, and therefore gives out a high and shrill sound. The sphere of the Moon, on the other hand, which is the lowest, resounds with a low tone. The Earth, the ninth sphere, is immovable at the center of the universe. But the other eight spheres produce at distinct intervals seven different sounds; two of them, however, have the same tone. The number seven, incidentally, is the key to the whole universe.

"Skillful artists have imitated this celestial harmony on stringed instruments and with their voices, and have thus opened for themselves a way back to this heavenly place. And those men of brilliant mind who have devoted their life on earth to study of the divine sciences have done the same.

"But the ears of mankind have been to some extent deafened by the amazing volume of this sound; indeed, hearing is the dullest of all human senses. Similarly, the people who live near the cataracts of the Nile, where the river flows down from the high mountains, are made deaf by the tremendous noise of the falling water. So the sound produced by the rapid motion of the whole universe is too great to be borne by human ears, just as you cannot look directly at the sun because its rays dazzle your vision."

But with all my admiration for this wonderful sight, I could not help looking again and again at the earth. When he noticed this, Africanus said: "I see you are still interested in the human race and the planet it inhabits. If it appears to you as small as it really is, you should despise it and turn your eyes forever towards heaven. For what sort of glory or renown can you expect to win among men? As you see, the earth is habitable only in certain regions, and even there is but sparsely settled, with wide stretches of desert between. The inhabitants of the earth too are not only separated from one another so that no communication between them is possible, but they do not even move on the same plane. Some live at an angle to you, some perpendicularly, others even upside down. Surely you cannot expect to gain glory from them.

"You observe, finally, that this earth of yours is divided into what may be called zones. The two farthest apart, the one on top and the other at the bottom, are, as you see, frozen solid. The central zone, on the other hand, which is by far the widest, is scorched by the Sun's fierce heat. Only two zones are habitable. The southern one, whose inhabitants walk upside down compared with you, has nothing to do with your people. Of the northern zone in which you live, only a very small part, as you see, constitutes your Roman empire. For the land your people cultivate is hemmed in by high mountains in the north and south and is but little wider in the east and west. It is a small island, so to speak, surrounded by the sea which you on earth call the Atlantic, the Great Sea, the Ocean, but which, in spite of its name, is far from large, as you can see for yourself. Even within these civilized and known regions, has your fame, or that of any of us, ever passed beyond the Caucasus mountains or the river Ganges? Who in the extreme east or west or north or south will ever hear your name? Leave those lands out of your survey and you see how narrow indeed is the area in which your glory can spread. And will even the few who now speak of us continue to do so for any length of time?

"Or, assume that some future generation should really desire to transmit to their descendants the memory of some one of us of whom they had heard from their ancestors; even this process could not go on indefinitely. For floods and volcanic eruptions, which inevitably occur at set intervals, would keep us from achieving long-lasting, let alone eternal, glory. After all, what matters it if those who are born here-after talk of you, when those who lived before you, whose number was perhaps as great and whose merit was certainly greater, did not so much as know your name?

"Especially is this true since not a man of those who shall hear of us can hold in his memory the events of a single year. Men generally, indeed, measure the length of the year by the return of the Sun, which is, after all, only one of the stars. We should, however, call the year truly over when all the stars have completed their courses and returned at the end to the position they originally occupied. I hardly dare say how many centuries of earth are comprised in such a year. Long ago there was an eclipse of the Sun when Romulus' soul ascended to this Heaven. When the Sun shall suffer another eclipse of exactly the same kind, and all the heavenly constellations shall have returned to the position they occupied on the former occasion, then a full year will be completed. Mark my words, of this year hardly a twentieth part has yet elapsed.

"If, then, you have no hope of returning here, where great and famous men are granted all their desires, of what good

213

is that ephemeral glory among men, which cannot last even for one brief portion of a single year? But if you raise your eyes upward to contemplate this everlasting, heavenly seat, you will pay no heed to the talk of men, nor set your heart on the rewards given you by mortals for your achievements. Virtue herself must attract you by her beauty to true honor. Let others speak of you as they may, for speak they will. Their chatter will not be spread beyond those narrow regions you see below, and will not last long. For it will perish with those who utter it, and be lost in oblivion through the forgetfulness of future generations."

When he had finished, I spoke. "You say, Africanus, that those who have worked for their country's good find the door to Heaven wide open. I myself, from childhood, have always followed the fine example you and my father set me, but from now on I shall push forward more eagerly, thinking of the final reward."

"Do so," he replied, "and remember it is your body and not you that is mortal. For your true being is not shown in your outer appearance, but in your mind; the person to whom someone else can point with his finger is not your true self. You must realize that there is divinity in you, for the being must be godlike who lives, thinks, remembers, and foresees, who rules, controls, and moves his body, even as the supreme God rules the world of which he is master. And as the eternal God sets this world, which is partly mortal, in motion, so does man's immortal soul rule over his fragile body.

"You know that whatever moves unceasingly is eternal, but whatever is set in motion from outside will, of necessity, come to rest and perish, as soon as the motion ceases. Only that which moves by its own power will never stop, since it never loses contact with itself. It is the source of motion also for other moving things and is therefore the origin of all motion everywhere. This principle can have no beginning, for, since everything develops out of it, it cannot be the product of anything. The very name, principle, implies that it has no origin. And whatever has no beginning will also have no end. For were it once extinguished, it could not be reborn, nor could it create anything of itself. All things then are necessarily derived from this principle. It is clear too that the source of all motion must lie where motion creates itself; then it is never newly created, nor can it be destroyed. Were this not so, Heaven would collapse, and all nature perish, nor could they ever be reborn and gain that strength which their continuing life requires.

"Since it is now clear that whatever moves by its own power is eternal, who will deny that this quality is characteristic of the soul also? For whatever is set moving by an external power is, by definition, inanimate. But the essential characteristic of a living being is its ability to move itself, an ability due directly to the nature and power of the soul. Since this power alone is able to move itself, it can have no beginning, and must be everlasting.

"This power of the soul, Scipio, I urge you to employ in all your actions. Work, first of all, for your country's welfare and your soul will the sooner return to this heavenly place. It will do so even more quickly if, while still enclosed in the body, it already makes itself independent, and succeeds as far as possible in separating itself from the body.

"As for the men who indulge in physical dissipations, whose souls have served as slaves of their bodies in their search for low pleasures, they have violated the laws of God and man. Once their souls are released from their bodies, they are forced to hover continually around the earth, and only after many centuries return to this heavenly place."

Africanus departed and I awoke from my dream.

215

ON THE LAWS

Cicero's book on *Laws* continued the work he had begun in the *Republic*, just as Plato's *Laws* might be taken as a sequel to his *Republic*. In fact it may have been this alleged relationship between Plato's two great political dialogues that influenced Cicero to follow his treatise on government with a discussion of law. We know that he was working on this book even before he had completed his *Republic*, in the summer of 52, though the manuscript of the *Laws* was not made public until after his death. It was found then unfinished and circulated in that state in antiquity. Today it is even more fragmentary, for we have only portions of three books, along with a number of brief passages that cannot be accurately placed. There are allusions in other authors to a fourth and a fifth book.

Both Plato's and Cicero's dialogues on the *Republic* were frankly imaginary conversations. And in his *Laws*, Plato dispensed with all pretense to an historical date and even with individualized interlocutors. Cicero, on the other hand, brought the conversation which comprised his *Laws* closer to concrete reality by placing it in that very summer of 52, at his own estate in Arpinum, and giving himself the principal part in it, the other two speakers being his brother Quintus and his intimate friend Atticus.

In spite of certain superficial similarities, the contents of the two works are entirely different. Plato, rather reluctantly, replaced his ideal state, governed by an extraordinarily gifted and trained class of rulers, by a "second best" state, in which less discretion was allowed to the rulers and an elaborate code of law was supreme. His *Laws* thus presents an alternate solution to the problem of government. Cicero, on the other hand, simply went on with his discussion of the constitution he had already envisaged in his *Republic*, dealing in his first book with the theoretical questions of the origin and sanctions of law in general. His material here he drew from Plato and the Greek Sophists and Stoics. The legislation listed in the later books he intended for Roman citizens, not Greek. It is based accordingly on Roman custom and belief and political experience in Cicero's day. The books are therefore more original in character and the fragments we have of them are valuable for the Roman historian and antiquarian.

It was, however, the first book that influenced later political theory. In it Cicero enlarged still further on certain themes on which he had lightly touched in his *Republic*, in particular on the universal and unchangeable law of Nature, right reason or conscience, innate in the heart of every member of the human race, that, in the words of the *Republic*, "summons to duty by its command and restrains from evil by its prohibition. . . . Nor may any other law override it, nor may it be repealed as a whole or in part, nor have we power through Senate or people to free ourselves from it. . . . Nor is it one thing at Rome and another at Athens, one thing today and another tomorrow, but one eternal and unalterable law, that binds all nations forever. It is the one universal lord and ruler of all, and God himself is its author, promulgator and enforcer. And he who does not obey it flees from himself." On this Stoic concept of a law of Nature, a sense of simple justice or right and wrong, recognized by men everywhere, Cicero would erect his structure of laws for a reformed Roman republic. To a similar concept of "the Laws of Nature and Nature's God," thirteen colonies, some eighteen hundred years later, were to appeal against the injustices of the rule of their king, George III.

217

ON THE LAWS

[De Legibus]
Book One

ATTICUS: I recognize this as the very grove with the famous oak of Arpino, often mentioned in your poem on Marius. If that oak still stands, this surely is it, for it is certainly old.

QUINTUS: Yes, Atticus, it still stands and always will, for it was planted by genius. No such long-lived stock can be produced by the labor of a well-trained gardener as can be sown by the verses of a poet.

ATTICUS: What do you mean, Quintus? What sort of seed do poets sow? While praising your brother you seem to me to be putting in a compliment for yourself.

QUINTUS: You may be right. Nevertheless, as long as the Latin language is spoken, some oak called Marius' will always be standing here; and, as Scaevola said about my brother's poem, *Marius*, "it will live on through the centuries to a venerable old age." Or do you perhaps believe that your fellow Athenians have really been able to preserve forever green that olive tree in your citadel? Or do you think the tall, slender palm tree, which Homer's Ulysses said he saw at Delos, is the very one the Delians point out today? In many places memory keeps alive many things for a longer time than they could ever have survived naturally. Therefore this acorn-bearing oak may be the actual one from which there once flew forth

"the golden bird of Jupiter, wonderful to see."

But when storms and the passing years have wasted it away, there will still be a tree here called the oak of Marius.

ATTICUS: I do not doubt it in the least. But now I am questioning not you, Quintus, but the poet himself. Did your poem make this oak famous, or do you really believe the story you told about Marius?

MARCUS: Certainly, I shall answer you, Atticus, but not before you have replied to my question. Did Proculus Julius actually meet Romulus after his death walking about near where you now live? And did Romulus tell him that he had become a god named Quirinus, and order a temple dedicated to himself in that place? Furthermore, did Boreas, not far from your former home in Athens, really carry off the nymph Orithyia? For so the story has it.

ATTICUS: Why are you asking these questions?

MARCUS: For no reason at all, except to show you that we should not inquire too carefully into stories that have been handed down in this way by tradition.

ATTICUS: Yes, but you make many statements in your *Marius*, about which people argue whether they are fiction or fact. They expect strict accuracy from you, because the events you relate are recent and concern a native of Arpino.

MARCUS: Of course I do not wish to be thought a liar. Nevertheless, Atticus, those people are stupid to demand literal truth in such a work, as if the story were being told not by a poet but by an eyewitness. No doubt they think Numa actually conversed with the nymph Egeria, and that an eagle dropped a crown on Tarquin!

QUINTUS: I understand you, brother; you think that one set of conventions must be observed in history and another in poetry.

MARCUS: Certainly; since the principal object of history is truth, and the principal object of poetry is enjoyment. Yet Herodotus, the father of history, and Theopompus give us countless myths.

219

ATTICUS: I have found now an opening I was waiting for, and I shall not miss it.

MARCUS: What opening, Atticus?

ATTICUS: For a long time now people have been asking, even begging, you to write a history, for they think you could do it well, and that in this branch of literature too we should prove that we are not inferior to the Greeks. Listen, please, to my views on the subject. I think you owe this service not only to the lovers of good literature, but to your country, because the same man who saved her should glorify her. Historical writing, as I have often heard you say, and as I myself know, is not represented in our literature. You, too, are better qualified than any other author, since, as you used to say, that type of literature especially demands an oratorical talent.

So I beg you to undertake the task and give your time to a subject of which our countrymen until now have been wholly ignorant or else neglectful. For after reading the annals of high priests, which are exceedingly dry, one comes next to the works of Fabius, or of that author whose name is always on your lips, Cato, or else Piso, or Fannius, or Venonius.[1] Yet though one may write somewhat better than another, they are all very defective. Coelius Antipater, to be sure, the contemporary of Fannius, wrote in a somewhat more vigorous style. He had a rustic, uncultivated enthusiasm without much polish or skill. However, he might have served as a warning to his successors to write with greater care. But his successors, Gellius, Clodius, and Asellio, instead of following what was good in his example, copied the dullness and stupidity of the earlier writers.

Why mention Attius? He is garrulous and lively, qualities he learned not so much from the great treasury of Greek litera-

[1] The works of these early Roman historians have for the most part been lost.

ture as from the Latin scribblers. But he uses most unsuitable diction in reporting speeches, high-flown and unbecoming language. His friend, Sisenna, is easily the best of all writers up to our time, unless there are some who have not yet published their works, about whom we cannot judge. Yet as an orator he never had your renown, and in his historical writings he shows his immaturity. Clitarchus is the only Greek writer he seems to have read, and he is content to imitate him exactly. Even if he could succeed in that, he would still have a poor style. So the task falls on your shoulders; we shall expect it of you, unless Quintus makes some objection.

QUINTUS: I have no objection. We have often discussed the subject; but there is a slight difference of opinion between us.

ATTICUS: What is it?

QUINTUS: With what era he should begin his history. I think he should begin with the very earliest days, since that period has been so badly treated that one avoids reading about it. He, on the other hand, prefers contemporary history, so that he may describe just the actions in which he himself took part.

ATTICUS: I am rather inclined to agree with him, for the greatest events of the age are happening right now in our own lifetime. Besides he will be singing the praises of his good friend, Gnaeus Pompey, and casting light on his own memorable year as consul. For myself I should prefer to have him tell us about these things rather than about Romulus and Remus, as they say.

MARCUS: To be sure, Atticus, I know this task has been required of me for a long time. If I had any leisure, I would not refuse it. But I cannot undertake such an extensive work while my mind is burdened with other matters. For I should have to be free from care and not involved in business affairs.

ATTICUS: Did you ever have free time for your other compositions? Yet you have written more than any other Roman author.

MARCUS: I have had some spare time, which I have not permitted myself to waste. For example, if I planned to spend some days in the country, I would use them for writing on a variety of subjects. But one cannot begin a history until he has previously set aside time enough for it, and such a work cannot be completed in a few days. I grow confused when I am forced to change from something I have begun to something different and I cannot easily correlate passages that have been interrupted, so as to bring it all to a right conclusion.

ATTICUS: That speech is certainly a petition for an appointment as ambassador or to some similar, leisurely and peaceful post.

MARCUS: Indeed I have rather been hoping, because of my age, to retire from public life, especially as I would not renounce our ancestral custom of giving advice to clients. I should thus be performing simply the pleasant, honorable duty of an active old man. And then I might perform the task you ask of me, and as many other large and important works as I might wish.

ATTICUS: But I fear that nobody will accept that excuse from you, and that you will be obliged to keep on with public speaking as long as you live, especially since you have been changing your style and trying a different kind of eloquence. Just as your friend Roscius, in his old age, simplified the meter of his songs, and called for a slower tempo in the flutes, so you are every day departing a little further from the elaborate style you used to employ. Now your style is not unlike that of a quiet, philosophical discourse. And since even as an old man you seem capable of making such an effort, I think you can hardly be allowed to retire on that ground.

QUINTUS: But I imagine the public would consent to your

confining yourself to pleading legal cases. So I think you might make that attempt, whenever you please.

MARCUS: I would do it, Quintus, if there were no danger in making the attempt. But I fear that while I am aiming to lessen my work, I may instead be increasing it, for I never start to plead a case without long thought and preparation. That labor would be added to my interpretation of the laws, a task not in itself so very arduous, but which would give me less time for the careful planning of my speeches, without which I have never yet dared to undertake any major law case.

ATTICUS: Why then do you not in your spare moments, as you say, explain just those very subjects, and write on civil law more fully than your predecessors have done? For from your early youth, as I remember, you were interested in law, ever since I used to go with you to Scaevola's school.[2] Nor have I ever thought that you concentrated on oratory to the extent of slighting civil law.

MARCUS: You are dragging me into a long discussion, Atticus. However, I shall attempt it, unless Quintus prefers some other subject. Since we have the leisure, I could discuss it.

QUINTUS: Of course, I should be delighted to listen to you. For what would I rather do, or how could I spend a day to better advantage?

MARCUS: Let us go then to our promenade and our benches. When we have walked about enough, let us sit down. We shall find it quite entertaining, putting questions to one another.

ATTICUS: Yes, indeed, if you are willing to discuss the subject, let us do it here, strolling along the shady riverbank of the Litis. Begin, please, by giving your opinion of the nature of civil law.

---

[2] A school of law, headed by Scaevola, who was killed in 82 B.C. during the civil war between Sulla and the party of Marius, after Marius' death.

MARCUS: My opinion? Why, the greatest men in our state have frequently rendered decisions and opinions on civil law to the people! However, though they called the subject great, they have concerned themselves more with its minor technicalities. For what is so important as the law of a state? And what is so petty as the profession of a private lawyer, necessary as it is for the citizens? I do not suppose that the men who practice this profession are wholly unfamiliar with universal law, but they make use of what they call civil law only insofar as it serves their aim, and set themselves above the general run of the people. Few of them grasp the true concept of civil law, even though they need it in actual practice.

So now, what are you asking or encouraging me to do? Write pamphlets about the law of drainage and the partition walls of houses? Or compose formulas for contracts and judgments? But those are subjects thoroughly treated by many persons, and more commonplace than the pronouncements I imagine you are expecting from me.

ATTICUS: You ask what I expect? You have written about the ideal state, and it seems logical that you should write about its laws. I notice that this was done by your much-admired Plato, whom you consider the greatest of them all and especially enjoy reading.

MARCUS: Would you like me then to discuss the subject as Plato did on Crete, with Clinias and Megillus from Sparta? He describes the summer day amid the cypress groves and the wooded lanes of Cnossus.[3] While discussing the best possible laws, he often criticizes and occasionally commends the existing laws of states. So while we are talking and resting among these stately poplars, on this green and shady riverbank, shall

---

[3] The setting for Plato's book on *Laws*.

we inquire more fully into these matters than the mere formal practice of law requires?

ATTICUS: I am truly anxious to hear this discussion.

MARCUS: What does Quintus say?

QUINTUS: There is nothing I should like better.

MARCUS: Well said! Can you imagine any other field of debate that provides as much scope for considering the topics of man's natural endowments, the capacity of the human mind to realize those noble projects we were created to initiate and perfect, the relationships of men to one another as individuals, and the natural groupings of men into communities. In trying to explain these phenomena we may discover the first principles of law and justice.

ATTICUS: You believe, then, that the fundamentals of justice should be deduced not from a praetor's proclamation, as many now assert, nor from the Twelve Tables of the Law,[4] as our forefathers maintained, but from the innermost depths of philosophy?

MARCUS: Well, Pomponius Atticus, in this discussion we are not trying to answer the questions of how to protect our clients in a lawsuit, or what advice to give our consultants. That may be an important matter, as indeed it is. Many a famous man of the past has thought it was, and one lawyer of great prestige and knowledge still does.[5] In our discussion, however, we shall embrace the whole realm of universal law, in such a way as to leave the so-called civil law to its proper narrow sphere. For first we must discover the nature of justice itself, and that is to be sought in the nature of man. We must,

---

[4] This was the first Roman code of law, enacted about 450 B.C. The text of the code has not survived except in fragments, although in Cicero's time it was customary for boys to learn it by heart.

[5] Servius Sulpicius Rufus, against whom Cicero made his plea for Murena.

next, consider the laws by which countries rightfully ought to be ruled. And then we must treat the laws and ordinances, known as civil law, which other peoples have formulated and recorded, not omitting those of our own country.

QUINTUS: You are probing deep, brother, into the problems we are to investigate, and you start, as we must, with first principles. Those who treat of civil law in other ways are exploring not so much the paths of justice as the roads to litigation.

MARCUS: That is not quite true, Quintus. Ignorance rather than knowledge of the law is the cause of lawsuits. But we shall talk of those things later. Let us look now for the first principles of right.

Many learned scholars have assumed that right springs from law. Perhaps they are correct when they define law as innate reason in the highest form, which tells us what we ought to do and forbids the contrary. When this same reason is established in men's minds, it becomes law. So they call law the wisdom which orders us to do right and forbids us to do wrong. They think too that the concept of law is derived in the Greek form from the word "nomos," which implies that each person is given his share. I, however, prefer the derivation in the Latin from our word "lego." The Greeks place the stress on equality; we place it on choice.[6] Nevertheless both these qualities are attributes of law. If this reasoning is correct, as, for the most part, it seems to me to be, the source of right must be found in law. For this is the meaning of natural law; it is a wise man's soul and reason; it is the measuring stick of right and wrong.

However, since we are assuming an ordinary type of reason-

---

[6] According to Cicero here, the Greek noun *nomos*, law, is derived from *nemein*, to distribute, and the Latin word *lex*, law, from *legere*, to choose.

ing throughout, we shall need sometimes to use colloquial expressions, and call law that which acquires authority from being written down, or, again, that which expresses its will through commands or prohibitions. But we will trace our history of jurisprudence from that supreme law which existed through the ages, before the mention of any written law or established state.

QUINTUS: That would be more fitting and suitable for the type of discussion we have undertaken.

MARCUS: Do you wish us then to seek the origin of justice at its source? After we have discovered that, there will be no doubt of the standard by which our questions should be measured.

QUINTUS: I believe we should do it that way.

ATTICUS: Put me down as agreeing with your brother.

MARCUS: And since we must maintain and preserve that republic which I had Scipio show, in my six books,[7] was the best possible state, all our laws must be appropriate for such a state; and there should even be some suggestions for manners and morals, though those details are not important enough to require recording. But I shall now examine the law of nature for the source of right; with it as guide, we should be able to carry through our discussion.

ATTICUS: You will be right. With such a guide, we can make no mistake.

MARCUS: Do you grant me this, then, Pomponius Atticus—for I know my brother Quintus' opinion—that the whole universe is governed by the energy of the immortal gods, by their special nature, their rational faculties, their power, their intelligence, their will, or whatever other word may be chosen

---

[7] The reference here is to the six books of his *Republic*, which Cicero was just finishing when he wrote this. In the *Republic*, Scipio Africanus the Younger was the chief speaker. See above, p. 207.

to express more clearly what I want to say. If you do not agree, we must begin the argument at this point.

ATTICUS: I grant whatever you ask. For the chirping birds and rippling streams make it unlikely that any of my fellow scholars will hear me.[8]

MARCUS: You are right to be cautious, for even good men sometimes lose their tempers; and they would be highly indignant if they heard you betraying the first principle of noble Epicurus, "God takes no care either of himself or of anyone else."

ATTICUS: Go on, I beg you; I am waiting to see where my concession will take us.

MARCUS: I shall not keep you waiting any longer. This is the logical deduction: that the animal called man, who is prudent, intelligent, complex, and keen, capable of remembering, of reasoning, and of planning, has been created in his magnificent state by the supreme God. He alone out of so many kinds and species of animals is able to reason and reflect, while all other creatures are incapable of it. What faculty more godlike than reason can be found, whether in man or anywhere, in heaven or earth? When this gift is mature and perfected, it may rightly be called wisdom. Inasmuch as there is no attribute superior to reason, and it is present in both God and man, it must be the essential basis for communion between man and God.

Since reason then is common to them both, the sense of right is also common to them. As the latter is, in reality, law, we should think of men and gods as linked together by law. Furthermore, those who are partners in law are necessarily also partners in justice, and those who share the same law and the same justice must be considered members of the same

8 Atticus was an Epicurean, and so could not consistently accept the doctrine of divine governance of the universe.

commonwealth. If, in addition, they obey the same supreme power and authority, their association is even more close. Now they do all obey the celestial order, the divine mind, the all-powerful God. Therefore, the whole universe should be regarded as one commonwealth of men and gods.

In commonwealths a certain order, which we shall discuss in its proper place, distinguishes ranks on the basis of family lineage. But the order of nature is much more glorious and splendid, since, according to it, men are the direct descendants and kindred of the gods. For whenever we consider the nature of the universe, we always, of course, say that once in the order of the endless progressions and revolutions of the heavenly bodies a period arrived suitable for the creation of the human race. The species spread far and wide over the earth, and was blessed by the divine gift of a soul. His other weak and frail qualities man acquired from his mortal nature, but his mind came from God. Hence we may claim we are kin, relatives or offspring of the celestial deities.

And out of many species of creatures, there is none but man that possesses any notion of God, whereas among men there is no nation either so effete or so savage as not to know that it must believe in a god, even if it does not know what sort of god he should be. From this fact we conclude that God is acknowledged by man, who almost remembers and knows his true origin. Moreover, the same moral excellence is characteristic of man and of God, and not of any other species. This excellence is simply Nature developed and brought to her fullest realization. In such ways does man resemble God. What affinity could be closer or more plain?

Nature has bestowed her gifts so liberally for man's convenience and enjoyment that it looks as if the produce of the earth had been provided for us intentionally, not accidentally. This observation applies not only to the fruits and vegetables which spring from the bosom of the earth, but to the animals also, since manifestly some of them are intended for man's service, others for breeding, and still others for meat. Under Nature's guidance we have discovered many methods of cultivation, and by intelligent imitation have found out precisely the things essential for our life.

Nature has, furthermore, equipped man with a quick mind, and given him the senses as servants and messengers. She has, besides, revealed to him the necessary knowledge of many obscure facts, which are, as it were, the fundamental principles of knowledge. She has given him a carriage adapted to his body and proper for the human intellect. For whereas she keeps the eyes of other animals cast down toward their fodder, she has made the posture of man alone erect, and has stimulated him to observe the heavens, in recollection of his former home. She has fashioned the features of his face in such a way as to disclose his most secret feelings within. Our remarkably eloquent eyes declare our sentiments, and our expressions, seen in no living being but man, betray our dispositions. The Greeks certainly recognized the significance of this fact, though they had no word for it. I only mention the other faculties and features of our body, the modulations of the voice and the power of speech, which is the chief means of communication in human society. For this is neither the place nor the time to discuss all these points properly, and I think that Scipio has brought them out sufficiently in books you have read.

Thus God created and equipped man, because he wanted him to be ruler of the universe. It is also obvious, without argument, that human nature by itself has made great advances. It has progressed without a teacher, by means of the principles recognized by its primitive and untrained intelligence. Through his own efforts man has strengthened and perfected his reasoning power.

ATTICUS: Immortal gods, how far back you have traced the principles of justice! And you have done it in so fascinating a way that I have not grown impatient for the discussion of civil law that I was expecting, but could easily let you spend the whole day in talk of this sort. For the topics you have introduced, perhaps as a preface to your other subjects, are more sublime than those for which they prepare the way.

MARCUS: The topics I have been discussing are indeed momentous. But of all the ideas propounded by learned scholars none is more important to understand clearly than this, that man was born for justice, and that justice was established not by the judgment of men but by Nature. This truth will become even more manifest if we study the kinship of man to his fellow man. For no one object is so like another as we men are like one another. If corrupt customs and fickle prejudices had not diverted weak minds from their proper lines of development, there would be no closer likeness between the various sides of one man's character than between men themselves everywhere. Hence whatever definition we give a single man applies to all men.

So the statement that there are no differences dividing the human species is sound; for one definition would not include all men if there were a difference. Certainly the power to reason, in which alone we surpass the beasts, and by means of which we can infer, argue, refute, converse, and bring an enterprise to completion, is common to all men. We have an equal chance to learn, although the kind and degree of our knowledge may differ. In all of us, the senses perceive the same objects and are affected in the same manner. The fundamental principles of knowledge impressed on the mind, of which I have already spoken, are impressed alike on the minds of all.

The faculty of speech, also, which is the interpreter of the mind, expresses everywhere the same ideas, although it may differ in the actual words used.

Thus too, there is no member of any nation who cannot attain true virtue, if he takes Nature as his guide. And human beings are conspicuously like each other not only in their goodness, but also in their shortcomings. For all men are attracted by pleasure, which has a certain resemblance to natural good, although it may lead to disgrace. Its charm and sweetness make it delightful, and so through a mental error we grasp it as beneficial. In our ignorance too we all shun death as if it were a violation of Nature's law, and cling to life, since it keeps us in the environment into which we were born. We all consider pain the greatest of evils, not only for the actual discomfort it gives us, but also because it implies the approach of death. Because too there is a resemblance between nobility and honor, men who are honored we consider happy, and obscure persons wretched. Troubles, joys, desires, and fears pervade all our minds in the same way.

People differ in their beliefs, but is it not merely that those who worship the cat and the dog as gods labor under a different superstition from that which flourishes in other lands? What nation, however, does not hold in high esteem courtesy, kindness, gratitude, and appreciation? What nation does not shun or detest the proud, the malicious, the cruel, and the ungrateful? We may thus conclude that, since the whole human race is so unified in itself, the same system of right living makes all men better. If you approve these remarks, I shall go on to others, but if any doubts occur to you, we would better clear them up first.

ATTICUS: We agree to everything, if I may answer for the two of us.

MARCUS: It follows then that Nature created all mankind to share and enjoy the same sense of right, and I wish it understood throughout our discussion that the right of which I may speak is derived from Nature. However, the corruption caused by our bad habits is so powerful that it puts out the fires of virtue kindled by Nature, and contrary vices spring up and grow strong. But if wise men, prompted by Nature, would agree with the poets that whatever touches humanity concerns them too,[9] then everyone would cultivate justice. For all to whom Nature gave the power of reasoning have received from her also the ability to reason correctly. Thus has arisen law, which is right reason as expressed in commands and prohibitions; and from law has come justice. Therefore, since Nature gave us all the ability to reason, she gave us also justice. Socrates was right in denouncing the man who first separated his personal advantage from justice; he used to complain that this separation had been the source of all evil.

Hence we may go on to assert that when one wise man feels that warm emotion which is everywhere pervasive for another equally virtuous person, there follows the inevitable result, which some find unbelievable; he loves the other man no less than he loves himself. For what difference can there be between them, when all their interests are the same? But if one makes the slightest room for his own private interest, it is the end of even nominal friendship. We all know that as soon as one wants something for himself more than for the other, there is no friendship.

I have said all this in preparation for the rest of the discussion, that you may more clearly perceive that Nature is the source of justice. After a few more words on the subject, I

---

[9] Probably a reference to the famous line in Terence, "Nothing human is alien to me."

shall proceed to take up the civil law, the starting point of our whole conversation.

QUINTUS: You will need very few more arguments. For I am convinced from what you have said to Atticus that Nature is the source of justice.

ATTICUS: How could I think anything else, now that you have so firmly established all your points? First, that we men are bountifully equipped by the gifts of the gods; second, that all mankind follows the same plan of life; finally, that all are bound together both by a natural sense of good will, and by a common law. Now that we have acknowledged that all these points are, as I believe them to be, correct, we cannot consistently separate Nature from law and justice.

MARCUS: You are quite right, and our argument is a consistent one. But the practice of modern philosophers, who set up their factories of wisdom, is to draw sharp distinctions between subjects which were once considered freely as a whole. They would not be satisfied with our present discussion, unless they had a special demonstration that justice is an actual part of Nature.

ATTICUS: You seem to have lost your freedom of judgment. Can it be that you are obeying other men's rules instead of your own principles, which have always been your guide in debate?

MARCUS: Not always, Titus Atticus. But you see the main line of my reasoning. Through this whole conversation my aim is to increase the authority of commonwealths, and to stabilize and embolden their populations. So I hesitate now to proceed with my argument for fear that the principles I started with have not been thoroughly examined and carefully considered. Not that I expect all the world to agree with me, for that is impossible. But those who believe that right and honorable things should be pursued for their own sake, and that nothing

234

should be counted good, and certainly not great good, unless it is admirable in itself, will be in accord.

Many have already agreed with me, the philosophers of the Old Academy [10] in the times of Speusippus, Xenocrates, and Polemon, the pupils of Aristotle and Theophrastus,[11] who held similar views, though they differed a little in method, and who, as Zeno,[12] thought, changed only the names they applied to the immutable principles, and the followers of the difficult and austere school of Ariston,[13] by now generally refuted, who taught that, except for virtue and vice, everything could be counted equal.

But some we shall advise to confine their talking to their own little gardens [14]—those, I mean, who pamper their bodies, and rely on the tests of pleasure and pain to decide the desirability or undesirability of everything. Even if they speak the truth, we need not discuss that question here. We will ask them to abstain from all participation in affairs of state, of which they know nothing and have never wished to know anything. We will also implore the New Academy of Arcesilaus

[10] The original school of teachers of Platonic doctrines. Speusippus (c.407–339 B.C.), Xenocrates (396–314) and Polemon (d.273) were in turn the successors of Plato (427–347) in the headship of his Academy.
[11] Aristotle (384–322), though differing in many respects from his master Plato, agreed with him in his belief in a divine cause of the universe, in eternal principles of right and wrong and in man's likeness to God through his reason. Theophrastus (c.372–287), a pupil of Aristotle, followed him as head of the so-called Peripatetic school or Lyceum.
[12] Zeno (d.c.264), founder of the Stoic school at Athens, believed that a divine providence governed the world, and that conformity to Nature or virtue was the chief end toward which man should strive.
[13] Ariston of Chios (d.250), a follower of Zeno, laid even more stress on ethics, insisting that it alone was the proper subject of philosophy.
[14] Cicero is jibing at the Epicureans. The school of Epicurus (342–270) at Athens was situated in a garden. Its founder denied the existence of any divine governance of the world, taught an atomic theory of matter, and declared pleasure to be the only rational goal for human life. He advised abstention from politics as one way to preserve serenity of mind.

and Carneades [15]—disturbing force that it is—to be silent. For if it should attack these principles, which to us seem so well established, it would bring us to utter confusion. I should like to placate them; I do not dare to order them off. . . .[16]

In some situations we may be cleansed without fumigation. But for the crimes of man against man and for impiety there is no purification. The guilty pay the penalties meted out by the courts, though in old times courts were non-existent, and even today they are unknown in many places, and, where they do exist, are often faulty. More surely they are punished by the Furies, who harass and pursue them, not with the burning firebrands of mythology, but with the pangs of conscience and the torments of disgrace. But if men were kept from wrong-doing by penalties only and not by their innate goodness, what anxiety would trouble the wicked, if once they lost their fear of punishment? For no wrongdoer, however hardened, denies that his deed was a crime, but he invents some good excuse for a justifiable grievance, or tries to defend his act by appeal to natural law. If the wicked dare to appeal to that law, should not good men strenuously uphold it?

If punishment or fear or suffering is all that keeps men from a wicked and evil life, and not the baseness of the conduct itself, then no one is really unjust, and the greatest sinners should be called unwise rather than wicked. Likewise, those of us who practice virtue do it not for herself alone but for motives of advantage and profit, and are shrewd and not good. For what will the man who dreads nothing but a

---

[15] Arcesilaus (c.316–241) and Carneades (c.213–129) were followers of Plato who emphasized the skeptical features in his philosophy. The New Academy, started by Carneades, took a radically questioning or skeptical attitude toward all assertions of human knowledge in the philosophic field. Cicero himself was considerably influenced by the New Academy. [16] There is a break here in the Latin text.

witness or a judge do in the dark? What will he do if in the desert he finds someone weak and alone, whom he may rob of a big sum of gold. A man who is naturally just and good will speak to him, help him, and escort him on his way. But you can see what will be done by that other man, who never does anything for a fellow creature and measures everything by his own advantage. If he says he would not take the weaker man's life or steal his gold, the reason for his denial can never be that he regards the act as intrinsically base, but that he is afraid he might be caught and suffer the consequences. Of such an attitude not only wise men, but even simple folk would be ashamed.

It is, however, quite absurd to call just every article in the decrees and laws of nations. What if those laws were enacted by tyrants? Suppose the Thirty Tyrants at Athens [17] had set up laws which pleased all the Athenians; merely for such a reason could those laws be considered just? No more just, I believe, than our law, instituted during the interregnum, that a dictator could with impunity put to death any citizen he chose without a hearing.

The essential justice that binds human society together and is maintained by one law is right reason, expressed in commands and prohibitions. Whoever disregards this law, whether written or unwritten, is unjust. But if justice is defined as mere compliance with the written laws and decrees of nations, and if too, as the same school affirms, all actions are to be measured by their utility, a man who thinks to gain advantage thereby will disregard the laws, if he can. It follows that the only real justice is that based on Nature, and that any

---

[17] A ring of despotic oligarchs, set up by the Spartans to rule democratic Athens, after the Spartan victory in the Peloponnesian War. The Tyrants were expelled after a year of power, 404–403 B.C. by an uprising of the Athenian democrats.

law enacted merely for utility's sake can be abrogated by some other utility.

If Nature does not endorse our law, all virtue will be thrown to the winds. For what except Nature can inspire us to generosity, patriotism, piety, charity, or gratitude? All such virtues spring from our natural inclination to love one another. This is the basic principle of justice, and without it we should feel neither good will toward our fellow men, nor reverence for the gods. For the latter, I think, is not the result of fear, but of the kinship of man to God. But if laws are to be made by popular demand, official decrees, or judicial decisions, then it might become right to rob, commit adultery, or bear false witness, wherever such acts were approved by the votes and decisions of the multitude. If the ideas and desires of foolish men can subvert Nature by a simple vote, can they not compel us to treat evil and harmful actions henceforth as good and helpful? If a law can make justice the fruit of wrongdoing, cannot the same law make good come from evil? It is only Nature's precepts that teach us to distinguish between a good law and a bad.

But with Nature's help we can draw distinctions between right and wrong, and between honorable and shameful actions. Our own common sense gives us the first principles of understanding, and impresses them on our minds, so that we connect honorable qualities with virtue and all that is disgraceful with vice. It is folly to suppose that such judgments are matters of our own opinion and not natural instincts. Not by opinion, but by Nature do we judge the excellence of a tree or a horse. This being so, whatever is either honorable or shameful we must judge with the help of Nature. If virtue in general were but a matter of our opinion, the same opinion would recognize particular virtues. Yet no one can

judge by a man's external appearance, instead of by his conduct, whether he is wise and prudent. The basis of his reputation is our correct reasoning, which is certainly a faculty of
Nature. The same thing is true of all honorable qualities. We
judge truth and falsehood, the logical and the illogical, on
their intrinsic merits, not by external standards, and so do we
recognize the consistent plan of life, which is virtue, and
the inconstancy, which is vice.

Can we not judge the character of young men in the same
manner? Is there any way but the natural one to estimate their
qualities, and the virtues and vices which arise from those
qualities? And must we not measure by Nature's standards all
their other honorable or shameful traits? Whatever is praiseworthy must have some intrinsic good to be praised! Goodness
is not just a matter of opinion—what idea is more absurd than
that? Since then we distinguish good from evil by its nature,
and since these qualities are fundamental in Nature, surely by
a similar logic we may discriminate and judge between what
is honorable and what is base according to Nature.

We are troubled in men's disputes and differences of opinion, but since in our sense impressions we seem to agree, we
think those are infallible by nature. We consider it a decep-
tion of the senses when the same object appears different to
the same person on various occasions, although that may be
far from the case. But our senses are not perverted by our
parents, nurses, teachers, poets, or dramatic shows, nor are they
seduced from the truth by popular prejudice, whereas all sorts
of snares are laid for our minds by the things I have just mentioned, which take possession of the young and uneducated
and soon influence and turn them as they will. Or pleasure,
that imitator of goodness and source of all evil, which lies in-
tertwined within our senses, corrupts us by its charms, so that

we do not sufficiently discern the things that are good by nature, because they lack a certain fascination and sensuousness.

The natural conclusion of this whole discussion should be evident from what I have just said. It is that both righteousness and honor should be pursued for their intrinsic worth. All good men indeed love justice and righteousness for their own sake, and no good man would make the mistake of loving something that did not deserve it. So we must seek out and cultivate the right for its own sake, and justice also. This being true, we must practice all other virtues too for their own sake.

What shall we say of generosity? Is it a free gift, or does it look for some reward? If it is kindness with no thought of recompense, it is a free gift; if it is kindness expecting a return, it is merely paid service. Certainly a person who deserves a reputation for generosity or kindness acts to do his duty, not to promote his own advantage. So justice too looks for no reward or profit; we choose it for its own sake. The same may be said of all the virtues and of our opinion of them. If we desired goodness for its reward rather than for itself alone, the only virtue in that attitude would properly be called shrewdness. For the more a man considers his own interest in what he does, the less good he is; those who measure virtue by its rewards think nothing is good unless it is shrewd.

Can anyone be called benevolent, if no one does a kindness for another? Can anyone feel gratitude, if he never meets a benefactor to thank? What will become of sacred friendship, if we are not to love our friend with all our heart for his own sake, as we say? Are we to desert him and cast him off, once we can get no more profit or advantage out of him? No behavior could be more inhuman than that. But if friendship is to be cultivated for its own sake, then human relations, equity, and justice, are also desirable for their intrinsic worth. If this were not so, there would be no justice at all; for to demand a reward for being just is the height of injustice.

What shall we say of sobriety, temperance, self-control, modesty, bashfulness, and chastity? Is it only fear of disgrace or dread of laws and penalties that keeps men from licentiousness? Do they practice self-control and modesty only to win a fine reputation? The truly modest blush at the mere mention of chastity. I am ashamed of philosophers who think it honorable simply to avoid notoriety, without avoiding vice itself. Can we call people virtuous who abstain from wickedness for fear of the disgrace which is the natural consequence of a base act? Can we praise or blame anyone at all, if we disregard the rule of Nature, which distinguishes between praiseworthy and blameworthy acts? Shall our physical disfigurements cause offense, but the deformities of our souls cause none, though moral corruption is clearly visible in a person's vices? Nothing is more foul than avarice, more hideous than lust, more despicable than cowardice, more contemptible than dullness and stupidity. Shall we consider persons wretched who are conspicuous for one or more of these vices, because they are perhaps suffering from certain handicaps, injuries, or ailments, or is their miserable condition to be attributed wholly to the ugly character of the vices themselves?

The opposite argument can be applied to virtue. If we strive after virtue for the sake of other advantages, it follows that something is preferable to virtue itself. Is it money then, or honor, beauty, or health? But even if we possess those advantages, they are unimportant, and we cannot know how long they will last. Or can it be that pleasure, which I blush to mention, is better than virtue? Yet we assume it is virtuous to repudiate pleasure. You can see now the interrelations of these topics and problems. I could continue indefinitely, if I did not check myself.

241

QUINTUS: Why should you stop, brother? I should be glad to follow any trend in your discussion.

MARCUS: I should eventually have to define honor and the means of achieving it. That is indeed a controversial subject, the cause of much dispute among the learned; still, it must be decided some time.

ATTICUS: Can we settle the problem, now that Lucius Gellius is dead?

MARCUS: How does that affect the matter?

ATTICUS: Phaedrus,[18] my teacher in Athens, told me about your friend Gellius, who had served as a pro-consul in Greece. He once called together all the philosophers in Athens and urged them to come to an agreement. He told them that if they were in the proper frame of mind and did not want to spend the rest of their lives in dissension, they could easily settle their difficulties. Moreover, he promised them his support to help them come to a genuine understanding.

MARCUS: It was a joke, Atticus, and an old one at that! For my part, I would aim only at an understanding between the Old Academy and Zeno's Stoic school.

ATTICUS: Why just that?

MARCUS: Because they differ on only one point, but otherwise agree remarkably well.[19]

ATTICUS: Do they disagree on only one point?

MARCUS: Yes, on one principle. All the ancient sages have defined the good as that which accords with Nature, and helps us in life. Zeno, on the other hand, thinks nothing is good but moral rectitude.

---

[18] An Epicurean philosopher under whom both Cicero and Atticus had studied in their youth at Athens.

[19] Cicero's harmonizing tendency appears again here. Plato's representatives in the Old Academy and Zeno, founder of the Stoic school, would hardly have agreed with him that they differed on only one point.

ATTICUS: But this is an inconsequential point of controversy, which certainly cannot be significant.

MARCUS: You would be quite right, even if the philosophers differed in principle and not just in terminology.

ATTICUS: You would then agree with Antiochus,[20] the friend with whom I lived, for I do not dare call him my master. He almost succeeded in tearing me away from our Epicurean gardens, and converting me to the Academy.

MARCUS: He was indeed a wise and intelligent man and highly accomplished in his way; he was, as you know, a friend of mine as well. I shall soon show whether or not I agree with him on all points. But I do say that this whole controversy could be settled.

ATTICUS: Why do you go into this question?

MARCUS: Well, Ariston of Chios considered moral rectitude the only good and baseness the only evil, and he thought all other things of equal importance, inasmuch as their presence or absence did not make the slightest difference. If Zeno had held the same views, then he would strongly disagree with Xenocrates, Aristotle, and the school of Plato. They would then be differing about a most important principle, and about the whole plan of living. Now Zeno does believe the only good is moral rectitude, called by the ancient sages the chief good. He likewise believes that the only evil is dishonor, which they called the chief evil. But he thinks wealth, health, and beauty are conveniences, though not good, and poverty, weakness, and grief inconveniences, though not evil. So he, after all, has the same opinion on the subject as Xenocrates and Aristotle, though he expresses himself differently.

The controversy over definitions arose from this difference, not of principle but of terminology. However, since the law

---

[20] Antiochus (early first century) taught an eclectic form of Platonism, one more in sympathy with the Old Academy than the New.

of the Twelve Tables requires a space of at least five feet of land between adjacent estates, let us not allow this crafty Stoic to trespass on the ancient property of the Academy. And, let us have not only one judge, as the Mamilian Law directs, but let the three of us, in accordance with the Twelve Tables, settle this question of definitions.

QUINTUS: What decision shall we hand down?

MARCUS: Let us resolve to discover and obey the definitions laid down by Socrates.

QUINTUS: That is an excellent suggestion, brother. Now, at last, you are using the terminology of civil law, the subject I have been waiting to hear you discuss. It is, as I have often heard you say, a very weighty matter. And we certainly are all ready to admit that the highest good is to live according to Nature, enjoying a life both temperate and virtuous, in other words, to follow Nature and live by her laws, doing everything as far as humanly possible to acquire the qualities she demands. That indeed is the most lawful and commendable mode of living. But I do not know that we can settle the controversy and I think not, if we continue to follow this line of argument.

ATTICUS: I, however, willingly digressed to this topic.

QUINTUS: We might go on with it at some other time. But now let us resume the original discussion, especially since the argument about the greatest good and greatest evil has nothing to do with it.

MARCUS: That is a sage observation, Quintus. But my earlier remarks were drawn from the very heart of philosophy.

QUINTUS: I am not eager to hear you talk of the laws of Lycurgus, Solon, Charondas, or Zaleucus,[21] nor even of our Twelve Tables and later decrees. I think that today you should

---

[21] Ancient and traditional lawgivers of Sparta, Athens, Sicily, and the Locrians.

outline the rules of conduct and the education proper both for nations and for individuals.

MARCUS: Indeed, Quintus, what you expect is most appropriate for our discussion, and I wish I were able to do it. In reality the law ought to penalize vices and commend goodness; hence correct rules of conduct should be drawn from the law. And the real mother of all good is wisdom, so loved by the Greeks that they composed the word "philosophy." [22] The immortal gods have given man nothing finer, more glorious, or more advantageous. For it is wisdom that teaches us, besides other lessons, the most difficult one, to know ourselves.[23] This precept is so important and so significant that it is attributed to no mortal, but to the god at Delphi.

For the man who knows himself will recognize, first of all, the godlike spark within him, and will realize that this innate quality was bestowed on him as a symbol of divinity. Thus he will always conduct himself in a manner worthy of this great gift of the gods. And when he has thoroughly examined himself, he will understand how well Nature has equipped him for life, endowing him with the means for attaining and acquiring wisdom. Even in the very beginning, the first principles of understanding were dimly imprinted on his mind and soul, and after wisdom has explained these principles, he then sees how he will become good and consequently happy.

Can anyone imagine a state more blissful than that of the man who has really achieved true virtue? He has discarded all gratification and indulgence of the body, has rejected pleasure as a thing dishonorable, and has overcome all fears of pain and death. He looks on all men as his brothers by nature, and affectionately seeks their companionship. He is a pious wor-

---

22 That is, love of wisdom.
23 The Greek maxim "Know thyself" was said to have come from the oracle at Delphi.

shiper of the gods, without yielding to superstition. He has made his mind and his eyes keen to select good and shun evil, a virtue which is called prudence because it looks ahead to the future.[24]

This same man examines the heavens, the earth, the seas, and the universe as a whole, aiming to discover the origin and destiny of living things, when and how they die, which of them is mortal and perishable and which divine and eternal. In the end he will come near to a comprehension of the Being who guides and regulates them all. And eventually he will realize that he himself is not confined by the walls of any one city, but is a citizen of the whole universe. In this magnificent situation, the result of his observation and recognition of Nature, he will know himself thoroughly, as the Pythian Apollo prescribed.

Then will he scorn, despise, and count as naught the prizes adored by the mob, and will protect his attitude by dialectic, an ability to distinguish truth from falsehood, and an understanding of formal logic. If he should feel himself equipped for public life, he will employ not only subtle persuasion, but also a more broad and enduring kind of oratory by which he may sway the populace and establish laws, punish the wicked and defend the good, sing the praises of famous men, and lay down rules of right conduct, suited to persuade his fellow citizens to aspire for glory and turn from disgrace. By it too, he may comfort the afflicted and record for everlasting recollection not only the deeds and counsels of the brave and wise, but also the infamy of the wicked. Wisdom is the mother of all these many great powers in mankind, which can be developed by those who wish to know themselves.

---

[24] The Latin word *prudentia* is a contracted form of *providentia*, which means foresight.

ATTICUS: Your praise of wisdom is excellent and justified. But whither do your remarks lead us?

MARCUS: They lead first, Atticus, to the important topics we shall now discuss. For the conclusions would not be so lofty unless the original premises were also noble. I shall discuss these conclusions willingly, and, as I hope, correctly, because I could not pass over in silence that enthralling study which has made me whatever I am.

ATTICUS: The subject is worthy of what you have truthfully said. And, as you say, the conclusions had to be reached by the way of this discussion.

LETTERS RELATING TO
HIS GOVERNORSHIP

Though the trial of Verres [1] had exposed something of the pre-
vailing corruption of Roman provincial administration, conditions after it did not much improve. Suitable candidates for
the many provincial governorships were increasingly hard to
find among those who had just held the office of consul or
of praetor. This difficulty was one though by no means the
only reason for a new law proposed by Pompey in 52 B.C.,
which prescribed that provincial governors must be chosen
from among the ex-consuls and ex-praetors who had served
more than five years previously. The measure was unquestionably designed in part to prevent Caesar from continuing his
prolonged conquests in Gaul, since it was known he intended
to be a candidate for the consulship in 48. Incidentally it
made Cicero eligible for a governorship.

The province assigned to Cicero was Cilicia and various con-
tiguous parts of southern Asia Minor, including the island of
Cyprus. The strategic importance at this time of this usually
peaceful area lay in its proximity to the region in which the
Parthian War was going on. Cicero did not look forward to
his term as governor, as one may see from Letter xii below,
though it proved to be one of his most successful political
ventures. He was most anxious to be kept well informed about
the situation at Rome during his absence, and his young
friend, Marcus Caelius,[2] undertook the task of collecting gossip, rumors, and news of all sorts for him. Letter vii from him
to Cicero, dated in May of 51, was the first in a series, of

---

[1] On Verres, see above, pp. 13–17.
[2] On Caelius, see above, pp. 157–160.

which Letter XI was a continuation. They show how conscientiously Caelius started to fulfill his promise.

On his way to his province Cicero stopped in Athens and
wrote from there Letter VIII to Memmius, who happened to
be away from Athens at the time. It is generally supposed
that this Memmius was the man to whom the Epicurean poet
Lucretius, a few years earlier, had dedicated his masterpiece
On the Nature of Things, the first great poem in the Latin
language. Cicero's contacts with the Epicurean school in
Athens dated back to his student days with Atticus in that
city, when he had attended the lectures of the Epicurean
Phaedrus and his successor Patron. We do not know whether
Cicero's appeal to Memmius was successful or what Memmius
decided with regard to the house that had once belonged to
Epicurus.

Cicero's predecessor as governor of Cilicia had been Appius
Claudius Pulcher, who, we learn from Letter IX, had left the
province in a bad way financially. Since Claudius, however,
was an influential member of the Roman nobility, Cicero
preferred to keep on good terms with him, even when his
own son-in-law, Dolabella, as he says in Letter X, brought a
suit against Claudius into court. Throughout his own administration Cicero was a model civil governor, as might have been
expected from the prosecutor of Verres. Fortunately he was
not compelled to engage personally in any serious military
campaigns. In his one enterprise of the kind he was sagacious
enough to depute the authority to his more experienced lieutenants. But they performed so well their task of reestablishing safe communications between Cilicia and the war-torn
province of Syria that Cicero himself was acclaimed as imperator by the troops on the field of Issus, the place where
Alexander the Great had once won a brilliant victory.

This bit of military success and especially the shouts of

imperator, a title normally bestowed only on generals victorious in decisive battles, gave Cicero the idea of celebrating a triumph on his return home as the true crown of his eventful career. The right to offer a public sacrifice, or *supplicatio*, and to lead a military victory procession into the city, or *triumphus*, were the highest honors in the gift of the Roman republic. For years they had been awarded only to those whose names, it was presumed, would be forever connected with the greatness of the eternal city. Cicero, however, may be excused for seeking these honors on the score of a minor military exploit, if we remember that his more memorable deeds had brought him small return, save that of exile.

LETTERS

HIS GOVERNORSHIP

Letter Seven
From Marcus Caelius Rufus to Cicero, en route to Cilicia
[*Ad Familiares*, VIII, 1]

Rome, May, 51 B.C.

I PROMISED YOU when you left that I would write you at
length, and report everything that happened in Rome. I engaged a reporter, but he went into such detail that now I am
afraid he pushes his accuracy too far. On the other hand, I
know how interested you are and how pleasant it is to people
far away to be told about even the small incidents that happen at home. And I beg you not to condemn me for the way
I am discharging my duty, delegating the work to someone
else. I should have been delighted, of course, to be constantly
remembering you, but I am busy, and, as you know, a slack
correspondent. And I think you will readily excuse me when
you see the size of the manuscript I am sending you. I have no
idea how much time it may take even to read it all, let alone
write it all out. Here it is—all the decisions of the Senate, all
the edicts, all the gossip, and all the rumors. If, by chance,
you do not like this sample, please let me know, so I shall not
go on unnecessarily taxing both your patience and my purse.

If any political event should take place which secretaries
cannot very well report adequately, I shall write you myself
and tell you how it happened, what was thought of it after-

251

wards, and what may be expected of it. At present nothing of importance is in the offing. These stories about the grant of citizenship to the people of northern Italy were hot news when I was in Cumae, but when I got to Rome I heard not a word more on the subject. Marcellus too has not yet made a motion on the new appointment for Gaul. In fact, he told me himself that he had postponed it until the first of June. He is obviously confirming those stories about him that were current while we were in Rome.

If you met Pompey, as you planned, please let me know what impression he made on you, what sort of talk you had with him, and what his wishes appeared to be, for there is usually a difference between what he thinks and what he says. But he is not clever enough to hide his true feelings.

The stories about Caesar are numerous, and none of them good. So far, they have been told in whispers, by new arrivals. One says he has lost his cavalry, which I think is certainly false. Another says that the seventh legion has been defeated, and that Caesar himself has been cut off from the army and besieged by the Bellovaci. But nothing is certain, nor are these rumors public talk. They are told as open secrets to a small group, the members of which you know—by Domitius, for example, who puts his finger to his lips.

On May 24th, some people around the Forum, confound them, spread a report that you were dead. The Forum and the whole town reverberated with a rumor that you had been murdered on your journey by Quintus Pompey.[1] I was unmoved by the story, for I knew that Pompey was starving at Bauli, and in such a state that I was sorry for him. In fact, I hoped that the lie might help to remove any dangers which might be threatening your safety. Incidentally, your dead

---

[1] This is Quintus Pompeius Rufus.

Plancus is in Ravenna, but though he has received a large gift from Caesar, he is neither wealthy nor well set up.

Your book on the *Republic* is in everyone's hands.

Letter Eight
To Gaius Memmius
[*Ad Familiares*, XIII, 1]

Athens, June or July, 51 B.C.

I WAS not quite certain whether the prospect of seeing you in Athens was painful or pleasant, for I was distressed by the injustice you have suffered, though proud of the philosophic attitude with which you bear it. Nonetheless, I wish I had seen you. For my sorrow is not diminished by not seeing you, and if I had, it would certainly have increased my pleasure— could I feel any at all. So I shall not hesitate to make an effort to see you whenever it is convenient. Meanwhile I shall take up now whatever can be discussed in a letter, and, I think, satisfactorily settled.

My first request is that you do nothing against your will even for my sake. If you think the matter important to me, and it makes no difference whatever to you, even then do not do what I ask unless you have previously convinced yourself that you do it freely.

I sympathize fully with Patron, the Epicurean, except in philosophy, where I hold opposite views. In the beginning, when he was paying special attention to you and your friends in Rome, he made a point of cultivating my acquaintance. More recently, when he had achieved all the privileges and rewards he wanted, he considered me practically his outstanding defender and friend. And now he has again been introduced and recommended to me by Phaedrus. In my boyhood days I once thought highly of the latter as a philosopher, before I knew Philo; later I saw he was simply a good, pleasant, and obliging man.

While I was still in Rome, this Patron sent me a letter, urging me to bring about a reconciliation between you and him, and to beg you to let him have some ruined house formerly belonging to Epicurus.[2] I did not write you about the matter, because I did not want my request to interfere with any building scheme of your own. When I arrived in Athens, Patron again asked me to write you and I have acquiesced, since all your friends agreed that you have abandoned your idea of building. If this is true and you are not at all interested in the subject, I wish you would take a kindly view of Patron's petition, either out of your own innate amiability or as a favor to me, in spite of whatever unpleasantness you have suffered at the hands of certain perverse persons, whose type I know. For my part, if you ask my opinion, I do not see why Patron should be going to so much trouble, nor why you should refuse him. Still it is easier to believe that he, rather than you, would stir himself up over nothing.

I am sure you know Patron's reasons for his plea. He declares he must safeguard his own honor and responsibility, the sanctity of a will, the renown of Epicurus, the instructions of Phaedrus, the house, the dwelling, even the footprints of a famous man. If we are disposed to criticize his efforts, we may as well jeer at his whole life and philosophical creed. But, on my oath, I feel no real antagonism to him or to others who choose that philosophy, and I think he should be forgiven for all the trouble he is taking. Even if he is wrong, it is because he is stupid, not depraved.

---

[2] The founder of the Epicurean school of philosophy had died over a hundred years before.

But to come to the real point—I must say it sooner or later
—I love Pomponius Atticus as a second brother. I consider
him my dearest, most delightful friend, and he is very fond of
Patron and has great esteem for Phaedrus, in spite of not belonging to their group, for he is well-versed in all humanistic
literature. He is an exceptionally unassuming man and never
at all importunate, but he is now soliciting this favor from
me with more energy than he has ever before displayed. He is
convinced that a mere nod from me would cause you to grant
the favor, even if you were thinking of building yourself. If he
hears now that you have refused my request, although you
have given up the idea of building, he will not believe you
were ungracious to me, but he will believe I was indifferent to
him. So I beg of you, write to your friends that you are willing
to have the decree of the Areopagus, called the memorandum,
annulled.[3]

But to return to what I said at the beginning. Before you
do this, I wish you to convince yourself you are doing it
willingly, for my sake. And be sure of this: if you do what I
ask, I shall consider it a very great favor.

Letter Nine
To Atticus
[*Ad Atticum*, V, 15]

Laodicea, August 3, 51 B.C.

I ARRIVED in Laodicea on July 31st. You will reckon my year
in office as beginning on that day. My arrival was much desired and I was warmly welcomed, but you will find it hard to
believe how weary I am of the whole business; for my mind

---

[3] The Areopagus was the chief administrative body in Athens.

and my energy, with which you are acquainted, do not have enough exercise, and I accomplish nothing worth while. Imagine me holding court at Laodicea while Aulus Plotius does the same in Rome, and me in nominal command of two insignificant legions, while our friend has a fine army! I do not really miss those things, but I long for public life, the Forum, the city, my home and you. I shall stand it as best I can, provided it lasts only a year. It would kill me if my term were extended. But that can be prevented if you are in Rome.

You ask what I am doing. As true as I live, I am spending money at a great rate, and am much pleased with that arrangement. The liberality I learned at your bidding is so remarkable that I fear I may have to pay your debt by asking for a new loan. I am not reopening the wounds inflicted by Appius,[4] but they are obvious, though not to the naked eye.

I leave Laodicea on August 3rd, the date of this letter, to go to the camp in Lycaonia. From there I plan to go on to the Taurus to see if I can settle the matter of your slave in a pitched battle with Moeragenes.

"The saddle bags are on the ox; 'tis clear we'll have no trouble."

But I will endure it, provided you do your best to see that my term lasts only a year. You must be there at the right time to move the Senate. I am worried because I have not heard for a long time what has been going on. So, please, as I asked you before, keep me posted about politics as well as other things. I shall write more later.

This letter, I know, will take a long time to reach you; I am giving it to a dear family friend, Gaius Andronicus of Puteoli. But you can often give your letters to the tax-collectors' postmen, through the contractors for the pasture tax and harbor duties in our districts.

---

[4] Appius Claudius Pulcher, Cicero's predecessor.

Letter Ten
To Publius Volumnius Eutrapelus [5] in Rome
[Ad Familiares, VII, 32]

Cilicia, 51 B.C.

SINCE you used a familiar style in your letter to me, as well you might, and dropped your first name, I wondered at first if it were not from my good friend Volumnius, the senator. But as I read on, your humorous banter revealed your identity. I was much pleased by everything in your letter except your neglect of your duty as my agent to protect my mines of Attic salt.[6] For you say that ever since my departure everybody's witticisms, even Sestius', are attributed to me. Why do you permit that? Are you not my defender, out to refute it? For my part, I had hoped that my witticisms were so distinctive that they would easily be recognized.

However, the level of taste in Rome is now so low that no matter how awkward a phrase may be, someone will consider it graceful. If you are my friend, show your disapproval, and make it plain beyond doubt that I am not responsible—except when some pointed innuendo, effective exaggeration, neat pun, or amusing revelation are well and cleverly expressed. The same applies to all other types of witticism, such as I have put in Antony's mouth in the second book of my *Orator*.

Your complaints of the law courts do not especially disturb me. For all I care let each defendant be dragged in by the heels! Let Selius be eloquent enough to prove he is a free man; that does not trouble me. But do let us defend my title to wit by every kind of injunction! In that line you are the only rival I fear; I despise the rest. Do you think I am making fun of you? I do now appreciate how smart you are. And, all

---

[5] A wealthy Roman knight, prefect to Antony.
[6] Delicate wit in the Greek manner.

joking aside, I did think your letter very humorous and well phrased.

But these tales you report, laughable as they are, got no laugh out of me. I sincerely hope our mutual friend will behave with real dignity while he is tribune, not for his own sake only (as you know I am very fond of him), but more especially for the sake of the country. Ungrateful though it may be to me, I shall never cease to love it.

Now that you have started this correspondence and find me pleased with it, do write me, dear Volumnius, as often as you can about affairs in the city and the political situation. I like the conversational tone of your letter. I gather that Dolabella [7] is anxious for my good opinion and favorably disposed toward me. Do encourage him, strengthen this feeling in him and make us both fast friends. Not, understand, that he has disappointed me in any respect, but I want his friendship badly and think my concern is not exaggerated.

Letter Eleven
From Marcus Caelius Rufus to Cicero in Cilicia
[Ad Familiares, VIII, 9]

Rome, September 2, 51 B.C.

"Is THAT the way you have treated Hirrus?" you say. Why, if you knew how easy it was, how little opposition he put up, you would be ashamed that he even dared come forward as your rival candidate! Now that he is defeated, he keeps on smiling, plays the good citizen and casts his vote against Caesar, finds fault with the delay and scolds Curio really vio-

---

[7] During Cicero's absence, his daughter Tullia, then a widow, married the profligate and spendthrift, P. Cornelius Dolabella.

lently. The defeat has completely changed him. He never used to appear in the Forum and seldom bothered with the law courts, but now he pleads cases for slaves wanting their freedom, though not often in the afternoon.

I wrote you that the matter of the provinces would be taken up on August 13th, but the trial of Marcellus, the consul-elect, has interfered with that. The subject was postponed until September 1st, but even then they could not get a quorum. I am sending this letter September 2nd, up to which date nothing has been done. As I see it, the question will be postponed, untouched, until next year, and, as well as I can guess, you will have to leave someone behind you to manage your province. For the matter of succession is being complicated by a suggestion that the Gallic provinces be considered in the same class as the other provinces—which will certainly be vetoed. I am sure of that. I have written you especially about it, in order that you might prepare for that eventuality.

In almost all my letters I have mentioned to you the subject of panthers.[8] It is a shame to see that Patiscus has sent Curio ten panthers and you have not sent me many times that number. Curio has given me those animals and ten more from Africa. So do not imagine that his only gifts are country estates! If you will only remember and send word to the people in Cibyra and at the same time write to the people in Pamphylia—for they say most of them are captured there—you will get what you ask. I am more anxious about this now, because I think I shall have to provide the show without help from my colleague. I beg you to take my request seriously. Ordinarily you are glad to take trouble for anyone, while I usually take none. And in this business you need only speak, that is, give a few orders and instructions. For as soon as the

---

[8] Panthers and other wild beasts were much in demand for the games at Rome.

animals are caught, the men I sent to see about the matter of Sittius' bond are there to feed and transport them. I am thinking too, if your letter gives me some hope, of sending more men.

I commend to you a fine, active young man, Marcus Feridius, a Roman knight and the son of a friend. He is coming to your province on private business and I ask you to treat him as one of your friends. He would like you to grant a tax-exemption to some lands from which certain towns draw their revenues. It is a favor you can easily and honorably grant, and you will oblige good men who will prove themselves grateful to you.

I should not like you to think that Favonius was defeated by the corner loafers only; all the best citizens abstained from voting for him. Your friend Pompey is plainly opposed to Caesar's holding a province with an army and being consul at the same time. Scipio moved that the question of the Gallic provinces be considered on March 1st, and that no other question be combined with it. The motion upset Balbus Cornelius, and I know he protested to Scipio. Calidius was most eloquent in his own defense, but rather indifferent as a prosecutor.

Letter Twelve
To Marcus Caelius Rufus in Rome
[Ad Familiares, II, 11]

Laodicea, April 4, 50 B.C.

WOULD you ever have thought it possible that words could fail me—not only those rhetorical words you public orators use, but even this everyday language I speak? That, however, is the case, because I am filled with apprehension as to what kind of decrees may be passed regarding the provinces. Strange as it may sound, I am yearning for Rome. I long desperately for my friends and particularly for you. I am tired of my province. I may feel this way because I have already achieved—so it seems to me—such an amount of fame that I do not need to work to increase it, and must rather dread a reversal of fortune. Or it may be that I feel the whole position unworthy of my powers, because I can and have performed more important duties in the state. On the other hand, my discontent may be caused by fear of the threatening great war, which I shall probably escape if I leave on the day appointed.

The matter of the two panthers is being diligently attended to by the professional hunters, acting on my orders. But there is a remarkable scarcity of the beasts and the panthers that exist are said to be complaining bitterly that in my province traps are set for no other creatures but them, and so they have decided to emigrate to Caria. But, nonetheless, the matter is being diligently attended to, especially by Patiscus. Whatever panthers there are you shall have, but how many there will be I of course do not know.

I am greatly interested in your aedileship, I assure you. The date reminds me of it, for I have written this on the very day of the Megalensia. I wish you would write me full details of the political situation, for I shall consider any information you give me entirely trustworthy.

LETTERS ON THE CIVIL WAR

When Cicero returned from his governorship, hoping to obtain his much desired triumph, he found Rome on the eve of another civil war, with little interest to spare for triumphs for victories in Cilicia. Already, in Athens, on his way back to Rome, Cicero had heard of the mounting hostility between Caesar and Pompey. Letter xiii to Atticus, written at that time, reveals that he at once realized the difficulty of his own position between the two combatants, which, as long as the conflict lasted, he was unable to improve. His heart was with Pompey, or rather with Pompey's party, as he makes clear in Letter xiv, while he detested most of Caesar's supporters, though he felt no hate for Caesar personally. At the same time, as an elderly man, he remembered only too well the disastrous effect of the war between Marius and Sulla and earnestly desired to work for peace and understanding. It was tragic that Pompey and his friends, as time went on and their chances of victory dwindled, became only more and more opposed to all attempts at a peaceful settlement, while Caesar, the enemy, welcomed and appreciated Cicero's conciliatory attitude; for Caesar saw how much might be gained by peaceful methods.

The role played by Cicero during the war might seem absurd, if one failed to remember that he had always been a man of words rather than of deeds. His many letters preserved from this period give a much fairer indication of his mental struggles than do his acts, which were usually the results of external circumstances rather than of his own volition. After the open break between Caesar and Pompey and Caesar's crossing of the Rubicon, on January 17, 49 B.C., Cicero stayed on for a while in Italy. He assured Pompey of his allegiance and was appointed commander of an unimportant region, as we learn from Letter xv. At the same time, however, Letters xvi, xvii, and xviii show us that he was in correspondence with Caesar, and even had a personal conference with him. Yet he refused to go to Rome and say publicly there what he told Caesar in private. On June 7, 49, he slipped out of Italy and went to Salonika, where he acted the part of onlooker friendly to Pompey, criticizing his strategy from a distance.

After Pompey's defeat at Pharsalus in August of 48, Cicero as the oldest ex-consul on the spot should have at once assumed the army command. He not only refused to do so, but was the first to rush back to Italy to surrender to Caesar. For nearly a year he presented an ignominious spectacle, confined to the city of Brindisi, and waiting until Caesar should finally return from Egypt. During that year he tried eagerly to win Caesar's forgiveness, calling on every last acquaintance he had in the dictator's camp to intercede for him. Among them was Cicero's own scoundrelly son-in-law, Dolabella, who had been mistreating his daughter, Tullia. Yet to ensure his own safety Cicero delayed sending Dolabella a letter demanding divorce, and even continued to pay him instalments of Tullia's dowry. The situation seemed all the more tragic in that Cicero had actually shown clear foresight in admitting the ruin of Pompey's cause immediately after Pharsalus. However, Caesar's military and political difficulties throughout that year made it always seem possible, and at times even likely, that his enemies might still win in the end and Cicero find himself once more on a losing side.

The gracious friendliness with which Caesar forgave Cicero, when at length they met at Brindisi, removed all the latter's fears for his own security, but from the standpoint of his political dignity, it was a disappointment. As long as Cicero could anticipate paying dearly for his friendship with Pompey he could feel like a hero, but after he was assured that Caesar had no intention of taking vengeance on him, he grew conscious of his own increasing personal insignificance in the new era that was obviously beginning for the Roman state. He was able to exert just enough influence on Caesar and his ruling clique to procure clement treatment for members of Pompey's defeated party.

The following years, down to the Ides of March, 44, saw Cicero filling nominally the role of general counselor and elder statesman, but in fact devoting most of his time to private literary activity. In close association with his friend Varro,[1] as we see from Letter XIX, he composed some of his most important philosophical works and essays on morals, presenting in easy, dialogue form, adapted to the Roman reading public, the teachings of the Hellenistic philosophers, which he knew so well. Since the Greek originals were later almost entirely lost, it was Cicero who preserved something of their substance for posterity. Only one of the books extant which he published during this period made any mention of politics. This was his *Brutus*, a treatise on oratory, in which the republican ideals for which he had fought were described once more in exalted terms.

The death of his beloved daughter, Tullia, in February, 45, was a shock from which he never really recovered. Little more than a year earlier, for reasons unknown, he had divorced his wife Terentia and married the young and wealthy Publilia. He now suspected Publilia of not sharing his grief at Tullia's death, in consequence of which they became estranged and were eventually divorced. Letter XX shows him

---

[1] On Varro, see above, p. 202, fn. 1.

trying to overcome his desperate sorrow by increased literary industry and by planning a worthy monument to Tullia's memory. This was to have been erected in some gardens, which he was to purchase with Atticus' help, but nothing ever seems to have come of the idea.

LETTERS

CIVIL WAR

Letter Thirteen
To Atticus in Rome
[Ad Atticum, VII, 1]

Athens, October 16, 50 B.C.

THOUGH PRESSED for time, I did in fact give Lucius Saufeius a letter just for you, because I did not want such an intimate acquaintance of yours to appear without a word from me. But considering the pace of philosophers, I suppose this letter will reach you first.

If you have already received my earlier letter, you will know that I arrived in Athens on October 14th, and disembarked at the Piraeus, where your friend Acastus handed me the letter from you. I was greatly disturbed, I wrote, to learn you had arrived in Rome with a fever, but was encouraged by Acastus' welcome news of your recovery. On the other hand, I was horrified at your report on Caesar's legions. I begged you to prevent our ambitious friend Philotimus from doing us any harm, and explained briefly another matter we discussed long ago—why I had not put my brother in charge of the province. Later that good fellow Xeno wrote me that Turranius had told you the wrong story at Brindisi. This was practically the substance of my other letter. Now hear what follows.

In heaven's name, please devote all the love you have poured out on me and all your remarkable sagacity to a consideration of my position. For I believe I foresee a struggle of violence without precedent, unless the same god who saved us—beyond my wildest hopes—from a Parthian war now again shows some pity for our country. True enough, I would be sharing this misfortune with the world at large. But I am not asking you to consider the situation as a whole, but imploring you to solve my own problem.

It was on your advice, you see, that I made friends with both of them. How I wish I had listened to your kindly warnings at the beginning.

"But never did you convince my stubborn heart." [1] Finally, however, you did persuade me to accept the one, because he had done me many favors, and the other, because he was so powerful. I accordingly did so, and humored them to the point of being the best of friends with each of them. I figured that an alliance with Pompey would not necessitate any political break, and an agreement with Caesar would not entail any quarrel with Pompey; the two were linked so closely together. Now, as you point out and as I see for myself, a desperate struggle between them is imminent. Each of them, moreover, considers me as his friend, unless, possibly, Caesar is pretending. Pompey has no doubts, believing correctly that his present attitude in politics has my complete approval. In the same mail with your last letter came two from them, each one implying that its writer thought more highly of me than of anyone else in the world.

Now what am I to do? I ask no advice about my final decision, for if it comes to open war, I prefer to lose with Pompey than win with Caesar. But what about the questions that will be under discussion in the Senate when I return? Should the candidacy of a man away from Rome not be counted, and must he disband his army? "Speak, Marcus Tullius!" What shall I say? "Wait, please, till I consult Atticus"? I shall not

---

[1] *Odyssey*, IX.

be able to evade the question. Vote against Caesar? What about our previous pledges? For when Caesar asked me at Ravenna, I helped him to obtain his privilege by speaking to the tribune Caelius. Was I asked by Caesar? Yes, and by our friend Pompey too, during that immortal third consulship!

Shall I decide in the other's favor? "I fear"—not only Pompey, but also "the men and women of Troy." "Polydamas will be the first to find fault." [2] Who is he? Why you, who are always praising my acts and writings. Did I escape this trap only to fall into the snare now? I shall let someone else be the first to vote. I should vastly prefer to be busy with my triumph, which would give me the best possible excuse for staying outside the city. However, they will do their best to make me express my opinion.

Perhaps you will laugh at all this. I wish to goodness I were still in my province. I would certainly have stayed on, if I had known this trouble was threatening. And yet it would have been depressing. I want you, by the way, to know that all those fine qualities I displayed at the beginning, which you in your letters praised to the skies, were only superficial. True virtue is far from easy and it is difficult even to pretend to it for any length of time. I thought it would be a fine and noble act to give Gaius Caelius, my quaestor, enough money to last a year and then pay back to the treasury a million sesterces [$50,000] out of the annual allowance assigned me by decree. But my whole staff thought that the money should have been distributed among them, and complained that I was a better friend to the treasuries of Phrygia and Cilicia than to our own. However, I was adamant, because my reputation is more important to me than anything else, but I have taken pains to honor these men in every way possible. These remarks are a

---

[2] *Iliad*, vi and xxii.

digression, as Thucydides would say, though not mere idle words.

But please think about my predicament! First, what trick will help me to keep Caesar's good will? Then there is the matter of my triumph, which I still think can be easily arranged, unless some critical turn in the situation at Rome prevents it. This I gather from the letters of my friends, as well as from the public thanksgiving decreed in my honor. The man who voted against that voted actually for more than if he had awarded me all the triumphs in the world. One of his adherents was my friend Favonius, the other my enemy Hirrus. Cato himself saw the drafting of the decree and sent me a very pleasant letter about his vote. Then Caesar sent me his congratulations on the thanksgiving, making much of Cato's vote without mentioning the latter's speech on the occasion. He merely stated that Cato voted against my having a thanksgiving.

To come back to Hirrus, you have begun to reconcile him to me; finish the process. You are a friend of Scrofa and Silius. I have already written to them and to Hirrus as well. In an informal conversation with them Hirrus remarked that he could have prevented the decree, but did not wish to do so. He said that he agreed, nevertheless, with my dear friend Cato, when the latter cast his vote, so flattering to me. He then complained that I had written to all the others, but not to him. He was right; the only persons to whom I had not written were he and Crassipes. But enough about politics! Let us return to domestic matters.

I wish to dissociate myself from that creature Philotimus. He is nothing but a bungler, a blood-brother of Lartidius.

"But let us forget the past, grieved though we be at heart." [3]

---

[3] *Iliad*, XVIII.

Let us settle the other problems, but this one first, because it causes me anxiety in addition to my distress. I do not want whatever money comes from Precius to be mixed up with my accounts, which Philotimus handles. I have written to Terentia and to Philotimus himself that I would deposit with you whatever money I can collect for my prospective triumph. That way I think no one will feel slighted, unless they so choose! Here is another task for you—how shall I begin? In your letter from Epirus or Athens you indicated certain steps to take, and I shall follow your suggestions in that respect.

Letter Fourteen
To Atticus in Rome
[Ad Atticum, VII, 6]

Formiae, December 17, 50 B.C.

I HAVE absolutely nothing to write—you know all my news. And I cannot expect anything from you. But let me keep to my old habit of letting no one go to you without a letter from me. I am in desperate fear for our country. So far I have met hardly anyone who does not think it better to accept Caesar's terms than to fight it out. His demands are, of course, brazen, more drastic than we had imagined. But why begin trying to stop him now?

"For no greater evil now menaces us—" [4] than when we extended his term of office for five years, or when we permitted him to run for office while still absent from Rome. Can it be that we then gave him these weapons so that we might now have to fight a well-armed adversary? You will say, "What then is your opinion?" Not the same that I shall ex-

---

[4] *Odyssey*, XII.

press. For I feel myself that everything should be done to avoid an open war. But I shall say whatever Pompey says, and I shall not do it out of servility either. On the contrary, the calamity threatening the state is so vast that it would not be right for me, even less than for others, to differ from Pompey on so momentous a matter.

Letter Fifteen
To Atticus in Rome
[Ad Atticum, VII, 11]

Campania, January 19, 49 B.C.

I ASK you—what is all this about? What is going on? I am completely in the dark. People say, "We are holding Cingulum! We have lost Ancona! Labienus has deserted Caesar!" Are we speaking of a Roman commander or of Hannibal? [5] Cursed madman, he never saw so much as the shadow of virtue! And he claims to be doing all this to protect his good name. Can a man without honor have a good name? Is it honorable to keep an army without the people's consent, to seize his fellow citizens' towns as a base for attack on his own country? Is it honorable to plot the cancellation of debts, the restoration of exiles and hundreds of other crimes,

"To achieve the boon divine, a tyranny?" [6]

Let him keep his fortune! By heaven, I should far rather have a well-earned holiday, basking in your sunny land, than any royal dominion of that kind. And I should rather die a

---

[5] The famous Carthaginian general and invader of Italy in the third century B.C.
[6] Euripides, *Phoenissae.*

thousand times than once plan such a scheme. "What if it happened to appeal to you?" you ask. Well, anyone may have a wish, but I regard this kind of wish as more shocking than a crucifixion. One fate would be worse—to realize such an ambition. But enough of this! A little philosophizing is a relaxation in the midst of these troubles.

To turn to our friend, what, in heaven's name, do you make of Pompey's plan? Why, I am asking, did he leave Rome? I am at a loss to explain it. Nothing could be more unreasoning. Would you desert the city? Would you do it if the Gauls were coming? "The republic," he says, "is not a matter of stones and cement." But it is a matter of altars and hearths. "Themistocles did the same." [7] Yes, because one city alone could not resist a horde of all the barbarians. Some fifty years later, however, Pericles did not desert Athens, even though he held nothing but the walls. Long ago our ancestors clung to the citadel, when the rest of the city was captured.

"Such were the glorious deeds of bygone days." [8]

On the other hand, Pompey's plan may work out successfully in the end. This I deduce from the resentment felt in the towns and from the conversation of men I meet. They do complain bitterly (I do not know if this is true at Rome, but please tell me) that the city has been left without magistrates and without a senate. But in general, Pompey's flight has moved me strangely. What do you think? The situation has entirely changed and people are now unwilling to grant Caesar any concessions. Please explain the significance of this.

My own duties are not exciting. Pompey wants me to be his inspector for the whole of Campania and the coastal area, in charge of the levy and other important business. So I expect to be on the move. You must be seeing by now in what

[7] Themistocles deserted Athens.
[8] *Iliad*, IX.

direction Caesar is going, how the people feel and the general state of affairs. Please write me about these things, and since they change rapidly, write often. My mind is at rest when I am writing to you or reading your letters.

Letter Sixteen
Julius Caesar to Cicero at Formiae
[Ad Atticum, IX, 6a]

On the road, near Brindisi, March 7, 49 B.C.

I HAVE already seen our friend Furnius, and I was unable to talk with him or listen to him conveniently, for I was on the march and in a hurry, having sent my legions on ahead. But I could not let an opportunity of writing to you pass, so I send him to convey my thanks. In the past I have done this often and in the future I expect to do it still more often; you are such a benefactor of mine. I hope to reach Rome shortly and beg you especially to let me see you there, that I may take advantage of your advice, influence, position, and help of every kind. To return to what I said first, kindly forgive my haste and the brevity of this letter. You may learn everything else from Furnius.

Letter Seventeen
Cicero Imperator to Caesar Imperator, Greetings
[Ad Atticum, IX, 11a]

Formiae, March 19, 49 B.C.

WHEN I read your letter, brought by our friend Furnius, inviting me to come to Rome, I was much surprised that you

273

wished to take advantage of my "advice and position," but I asked myself what you meant by my "influence and help." My hopes, however, lead me to believe that a man of your remarkable understanding desires to achieve tranquillity, peace, and harmony for our fellow citizens. For such an undertaking I do consider myself well suited by character and disposition.

If that is the case and if you are anxious to save our friend Pompey and reconcile him to yourself and the state, you will assuredly find no one more suitable for the purpose than myself. As early as I could I advised him and the Senate to keep the peace, and after the outbreak of hostilities I took no actual part in the war. I believed that you were being wronged in this war by men who were jealous of the honor conferred on you by the Roman people, and were working to deprive you of it.

But just as I then personally supported your position and advised others to stand by you, so now I am much concerned about Pompey's situation. Many years have passed since I selected both of you as objects of my admiration and friendship, as indeed you are. Accordingly, I ask you, or rather I pray and most earnestly beseech you, in spite of your pressing problems, to give some time to considering how, with your help, I may show my devoted gratitude for the favors I have received. Even if this matter were a concern of mine only, I should count on you to grant my request. But in my opinion, it is to the best interest of both you and the country to keep me, a friend of both parties and an ardent lover of peace, in a position to restore harmony between you two and among all citizens.

I have already thanked you for sparing the life of Lentulus, who once saved mine. After reading his letter, so full of deep gratitude for your generous kindness, I feel as much indebted to you as he is. If you can understand how grateful I feel in his case, please give me an opportunity of showing my gratitude to Pompey too.

Letter Eighteen
To Atticus
[Ad Atticum, IX, 18]

Arpinum, March 28, 49 B.C.

I DID both the things you advised. I spoke so as to win his[9] respect, though not his gratitude, and I refused to return to Rome. We were wrong in considering him easy to handle. Quite the opposite is true. He said other men would be slow to return if I did not come back and in this way my decision would harm him. I stressed the fact that I was in a different position from the others. After considerable discussion, he said, "Come, then, let us talk of the peace." "As I look at it?" I asked. "Am I to tell you what to say?" he retorted. I replied, "My position would be that the Senate should oppose your going into Spain and your taking the army into Greece. Moreover, I should express my regrets about Pompey." He replied, "I do not want any such speech." "That's what I thought," I said. "Neither do I want to go to Rome, for then I should have to say that and many other things which I could not help saying if I were there. The alternative is—not to go." The result was that he closed the conversation with a suggestion that I think things over. I could not refuse that request and we parted. But I think he does not like me. I, however, am more pleased with myself than I have been for a long time.

For the others, ye gods, what a crew! What a parade of lost souls, as you used to say! In this array Celer is one of the heroes. What a rotten enterprise of desperadoes! Think of it

---

[9] Caesar is of course the person referred to.

—sons of Servius and of Titinius in an army opposed to Pompey! Six legions! But his vigilance and courage are tremendous. I see no end to our misfortunes. Your advice is urgently needed. This has been the last straw.

His final words, which I almost forgot to mention, were bitter. He said, "If I cannot have the help of your advice, I shall ask whomever I can, and shall go to the limit. . . ." You will say, "Was he really as you describe him? Did it cost you a pang?" It did. But that is that! What next? He went straight to his villa at Pedum, I to Arpinum, to wait for your cheery answer. "Come," you will say, "do not cry over spilt milk! Even our leader has made many mistakes."

So I am waiting for your letter. It is too late now for your "Let us see how things turn out." This meeting was a critical event. There is no doubt in my mind that I have offended him, which is another reason for quick action. I am expecting your letter to be on the whole political situation. Indeed I am waiting for it very anxiously.

Letter Nineteen
To Marcus Terentium Varro at Tusculum
[Ad Familiares, IX, 2]

Rome, about April 20, 46 B.C.

WHEN our mutual friend Caninius came to me late one night and said he was going to see you early the next day, I said I should have something to give him and asked him to return in the morning. I wrote you a letter that night, but he did not come back. He must have forgotten. However, I should have sent the letter on by some of my men, had I not heard from Caninius that you were about to leave your Tusculan villa. But, a few days later, when I least expected him, Caninius showed up in the morning. He said he was then on his way to see you. My letter was stale, especially as so much had happened meanwhile, but I did not want my midnight effort wasted and so I gave him the old letter. At the same time I had a conversation with your learned friend, and I expect he has told you about it.

I advise you to do what I am advising myself—avoid being seen, even if we cannot avoid being talked about. For those who are glad of the victory look on us as beaten men, while those who regret our defeat resent our being still alive. You may wonder why, if the situation is so unpleasant here, I have not left Rome, as you did. You, of course, outdid me and the others in foresight and knew all that would happen; you made no mistake. But who has the gift of Lynceus [10] to find his way in such darkness without running into one obstacle?

I myself have thought for a long time that it would be a comfort to go away somewhere, so as to avoid seeing what is being done here and hearing all that is said. But I have constantly scolded myself and been sure that anyone I met then would feel justified in suspecting my motives, or, at any rate, would say, "The man is frightened, and that is why he is running away, or else he has a scheme in mind and a ship ready in port." Even those who perhaps know me best and suspect me least would still believe that I left because I could not stand the sight of certain persons. To prevent this suspicion, I am still in Rome. Long experience has at last hardened me so that I can stomach it. That is my reason for advising you as I do.

My advice to you then is this. Lie low for the time being wherever you are, until the celebrating calms down and we

---

[10] The Argonaut, famous for his keen sight.

hear how things have been settled, for settled they have been, I am sure. It will make a great difference what the state of Caesar's temper may be and what the outcome of the campaign. I think I know what is going to happen, but still I wait for the final event. I really do not want you to go back to Baiae until all this shouting is over and done with. It will be better for our reputation, even though we did leave there, if people think we went to mourn rather than to bathe. But you know this better than I do.

Only let us be firm in the resolution to spend the rest of our lives in study together. In times past we found merely pleasure in that occupation, but now it will mean self-preservation. Let us respond too to any request for help in the reconstruction of the state, be it as architects or even as laborers. Better yet, let us respond joyfully. If no one wants our help, let us read and compose essays on government. If our voices are no longer heard in the Senate and in the Forum, let us follow the example of the ancient sages and serve our country through our writings, concentrating on questions of ethics and constitutional law. This is what I am thinking. I should be very glad if you would write me about your plans and your views on these matters.

Letter Twenty

To Atticus

[Ad Atticum, XII, 52]

Tusculum, May 21, 45 B.C.

I THINK you will remember Lucius Tullius Montanus, who accompanied my son abroad. His brother-in-law now writes me that Montanus owes Plancus 20,000 sesterces [$1,000], which he gave as bail for Flaminius. I don't know what Montanus has asked you to do. Personally, I wish you could be of assistance, either by talking to Plancus or in some other way. I feel I owe that much to Montanus. If you, by any chance, know more about the matter than I do, or if you think I should approach Plancus, please let me know the situation and what I should do about it.

I am anxious to hear what you have done about the letter to Caesar. I do not care so much about Silius. You must try to get me either Scapula's gardens or Clodia's.[11] Somehow or other you seem to be doubtful about Clodia's plans. Is it a question of the date of her arrival or whether or not she will sell? What is this I hear about Spinther's getting a divorce?

Do not worry over my use of the Latin language! [12] You will say, "Look at the subject you are treating!" My reply is, "Those are translations and need little effort; I only supply the words, of which I have plenty."

---

[11] Cicero wished to acquire these gardens as a memorial in honor of his daughter, Tullia.
[12] Evidently Atticus had been criticizing Cicero's style in one of his paraphrases from the Greek.

LETTERS AFTER CAESAR'S ASSASSINATION

Cicero was present on March 15, 44 B.C., when Caesar was murdered, and was taken completely by surprise. His immediate reaction, however, was one of relief and joy at the liberation of the republic from the grip of the overweening dictator. Letter XXI, a short, excited note to Basilus, is always interpreted as referring to the gruesome event.

For the following weeks he and Antony were the leading men in Rome, Cicero as spokesman for the Senate, Antony as consul and executor of Caesar's will. But the two men had never been on cordial terms, and before long they were acknowledged enemies. The formal politeness with which they addressed each other, a little more than a month after Caesar's death, is illustrated by Letters XXII and XXIII on the subject of Sextus Clodius, the son of Cicero's old enemy Clodius,[1] who was closely related to Publius Clodius, Antony's step-son.

A few months later, Cicero delivered the speech known as the *First Philippic*,[2] which marked his open breach with Antony. At the same time, he wrote two letters—one of them Letter XXIV—to Cassius, who had taken part in Caesar's assassination, urging him and his comrade Brutus to start action in defense of the republic. Cassius had been a member of Pompey's party, to whom Caesar had showed clemency and granted favors. His "lean and hungry look" has since been immortalized by Shakespeare.

But the relationship between Cicero and the Liberators was quite one-sided; all enthusiasm, energy, and vitality on the part of the aging Cicero, all pessimism and cynicism on the

---

[1] See above, p. 118.
[2] See below, p. 296.

part of the younger men. The letters to and from Brutus belonging to this period reveal clearly the hopelessness of Cicero's aims to restore a system of government that had proved itself unable to meet the demands of a new, expanding age, and to enlist the interest of the young Octavian, Caesar's nephew and adopted son, in the attempt. Letter xxv is Cicero's own summary of his futile efforts during the year after Caesar's death.

281

LETTERS AFTER CAESAR'S ASSASSINATION

Letter Twenty-One
To Lucius Minucius Basilus
[Ad Familiares, VI, 15]

Rome, March 15, 44 B.C.

CONGRATULATIONS! I am overjoyed! I admire you and have your best interests at heart! I want you to return my affection, and I should like to know how you are and what is going on.

Letter Twenty-Two
Antony Consul sends Greetings to Marcus Cicero
[Ad Atticum, XIV, 13a]

South Italy, April 24, 44 B.C.

I WAS so preoccupied and you left so suddenly that I was unable to discuss the following matter with you in person. I am therefore afraid that you may take it lightly, since I cannot talk to you about it. But I should be delighted if you would prove as generous as I always thought you were.

I had asked Caesar to permit Sextus Clodius to return from exile, and he had granted my request. But even then I planned to take advantage of the favor only with your permission. I am anxious now to obtain your consent to it. If you are unimpressed by the wretched condition in which Clodius lives, I shall not argue with you, in spite of the fact that I think I ought to carry out Caesar's intention. On the other hand, if you want to take a more favorable and reasonable attitude towards me, you will be liberal in this matter.

You will also be glad to have the promising young Publius Clodius think you are not going out of your way to hurt friends of his father. Make it clear, I beg you, that your hostility towards his father was purely on political grounds, and that you bear no ill will towards the family. Such political enmities can be more readily and honorably dropped than a personal feud. Do allow me this opportunity to give the young man an object lesson, and show him at his tender age that quarrels need not be perpetuated from generation to generation. I am sure that you yourself, my dear Cicero, are entirely out of danger, but I believe you would prefer a quiet and honored old age to one shadowed by anxiety.

Finally, I think I am entitled to ask this favor of you, since I have done everything in my power to help you. But if you refuse, I shall not have Clodius recalled, just to show you how highly I respect your authority; besides, this assurance may make you more lenient.

Letter Twenty-Three
Cicero to Antony, Consul, Greetings
[Ad Atticum, XIV, 13b]

Puteoli, April 26, 44 B.C.

THERE is just one reason why I wish your request had been made in person rather than by letter. For then you could have seen my affection for you, not only from what I said but also from the way I said it. Indeed, I have always felt warmly toward you, first because of your interest in me, afterwards because of the favors I had from you. And now the political situation makes you more dear to me than anyone else. Your letter was written in such a friendly, even flattering tone that I felt more as if I were receiving a favor than being asked to grant one. You declared yourself unwilling, without my consent, to help a man who is your friend and my enemy, and this, though you could easily do it.

I am, of course, delighted, my dear Antony, to grant your request. I think you treated me in your letter with the utmost liberality and courtesy. Indeed, I should have agreed to any request of yours, whatever it might have been, under the impulse of my own natural kindliness. I was never a hard man, nor in any way severe beyond the requirements of my political position. Moreover, I never had any personal grudge against Clodius, and it was always my opinion that one should not bear malice against the friends of one's enemies, especially those of a lower class, nor should we deprive ourselves of such supporters.

As to young Clodius, I think it is your duty to imbue him "at his tender age," as you say, with the conviction that no enmity exists between me and his family. In my struggle with Publius Clodius, I represented our country, he, his own interests. Our controversy was ended by a public decision. Were he now alive, I should have no more quarrel with him.

Since while presenting your request, you protest that you will not use your authority against my will, you might, if you have no objection, grant this concession to the young man as a favor from me. Of course, a man of my age has nothing to fear from a man of his age, nor does a man in my position have to fear any quarrel. Pray do this, however, so that we two may become more friendly than we have been as yet. For as long as these feuds lasted, I was more often in your thoughts than in your house. But enough of this!

Let me add this one word. I shall always, without hesitation and with utmost diligence, do whatever is your desire and for your interest. Please be assured that I mean this sincerely.

Letter Twenty-Four
To Cassius
[Ad Familiares, XII, 2]

Rome, late September, 44 B.C.

I AM glad that you like the motion I made in the Senate and my supporting speech.[1] If I were permitted to do that sort of thing more often, we should have no trouble in restoring freedom and orderly government. But this man Antony is insane and corrupt and much worse than Caesar, whom you called the worst of the villains when you killed him. Antony wants now to start a blood bath. He accuses me of having been responsible for Caesar's death, merely in order to arouse against me the wrath of Caesar's veterans. But I am not afraid of that danger, which, in fact, only adds to my reputation the glory of your deed.

We can no more enter the Senate with safety, neither Piso, who was the first to attack Antony—but found no support— nor I, who repeated the attack a month later, nor Publius Servilius, who followed me. The gangster is out for murder and he expected me to be the first victim on September 19th. He came all set, having prepared himself for several days at Metellus' villa, though what sort of preparation could it have been, in the midst of women and wine? As I wrote you before, everyone could see he was spitting out words, not making a speech.

---

1 This was the *First Philippic*.

You write you are sure my popularity and eloquence will do some good. Well, considering the desperate state of affairs, it may help a little, for the people of Rome have now realized that three ex-consuls, outspoken patriots, cannot appear in the Senate with safety. But this is as far as it goes, and you can expect no more.   .

Your dear relative, Lepidus, enjoys his new marriage. He does not care for sports any more and is annoyed by the popularity of your brother. Another relative of yours has been cowed, because his name occurred in Caesar's memoranda. One could stand all this, but it is unbearable to see a man who thinks his son may be made consul rather than you and Brutus, who accordingly humiliates himself before this brute.

To mention a few names, my friend, Lucius Cotta, hardly ever comes to the Senate because, as he says, its doom is inevitable. Good, upright Lucius Caesar is suffering from ill health. Servius Sulpicius, who has great influence and a sound judgment, is away from Rome. I trust you will pardon me if I consider no one else deserves the consular rank but the two who are going to be consuls next year. And here you have our political leadership! In times of peace this would be a pitifully small number. What shall I say of it now, in this desperate situation? So you see, all our hope rests on you. But if you men hold aloof, just to be safe, we shall not be able to count even on you. If, however, you are planning some action worthy of your fame, please start on it while I am still alive. But even though this should not happen, our country will eventually come into its own through your efforts. I am helping your friends and relatives here and shall not fail to do so in the future, regardless of whether they come to me or not. My faithful affection for you will always remain the same. Farewell.

Letter Twenty-Five
To Brutus in Macedonia
[Ad Brutum, I, 15]

Rome, mid July, 43 B.C.

MESSALA is now with you, and I am sure that no letter of mine, however conscientiously composed, could explain to you the general state and trend of politics better than he can. For he is not only exceptionally well informed, but thoroughly capable of presenting any subject lucidly. I am about to say something about him, dear Brutus, which of course is well known to you, but I simply must remark on so much unique excellence in any one man. You know that no one can measure up to him in honesty, faithfulness, diligence, and patriotism. Compared with these great qualities, his eloquence, which is admirable, hardly deserves praise. Yet there is more in his oratory than one would think. For his sound judgment and fine feeling for style make him a real expert in rhetorical art. The minute care with which he prepares himself for his work sometimes distracts attention from his great innate talent.

But, alas, I am being carried away by my affection. It is not the purpose of this letter to praise Messala, not to Brutus, at any rate, who knows his qualities as well as I do, and appreciates even better the accomplishments of fine oratory. I was much grieved at his leaving. My only consolation is that he is going to you, who are a part of myself, that he serves in an important capacity, and that he will acquire much glory for himself. So much for that!

I should like to return now to a passage in an earlier letter of yours in which, after paying me compliments, you rebuked me for proposing an excessive number of public honors. That is your point of view. Someone else may complain of my

287

harshness in proposing punishments; or perhaps you would agree with that criticism too. If that is the case, I should like you to understand clearly the purpose behind my act. And what I am saying is not just borrowed from Solon, the wisest of the Seven Wise Men, and also the only one who actually functioned as a lawgiver. But he said that a political organization is kept together by two things—rewards and punishments. In either case, naturally, as in every other case, a certain moderation should be used. But that topic is too complex for a letter.

However, I think it my duty to explain the principles I have followed during the present conflict, whenever I raised my voice in the Senate. After Caesar's death, that is, after your memorable deed on the Ides of March, my dear Brutus, I pointed out some things you and your friends had omitted and the perils threatening the state. I hope you have not forgotten that. True enough, you did remove an evil blot from the annals of the Roman people, true enough, you have acquired a god-like glory. Yet the "royal" power did pass to Lepidus [2] and Antony! One of these two is the more unreliable, the other the more corrupt. Both are afraid of peace and hate quiet. We had no weapon in our hands to oppose their determined intention to create a condition of turmoil in the state.

Then the populace arose, resolved to maintain their liberty. I myself was perhaps too daring. You may have been more prudent in leaving the city you had liberated and refusing to look after Italy when you were asked to do so. But with the city in the hands of murderers and under the armed control of Antony, when neither you nor Cassius could stay there safely, I thought I too should leave town. I found it horrible

---

[2] One of the *triumviri* with Octavian and Antony.

to see our city ruthlessly crushed without any possibility of rescue. And yet my staunch patriotism would not permit me to leave my country in danger. So when on my way to Greece I was driven by the Etesian winds back to the Italian coast, a divine intervention to keep me from my journey, and I met you at Velia, I was greatly distressed. You, Brutus, were leaving, and I use the term "leaving" only because our Stoic friends claim that the wise man never flees. But I went to Rome and openly opposed Antony's enormities. I made him hate me, but I took steps tending towards the liberation of the state, and thus truly followed your family tradition.

The rest of the story is too long and must be omitted, for it has to do chiefly with my own actions. I will say this much: it was my idea to bring the young Caesar [3] to Rome and if it had not been for him—let us admit it—we should all now be dead. It is a fact that I proposed honors for him, but those, my dear Brutus, were not only well deserved, but also necessary. That was the time when we were beginning to regain our liberties. Decimus Brutus had not yet revealed his extraordinary wisdom. Young Caesar was the only protection for our necks from Antony's sword. Would any honor have been too great to grant him? All I actually did was praise him when I spoke, and that with moderation. I did vote to grant him unrestricted powers, which may seem too great an honor for a man of his age, but necessary, of course, for the commander of an army. For what use is an army, if its commander does not have full powers? Philippus proposed a statue for him. Servius suggested lowering somewhat the age-requirements for holding office; Servilius went even beyond that. At that time no honor seemed too great.

I do not know the reason, but it seems that frightened

---

[3] Octavian.

people are more apt to be generous; once victorious, they are ungrateful. When Decimus Brutus was freed, a glorious day seemed dawning over the city. Since the day happened to be Brutus' birthday, I proposed that Brutus' name be given to it in the official calendar. I was following the example of our ancestors, who granted that honor to Larentia,[4] on whose altar you priests regularly offer sacrifices. By proposing the honor for Brutus, I meant to immortalize that most welcome victory by entering it in our calendar. On that very day, however, I discovered that the ill-disposed members of the Senate outnumbered the grateful ones.

At the same time I was pouring honors, as you would say, on Hirtius, Pansa, and Aquila, too, all of whom were dead. But who can object to that, except a man who forgets a danger altogether once it is past. In thus commemorating their services in years gone by I had also in mind some benefit for the future, for I wanted to see established an undying reminder of the public wrath against cruel enemies of the state.

I fear you do not approve of one measure that was rejected by your friends, who are fine men, but politically inexperienced. I refer to my proposal to grant an ovation for young Caesar. I may be wrong, for I am not the kind of person who believes his own way necessarily right, but I think I took no more prudent step in the present conflict. The reason for my belief I cannot reveal, or else I might appear to be looking for future benefits, when I really am returning thanks for past favors.

I have already said too much, but notice some other points. I have mentioned the honors I proposed for Decimus Brutus and Lucius Plancus. Great minds in my opinion are stimu-

---

[4] Nurse of Romulus and Remus.

lated by the prospect of glory. The Senate itself wisely attracts men to the service of the state by every honorable means. In the case of Lepidus, I am criticized as being responsible for having his statue erected on the Rostra, but I was also responsible for having it removed. By giving him a public honor I tried to check him in his wild career. But the weakling's folly triumphed over my shrewd plan. However, the harm done by erecting a statue to him was outweighed by the good effect of removing it.

I have said enough about the rewards of public service. I should like now to say a few words about the punishments. In your letters I have often noticed your ambition to be praised for clemency to defeated enemies. You are indeed usually very reasonable, but while to waive all punishment for crime—and this is what clemency amounts to—may be permissible in some circumstances, in this war I think it would be disastrous. In all the civil wars I remember, whichever party won, some sort of political organization was still left standing. If we win in the present conflict, I cannot tell what sort of government we shall have, and if we lose, we certainly shall have none at all. It is for this reason that I propose the severe measures against Antony and Lepidus, not so much out of revenge, but in order to scare people for the moment from attempts at civil disobedience, and to establish a warning for the future, should anyone wish to copy their folly.

I myself, however, was no more responsible for this verdict than were all the others. It was cruel only in that it applied to children, who were actually innocent. But that is an old custom and common to every state; the children of Themistocles lived in poverty. And if such a penalty is prescribed for people condemned in court, how can we be more lenient to enemies of the state? And how can I be criticized, when it is obvious

291

that my enemy, had he been victorious, would have been far more cruel to me.

I have given you now the reasons for my various actions, as far as rewards and punishments are concerned. You have heard, I know, my views on other subjects and the steps I have taken to promote them. All this, however, is not so important as my conviction, dear Brutus, that you should come to Italy as soon as possible with your army. We are all eagerly waiting for you. Once you reach Italy, everyone will turn to you. If victory is at hand, your help will be needed to reestablish some sort of government. I might add that we should already have won a glorious victory if Lepidus had not chosen to ruin everything, including himself and his friends. If, however, the final decision should still lie ahead of us, we shall put our trust first in your personal influence and even more in the power of your arms. But pray hasten! You know how important it is to seize the right moment, when everything depends as now on swift action.

I hope you have learned from your mother's and sister's letters what great care I am taking of your sister's children. I do it as an act of friendship towards you who are so dear to me, and not, as some people think, out of mere loyalty. There is nothing in which I want to be and to appear more loyal than in my affection for you.

FIRST PHILIPPIC AGAINST MARK ANTONY

It is impossible to picture conditions in Rome after the assassination of Caesar (March 15, 44 B.C.), without remembering that the crisis was to be finally resolved by the rise of Octavian, later known as Augustus, and the establishment of the Empire. The futility of Cicero's last efforts to restore the republic is emphasized by the title of *Philippics*, given to a series of his speeches delivered between September 2, 44, and April 21, 43. That title recalls the eloquently patriotic but equally unsuccessful orations of Demosthenes, by which, three hundred years earlier, he had attempted to arouse Athens against the conqueror Philip of Macedon. It is said that Brutus, picking up a casual remark made by Cicero in jest, gave the name of *Philippics* to these speeches, for Brutus never deceived himself as to the improbability that the various factions opposed to Antony could ever be induced to unite.

Immediately after Caesar's death, when the consul Mark Antony presented himself as the executor of Caesar's will, there were apparently only two major political parties, the Caesarians, led by Antony, and the republicans, led by Brutus and Cassius, the assassins of Caesar. Antony appeared conciliatory, being still uncertain of his own strength and of his adversaries' power. Not long afterward, however, Brutus and Cassius left Rome and Italy to see to the situation in the provinces, and their departure strengthened Antony's position considerably. Cicero, though in fact deeply hostile to Antony, did not yet venture on an all-out attack. The first *Philippic* contained indeed a violent criticism of Antony's new legislation, but one professedly based on Caesar's own will, Cicero pointing out that the spirit of this legislation was opposed to the policy Caesar had pursued in life. And in spite of Cicero's principles and his friendship and admiration for Brutus and Cassius, his favorable estimates of Caesar's work were not all hypocritical. He had come by this time to the conclusion that the best prospect for peace at Rome lay in a union between the genuine republicans and the original followers of Caesar, under the leadership of young Octavian. The last year of his life Cicero devoted to an eloquent fight for this idea. He continued to believe in the possibility of its realization after all his sympathizers had given up hope.

Once the first Philippic had been delivered, there was no chance certainly of a settlement between Antony the consul and Cicero, the senior member of the Senate. It likewise looked as if Cicero had succeeded in splitting the forces of the Caesarians by his espousal of the cause of Caesar's adopted son, Octavian, who seemed to feel more secure with Cicero than with Antony. The next steps necessary were to declare Antony an enemy of the state, and to establish some sort of alliance between Brutus and Octavian. This last, too fantastic idea was outwardly accepted by Brutus, by Octavian, and even by several conservative members of the Senate, but undoubtedly with mental reservations. Brutus, however, did not object to seeing his two opponents at odds with each other. And since Octavian enjoyed the support of many republicans in his struggle with Antony, the Senate felt that it could only gain by this new alignment. None of them shared Cicero's belief in a speedy revival of the republic.

On the day when Cicero delivered his fourteenth and last *Philippic*, the battle of Mutina took place. The two consuls of that year, 43 B.C. were killed in combat, but the victory seemed that day on the side of the republic. Yet three months later (July–August), Antony was again at the head of a large army, and Octavian had entered Rome in force, meeting no opposition. Even Cicero by then must have foreseen the inevitable outcome. A reconciliation between Octavian and Antony took place, a new purge followed promptly, and Cicero's name headed the list sent out by Antony.

FIRST PHILIPPIC
AGAINST MARK ANTONY

[*In Antonium, I*]

SENATORS, before I speak on the state of the republic, as I now feel bound to do, I should like to explain briefly the reason why I left the city and why I have recently returned. As long as I could hope that a proper respect for your authority had been restored with the republic, I resolved to stay in Rome as a watchful observer in my capacity as senator and former consul. Indeed, I was not once absent, nor did I ever take my eyes off the political scene from the day we were summoned to meet in the temple of Tellus. I did my best there to lay the foundations for peace, following an ancient precedent of the Athenians. I even quoted the Greek phrase which the Athenians of the past used in settling their internal differences, and I declared that all discord should be once and forever forgotten.

Then Mark Antony made a brilliant speech, showing a surprising amount of good will. Accordingly peace between the leading citizens was established through his efforts and those of his sons, and the problems remaining were decided along the same lines. The political conferences held at his house were attended, at his request, by the most prominent men of the city to whom the most important matters were referred. At that time nothing had been found among the papers of Caesar which had not been known before; and Antony answered all questions with the greatest consistency. Were any exiles restored? He said that one had been, and only one.

Were any exemptions granted? He answered, none. He even wanted us to adopt the proposition of the senator, Servius Sulpicius, that no ordinance or grant made by Caesar should be published now that he was dead.

I pass over many other of Antony's remarkable statements, for I hastened to come to his one outstanding action. He abolished from the constitution the office of Dictator, which had by this time become monarchical. And on this measure there was no discussion. He introduced a senatorial decree, already drawn up, which formulated his proposal. Upon the reading of it, we all submitted eagerly to his authority in the matter, and expressed our gratitude to him in another resolution, phrased in the most complimentary language.

It was exactly as if a new life had begun for us, for not only the oppressive power to which we had been exposed but even the fear of its recurrence had been removed. When Mark Antony abolished the dictatorship, he seemed to be giving us a solemn pledge of his intention that the city should be free. The office had often been necessary in the past, but had become odious to us because of its continuous use. A few days later the Senate was relieved of the threat of bloodshed, and the runaway slave who had usurped the name of Gaius Marius was caught like a fish. All these things Mark Antony did in cooperation with his colleague. Other actions were taken by Dolabella alone; but had Mark Antony been there, the two consuls, I believe, would have acted together. For danger was creeping into the city on a large scale, and spreading day by day. A monument was set up in the Forum by those who had conducted the funeral that was no funeral. Rabble and slaves of the same ilk with increasing vehemence daily threatened houses and shrines. Under these circumstances Dolabella took rigorous action against the criminals, both slaves and citizens, and showed a courage in overthrowing that blasphemous monument that makes me wonder at his different behavior on subsequent occasions.

But, lo, on the first of June, when Mark Antony required our presence in the Senate, the whole situation changed. The Senate took no part in the many important decisions which were being made in the name of the popular assembly, although the people were not in favor of them, nor even present. The consuls-elect said they did not dare come into the Senate. The liberators of the country were away from their city, which they had freed from the yoke of slavery, though they were being praised by the consuls in every assembly. The war veterans, who had always been a special charge of the Senate, were encouraged to expect new grants instead of merely keeping what they had before. Since I preferred to hear these things rather than witness them myself, and since as an honorary ambassador I was free to leave, I went with the intention of returning before the first of January, when it was expected the Senate would reconvene for the first time.

I have now explained to you, senators, my reason for leaving the city. The reason for my return may, perhaps, seem more surprising. Since, for obvious reasons, I was avoiding the normal route to Greece via Brindisi, I set out for Syracuse, and arrived the first of August, for the crossing from there to Greece was said to be good. I spent only one night there, although I should have been glad to stay longer, for I am very much attached to that city, but I was afraid that my sudden appearance among my friends might cause some suspicion if I lingered. On my departure from Sicily the winds drove our boat towards Leucopetra, a promontory in the territory of Reggio. I reembarked there for the crossing, but we had not gone very far when the wind drove us back to the place from which we had started. And since the night was stormy, I spent that night in the house of Publius Valerius, an intimate friend of mine.

I remained there all the next day waiting for a favorable wind, and many inhabitants of Reggio, recent arrivals from Rome, came to see me. It was from them that I first heard of Mark Antony's speech, and after reading it I was so much pleased that I then for the first time thought of returning to Rome. Not long afterwards I received the proclamation of Brutus and Cassius, which seemed to be thoroughly fair, perhaps because I like those men even more for their policy than I do for personal reasons. My informants added that an agreement was in the offing. They said that the Senate would meet on the first of the month, and Antony had discarded his evil counselors, resigned the provinces of Gaul, and was about to submit again to the authority of the Senate. Men like to exaggerate in order to make their good news even better.

This report fired me with such eagerness to return that no oars or winds could be fast enough for me. I quite expected to arrive in time, but feared that I might have to wait too long to express my satisfaction with the state of affairs. I soon arrived at Velia, where I saw Brutus. I cannot tell you how grieved I was then. It seemed to be dishonorable of me to be trying to go back to the Rome which Brutus had just left, and to be willing to live in safety in a place where he could not stay. But I noticed that he was not so disturbed as I was, for he held his head high, conscious of his noble deed, and was distressed at your fate rather than at his own. He was the first to tell me of the speech of Lucius Piso in the Senate on August first. According to Brutus' report, Piso received little applause from those who should have supported him. According to the same veracious Brutus and all I heard later, he nevertheless gave a good account of himself. I therefore pushed on to Rome to give him the support he seemed to need. Not that I expected to accomplish anything important, but I thought if anything should happen to me, and, under the circumstances, this seemed quite possible, I should leave to my country an undoubted proof of my everlasting loyalty.

I trust, senators, that my reasons both for leaving and for coming back have met with your approval. But before I begin to speak of the political situation, let me first protest briefly against the insult offered me yesterday by Mark Antony. I am his friend, and I have never denied that I owe him a great deal. Why, then, did he so rudely force me to attend the Senate yesterday? Was I the only person absent? Have you not often had a smaller attendance than yesterday? Or was a matter of such importance under discussion that it was desirable for even sick men to be carried down? Hannibal, I suppose, was at the gates? Or a debate about peace with Pyrrhus was in progress, on which occasion, it is said, even the great Appius, old and blind as he was, was brought down to the senate house? No, discussion of a thanksgiving celebration was on the program, an occasion when senators are usually present, but which they are not compelled to attend; they simply appear out of deference to those about to be honored. The same is true when the discussion concerns a triumph. In either case, the consuls take no special measures to ensure a senator's attendance.

As I was aware of the custom, tired from my journey, and indisposed, I informed Antony, purely out of friendship, that I would not be there. But you are all witnesses to his declaration that he would take workmen and break into my house. He said this in a great passion, without stopping to consider. Was my crime so great that he should dare say in this assembly that he would enter and damage a house built at public expense on a vote of the Senate? Who else ever exerted such pressure, or inflicted such an injury as that on a senator? If he had known what opinion I would express, he would not have exerted such violent compulsion.

Or did you really suppose, senators, that I would vote for the resolution which you were so unwilling to adopt, to combine funeral obsequies with a public thanksgiving, introduce impiety into a state function, and decree religious honors to a dead man? I say nothing about the character of the man. Even if he had been the great Lucius Brutus, who liberated our country from royal domination and whose equally patriotic descendant, nearly 500 years later, performed a similar deed— even then I could not have been persuaded to include a deceased mortal in the worship of the immortal gods, or sanction public adoration of one whose actual tomb is extant, where funeral services may be celebrated.

On the contrary, senators, the opinion which I would express would easily clear me in the eyes of the Roman people, should any major calamity, such as war, pestilence, or famine befall the state. Some of these misfortunes, indeed, are already upon us, and others, I fear, are in the offing. I pray, however, that the immortal gods may forgive this sacrilege, for the Roman people do not approve of it, and the Senate unwillingly voted it. There are other evils existing in this city of which I might well speak. At all events, I have now and shall always have the right to defend my own honor and despise death. As long as I am able to come into the Senate, I shall never shrink from the danger of expressing my opinion.

I wish, senators, that I might have been present on the first of August; not that I could have accomplished anything, but at least one ex-consul would have been found worthy of his position and worthy of his country. I am especially grieved that men who have received and enjoyed the greatest honors conferred by the Roman people did not support

Lucius Piso, when he made his excellent proposal. Did the Roman people elect us consuls so that after we had held the position of highest honor we should take no more interest in the republic? Not one ex-consul raised his voice in agreement with Lucius Piso, or even looked as if he agreed with him! What means this voluntary servitude? In some cases it may have been necessary, but I should not expect it from all who speak from the consular bench. I draw a distinction between those whose silence I can condone and those from whom I expect an open expression of their feelings. I regret that the latter are now suspected by the Roman people not only of being afraid, which in itself is shameful, but of letting personal considerations keep them from living up to their position. For this reason I am intensely grateful to Lucius Piso who set his mind on doing not what he could but what he ought.

Next, I ask you, senators, if you do not dare to agree with me and follow my advice, at least to continue listening to me courteously as you have done so far. First of all, then, I think that Caesar's work should be preserved, not that I approve of it—for who indeed can do that?—but because I believe that peace and order should be our first concern. I wish that Antony were present, but without his legal advisors. I suppose, however, that he may be allowed to feel unwell, a privilege he did not grant me yesterday. He would then explain to me, or rather to you, senators, to what extent he would uphold Caesar's work. But shall we confirm all the orders he wrote or merely dictated that may be found in his memoranda, manuscripts, and notebooks? Or shall we not ratify his official pronouncements that he had engraved in bronze in which he affirmed the validity of his state edicts and laws? In my opinion, indeed, nothing is more worthy to be called the work of Caesar than his laws. Or shall the promises he made be honored which he himself was unable to fulfill? He did not, it is true, fulfill many of the promises he made. After his death there were more promises discovered than favors he had actually bestowed in his lifetime.

Those things, however, I do not propose to change. In fact, I wholeheartedly defend all his beneficial acts. And let the money, bloodstained as it is, remain in the temple where it was deposited, since it has not been returned to those to whom it really belonged, and it may be put to good use. Though this money too may be distributed, if any existing law requires it.

But what can be more properly called the work of a citizen vested with supreme authority than the legislation that bears his name? What was the work of the Gracchi but the Sempronian laws? What was the work of Sulla but the Cornelian laws? What was Gnaeus Pompey's achievement during his third term as consul? His laws, of course. And if you could inquire of Caesar what was his chief contribution as a politician, he would cite his responsibility for many excellent laws. His informal notes he might change or discard; at any rate he would not count them as part of his serious policy. I shut my eyes to those things, but that Caesar's outstanding accomplishment, his laws, should be nullified, I think intolerable.

No law is better, more useful, or more often cited in times of political probity than that which provides that an ex-praetor should not hold a province more than one year, or an ex-consul more than two. Do you think Caesar's work is being preserved if that law is ignored? Are we not abrogating all the laws of Caesar on judicial procedure by passing the law for the third class of judges? Do you think you can protect Caesar's work if you destroy his laws? Shall we preserve as an essential part of Caesar's system everything he put down in a notebook, even if it is unfair and useless, and discard his measures which received the approval of the assembled people? What is this third class of judges? "It consists of centurions," he answers. Was not this group admitted to the office of judge by the Julian laws, and even earlier, by the Pompeian and Aurelian laws? "Yes, but property qualifications were set up," he replies. Certainly, both for the centurions and for the Roman knights. Those brave and honest men who held commissions in the army are and have been functioning as judges. "I am not speaking about those men," he says, "but I want every former army officer to serve as a judge." Well, if you made such a proposal for everyone who has held the more honorable rank of cavalry officer, you would still get no support; for in selecting a judge one should consider a man's wealth and his reputation. "Never mind that," he says, "I am going to make judges out of the common soldiers of the Alaudae legion; for our friends tell me that only such a measure can help them." What an insulting compliment to those men you summon to act as judges without their knowing anything about their duties! The law is designed to put into the third class of judges persons who will not dare make an independent decision. Therein, by the gods, lies the great mistake of these legislators! For the poorer each man is, the more eagerly will he hide his poverty behind the severity of his decisions, and the more will he strive to appear to be a member of the better class of judges rather than of the low class to which he actually belongs.

Another law contains the proposal that men condemned for crimes of violence or treason may appeal to the people. Is that a law, or is it not rather an abrogation of all laws? Who is personally interested this moment in the enforcement of that law? Under it no one will be guilty and no one will be condemned; for no act of violence will ever be tried in a court of justice. However, you say the measure is popular. I wish you

304

would really support a popular measure, for, at present, the citizens all have but one opinion with regard to the preservation of the republic.

Why all this eagerness to pass a law which is both vicious and unpopular? Nothing is more vicious than letting a man who has worked to undermine the sovereignty of the Roman people and has been condemned by a court of law resume the crimes for which he was justly condemned. Why argue any longer about the law as if its sole object were to permit an appeal? In fact, the inevitable consequence of it must be that under no circumstances can anyone under that law ever be convicted. For what prosecutor would be so foolish as to get a defendant condemned and thus expose himself to the anger of an organized mob? Or what judge would dare condemn a criminal only to be assaulted by a hired gang? It is not, therefore, a law that gives a right of appeal, but one that abolishes two most salutary laws and modes of judicial investigation. It amounts to encouraging young men to become restless, seditious, and dangerous citizens.

From what crime will the rabid tribunes abstain, once indictments for violence and treason are abolished? Is this not an abrogation of Caesar's laws, which provide that all persons convicted of either violence or treason should be exiled as outlaws? If such men are given the right of appeal, are not Caesar's decrees annulled? Although, senators, I personally never approved of them, still I think they should be maintained for the sake of national unity. So, it has been my opinion that not only the laws passed during Caesar's lifetime should be kept in force, but also those which you have seen since proposed and confirmed.

The dead man recalled exiles; granted citizenship both to individuals and to tribes and whole provinces; he diminished our revenues by allowing countless exemptions. Shall we, then, sanction his posthumous measures, presented on the authority of a single, though admittedly excellent individual, and at the same time set about abolishing laws which he himself proposed in our presence, advocated, and carried? He was proud of the laws he had passed, and especially of those regulating the provinces and judicial procedure, on which he believed the safety of the republic depended. Shall we, who pretend to guard Caesar's memory thus revoke Caesar's laws?

We can at least argue about laws which have been proposed, but about those now alleged to have been passed, we cannot do even that. For they were passed without ever having been proposed or drawn up. But I should like to ask, senators, why I, or any one of you should be afraid of harmful laws as long as we have good tribunes? They are ready to step in, faithful to their oaths, ready to defend the republic. We should be strangers to fear. "But what do you mean by stepping in?" says he. "What do you mean by the faithful observance of oaths?" The safety of the republic depends on these things, but we neglect them and think them too old-fashioned and foolish.

Next the Forum will be surrounded, every entrance to it will be blocked; armed men will be stationed as guards at many points. Do you consider this the way to make laws? But after they have been passed in this fashion, I presume you will have them inscribed on bronze tablets. "The consuls consulted the people, as prescribed by law, and the people decided . . ." Is this the way of consulting the people we inherited from our ancestors? What people, moreover—what of those who are locked out? As prescribed by what law, a law polluted by armed violence?

But I am speaking of the future, for it is a friend's duty to point out what may still be avoided. If this situation never materializes, that will be the best refutation of my speech.

And I am speaking of laws which have been proposed, as to which you still have a free hand. I am pointing out defects; remove them! I am denouncing armed violence; away with that too!

Dolabella, you should not be angry with me for speaking in defense of the republic. I think you will not be, for I know your good nature. Your colleague, however, so proud of his position, is said to be offended. Without insulting him, I should like to suggest that he follow the example of his grandfathers and his uncle, when they were consuls. I understand what it means to be hated by a person who is heavily armed, especially at a time when men can use force with impunity. But I should like to make a fair proposition, which, I think, Antony will not reject. If I have insulted him personally, I shall not object to his becoming my bitter enemy. But if I have only been true to my past record in politics, that is, if I have only expressed my candid opinion on the state of the republic, I expect him not to feel insulted. If this is impossible, ask him, at least, to treat me in his anger as a fellow citizen.

He may use force, if it is necessary, as he says, in his own defense. But I ask him not to turn this force against those who have said what they thought was best for the republic. Can this be an unreasonable request? If, however, as one of his party told me, our friend is offended by any criticism, even though it involves no personal disparagement, we shall then have to get on as we can with his disposition. At the same time I was told, "You, as Caesar's enemy, must not speak with as much freedom as Piso, who is Antony's father-in-law." I was warned, also, to be careful, for it would be better to miss a session of the Senate because of illness than because of death!

As I look at you, Dolabella, my dear friend, I cannot help

pointing out the mistake you are both making. I believe, by the immortal gods, that you ambitious aristocrats are not, as some simpletons suspect, out for money, which men of nobility always despise. Nor are you after power based only on violence, which the Roman people will not endure, but you are working for glory and the affection of your fellow citizens. Now glory is praise deserved for meritorious public service, approved not by a few only, but by the many. I might describe for you, Dolabella, the reward of deeds that are good, but I know that you, more than anyone, are well acquainted with it.

Was it not the happiest day of your life when you went home after clearing the Forum of a dangerous mob, inflicting punishment on the ringleaders, and freeing the city from dread of fire and massacre? Were you not praised and congratulated by all classes and ranks of the population. Even I was thanked and congratulated by our good citizens, who thought you had acted on my advice. Remember, please, Dolabella, the unanimous applause in the theater, when the audience forgot their old grudge against you, and showed their willingness to forgive a past injury for the sake of your late patriotic service. I grieve to speak of it, but how could you, Dolabella, so readily forfeit this popularity?

And Mark Antony—I address these words to you, though you are not present—do you not value that one day when the Senate met in the temple of Tellus above all those months during which my opponents considered you happy? On that day you spoke brilliantly of national unity. You freed the city then from a great strain and anxiety. You forgot old enmities that day, disregarded the auspices you had made as augur, and accepted your present colleague. You sent your little son to the Capitol as a hostage for peace. Never was the Senate more relieved, or the people as a whole more delighted.

Never was the assembly better attended. Then, at last, we seemed to have been delivered by the acts of courageous men, for through their efforts freedom was succeeded by peace. On each day following, you bestowed some new benefit on the republic. The greatest of all was when you abolished the dictatorship, an act by which you yourself condemned the dead Caesar to everlasting ignominy. As once the crime of a certain Marcus Manlius caused the Manlian clan to decide that no member of their family should ever again be called Marcus, so the hatred for one man who bore the title of dictator prompted you to do away with it altogether.

When you did so much for the safety of the republic, you did not object to the consequent glory and the affection of your fellow citizens, did you? Whence comes this sudden change? Nothing can induce me to suspect you have been bribed! Everyone is free to say what he pleases, but I do not have to believe it, for I have never found anything wicked or base in you. Though a man's character is often corrupted by his subordinates, still I know the strength of yours. I only wish you could avoid the suspicion of the fault as successfully as you avoid the fault itself.

What I really fear is that you do not know the true path to glory, but believe you will win fame by being more powerful than everyone else put together, and prefer being feared by your fellow citizens to being loved. If you really believe that, you are ignorant of the true path. For fame comes from being a loyal citizen, serving the republic devotedly, earning praise, respect, and love. To be feared and hated is not only an odious and detestable state in itself, but is a sign of weakness and impotence. We see this is so in the play, where disaster overcomes the man who said, "Let them hate me, so long as they are afraid of me."

I wish, Antony, you could remember your grandfather;

though I have told you often a great deal about him. Do you imagine he would have aspired to win immortality by making men fear him for his illegal possession of arms? For your grandfather life and good fortune meant having only as much liberty as other men, but being their leader in uprightness of character. Without counting the happiness of your grandfather's days, I should prefer his cruel end to the terror of Lucius Cinna, by whom he was wickedly slain.

But how can I move you by my speech? If Caesar's fate cannot show you that it is better to be loved than feared, no words will have any effect on you. Those who once thought Caesar happy are most miserable themselves. No man is happy who lives in such a way that he can be killed not merely with impunity, but actually to the greater glory of his slayer. Hence, I entreat you, change your methods! Follow the example of your ancestors, and rule the state so that your fellow-citizens may rejoice that you were born, for without their affection no one can be happy or illustrious, however powerful he may be.

Indeed, the Roman people have already given both of you many indications of their attitude toward you. I am sorry that you are not sufficiently impressed. Remember the shouting crowds of citizens at the gladiatorial games, remember the popular songs, remember the ceaseless cheers before Pompey's statue, remember the applause for the two tribunes who dared oppose you. Is this not enough to show you how remarkably unanimous is the feeling of the whole people? Were you not affected by the applause at the festival of Apollo, that was tantamount to a popular expression of judgment? Those men, whom you forcibly prevented from being present, were nevertheless there, hidden in the hearts and souls of the Roman people. Or perhaps you thought they were applauding Accius, sixty years too late, and not Brutus, absent from his own play? By their continuous applause and cheering the Roman audience both showed their enthusiasm for the magnificent performance, and satisfied their desire for the absent liberator.

I myself have always felt a contempt for popular acclaim, but if the approval is expressed simultaneously by all classes, and if those who used to respect the popular opinion now disregard it, then I consider it not empty applause, but a deliberate verdict. If this serious attitude seems to you to have no significance, do you also despise the open affection the people show for Aulus Hirtius? Suffice it that he is notably esteemed by the people, and exceedingly dear to his friends and family; and do we know anyone for whom all good citizens have felt so much anxiety and concern? Immortal gods, can you understand the meaning of this attitude? Do you think your life is prized by a people who worship the men they consider saviors of the state?

I have been rewarded, senators, for my return, since, whatever happens, I have borne witness to my own steadfastness, and have found in you a gracious and eager audience. And if a similar opportunity arises more often in the future, without endangering either you or me, I shall take advantage of it. If not, I shall still devote myself as much as possible not to my own pleasure, but to the service of the state. My life has been full enough both of years and of successes. Any additional years shall be, not my own, but given to you and to the republic.

ON DUTY

The essay *On Duty* was written by Cicero during the last months of 44 B.C. He was then prudently absent from Rome after having delivered his first open attack on Mark Antony in the *First Philippic*. He said that the best way to use such a period of enforced leisure was to write books like this. By the time he returned to Rome on December 9th, he had finished it. Some flaws in the composition, however, suggest that it was probably never published in Cicero's lifetime. The same conclusion may be drawn from the passages of invective against Caesar, for he would hardly have made them public at a time when he was working for an alliance with Caesar's adopted son, Octavian.

The essay, as we have it, is addressed as a letter to Cicero's only son, Marcus, to whom it was apparently sent. Marcus, a youth of twenty-one, was then studying in the Peripatetic (Aristotelian) school of philosophy at Athens, the city to which Roman young gentlemen were now going for their initiation into the higher learning. Here were still Plato's Academy, Aristotle's Lyceum, the so-called Garden of Epicurus, and the Porch where Zeno had preached Stoicism. We may infer from allusions in the letters to extravagance and fast living that the conduct of his son was giving Cicero cause for concern.

The philosophic works of Cicero, of which the essay *On Duty* is the last and perhaps the greatest, transmit to us much material from Hellenistic philosophy, which would otherwise be almost entirely lost, and indicate the attitude of the various schools on many important problems, religious, moral, and political. He himself had studied under most of the leading teachers of the day and was well acquainted with their textbooks. He seems to represent them all fairly, except for a certain contempt he expresses from time to time for the materialistic school, of which his bosom friend Atticus was a distinguished member.[1] He himself in his metaphysics inclines generally toward the skeptical position of the New Academy under Carneades, a development from the skeptical elements of Platonism, to which Cicero had been converted by one Philo of Larissa, although occasionally he reverted back to Aristotle. In his moralizing, however, he remains consistently Stoic and faithful to the doctrines of the Stoic Posidonius, to whose school he had gone when he left Atticus at Athens. He was thus an eclectic with no passionate convictions as to the truth of any position. The best one could do, he thought, was to follow the teachings that seemed most probably right.

Stoicism, as set forth in the writings of Seneca, Epictetus, and the Emperor Marcus Aurelius,[2] is considered to be peculiarly the philosophy of the practical Romans. In this work of Cicero we possess a still earlier, indeed the earliest, surviving document of Roman Stoic ethics. The source which Cicero says he used in composing the first two books of his essay was a treatise on the same subject by a Greek philosopher, Panaetius of Rhodes, who had lived in the preceding century and been intimately associated with the circle of the Scipios and their friends in Rome's heroic age. Cicero makes no claim to originality, beyond that of having compressed the three books of Panaetius' treatise into two, and added a third of his own to deal with topics omitted by Panaetius.

The first book, which is here translated, is a discussion of

---

[1] See Cicero's scornful allusion to the Epicureans in his dialogue *On Laws*, p. 235, fn. 14.
[2] See Epictetus' *Discourses* and Marcus Aurelius' *Meditations*, both published by Classics Club.

what men must do in order to be morally good. The second book treats in similar detail of acts performed for profit and expediency. The third book describes the conflicts that may seem to arise between the two types of human behavior. Through it all, however, runs Cicero's own deep conviction, once beautifully expressed by Socrates, that there really is not and cannot be any conflict between the truly good and the truly useful and advantageous. For his third book, Cicero professes to have relied mainly on his own resources. In it indeed we find more abundant references to Roman history and echoes of his earlier philosophic work, On Ends. Yet a letter to Atticus informs us that before November was over he had received the sketch prepared for his use by the Stoic Athenodorus, for which, he says in Letter xxvii (p. 316), he was impatiently waiting. It is usually assumed that he followed the sketch rather closely, both in the plan of the third book and also in his critical appendices to the first and second books.

The essay On Duty, with several of the other essays on ethical and philosophical subjects which Cicero composed in the few years he spent in retirement before his death, were, as we have already said, practically all that was known of his writing in the Middle Ages. The essays On Friendship and On Ends, with their pleasant moralizing, the dialogue on The Nature of the Gods and the Tusculan Disputations, with their simplified interpretations of Greek philosophy for Latin readers, were preserved and copied by students of old literature in the better monastic and cathedral libraries. They kept a permanent appeal, when the rhetorical and political treatises, the speeches and the letters, no longer interested anyone and lay forgotten.

The essay On Duty is preceded by two letters to Atticus, in which Cicero discusses this work and other compositions that were engaging his attention at the time.

LETTERS RELATING TO ON DUTY

Letter Twenty-Six
To Atticus in Rome
[Ad Atticum, XV, 13a; postscript to XV, 13]

Puteoli, October 25, 44 B.C.

As I was writing this letter during dessert, I heard that our good friend Dolabella [1] had come to Baiae, but he had written me from Formiae and I had received his letter just as I left my bath. In that he claims to have done his best to assign the debts to me. He plays his hand like a good businessman and blames Vettienus for it all, but says that Sestius has undertaken to see to the affair. Sestius is a good man and a dear friend of mine. Still I wonder what Sestius can do in this matter which any one of us could not have done. However, if anything goes wrong, please let me know. And if, as I think, the situation is hopeless, please write just the same, for it will not disturb me.

I am spending my time here on philosophy—what else could I do? I am getting along nicely with my book *On Duty*, which I am dedicating to my son. Could a father dedicate to his son anything more suitable than a book on his duties? Afterwards I shall turn to other work. Do not be surprised if this excursion produces several books.

We are expecting Varro today or tomorrow. But I am hurrying on to Pompeii, not that there is any place more beautiful than the one where I am, but in Pompeii there will be fewer interruptions. Please let me know what charge was brought against Myrtilus and whether it was discovered who instigated the plot; I did hear that he was executed.

---

[1] On Dolabella, see above, p. 258, fn. 3.

As I write this, it occurs to me that you will have just received the text of my speech. Dear me, how I dread your criticism! And yet what does it matter, since it will not be published unless the free government is restored. My hopes as to that I dare not set down on paper.

Letter Twenty-Seven
To Atticus in Rome
[Ad Atticum, XVI, 11]

Puteoli, November 5, 44 B.C.

I RECEIVED two letters from you on November 5th, one of them dated the first, the other the day before. I shall answer first the earlier one. I am glad you liked my manuscript, and I think you picked the best passages. They look to me even better now since you chose them, for I was afraid of seeing the critical marks of your pencil. You are quite right about Sicca. I could hardly refrain from mentioning the subject, but now I shall just touch upon it, without compromising either Sicca or Septimia. I shall not beat about the bush like the poet Lucilius. Our children's children should know that Antony had children by Fadius' daughter.

I cannot wait for the day when the speech can be freely distributed, and find its way even into Sicca's house. I wish the good old days of the triumvirate were back! That is a mighty fine joke.[2] You must read my manuscript aloud to Sextus and tell me what he thinks. Better one good man than ten thousand imbeciles! On the other hand, be careful when you meet Calenus and Calvena.

---

[2] Cicero, of course, had done his best to protect republican liberties from what he then had considered the intolerable domination of the first triumvirs, Crassus, Pompey, and Caesar.

Are you really afraid that I think you too verbose? The longer your letters, the better. I feel about them the way that Aristophanes felt about Archilochus' poems. I not only tolerate, but enjoy your advice, even if it contains some criticism, because what you say is both wise and kindly meant. I shall therefore gladly change the passages you marked. I shall write "just as you got hold of Rubrius' property" instead of "Scipio's property," and I shall tone down my praise of Dolabella. Yet I think it was good sarcasm when I said that he was "three times in arms against his fellow citizens." I also prefer your "It is a disgrace that this man should be alive" to my original version, "What is more disgraceful. . . ." I do not mind praising Varro's potpourri.[3] So far I have been unable to get from him his book of dialogues in the style of Heracleides.

It is kind of you to urge me to write, but you must know that I am doing nothing else. I am sorry to hear of your cold. Do take great care of yourself, as you usually do. I am glad to learn that my book on *Old Age*, which I dedicated to you, does you good. The "men from Agagni" mentioned in my manuscript are Mustela, the brigadier, and the drunkard, Laco. I shall send you the book you ask for, but first I must polish the style a little.

Now for my reply to your second letter. I have finished the section of my essay *On Duty* that is based on Panaetius. That part will be in two books, though his work is in three. He made his division at the very beginning, pointing out that there were three types of duties to be analyzed, first the conflict of right against wrong, second, of the expedient against the inexpedient, and third, of right against expediency, when they clashed, as they did in the case of Regulus,[4] whose honor

---

[3] The name of Terentius Varro, the encyclopedist, and one of Cicero's best friends, has been mentioned several times already in these letters.
[4] On the story of Regulus, see below, p. 337.

required him to return, while self-interest urged him to stay. The first and second topics Panaetius discussed brilliantly, but his dissertation on the third topic, though promised, was never written. Posidonius did that later. I have tried to get hold of his book and have written to Athenodorus Calvus to send me an outline of it, but am still waiting. I wish you would urge him on and implore him to make haste. Posidonius deals with duties under special circumstances.

As far as the title is concerned, there is no doubt in my mind that the Greek word *kathekon* corresponds to the Latin *officium*. Have you a different idea? The full title then would be *De Officiis*. I shall dedicate the book to my son, which seems to me quite appropriate.

Your account of Myrtilus is clear and you certainly give a good description. And of all people it is Decimus Brutus who is involved! [5] Good riddance to them! I wrote that I was moving to Pompeii, but I did not. First of all, because of the abominable weather, secondly because of Octavian's letters, in which day after day he urges me to take a hand in politics. He wants me to come to Capua, to save the republic again—to come to Rome! To use Homer's phrase, "I hate to say 'No,' and am afraid to say 'Yes'." [6]

Octavian, however, has been vigorously active and is still going strong. He will enter Rome with a large army, but he is still only a boy. He thinks he can convene the Senate, but who will appear? And if they do, who will dare offend Antony as long as the situation is uncertain? Octavian's armed support may be helpful on January first, but perhaps the fighting will be all over by then. It is amazing what enthusiasm he arouses in the cities of Italy. On his way to Samnium he went to Cales and stayed at Teanum. A big crowd turned out and

[5] The reference is to the attempt on Antony's life.
[6] *Iliad,* vii.

cheered him. Would you believe it? This news may make me go to Rome earlier than I had intended. I shall write as soon as I have made my plans.

Although I have not yet seen the documents, for Eros has not yet arrived, I still hope you can finish the business on the 12th. It would have been more convenient for me to write directly to Catana, Taormina, and Syracuse, if my local agent, Valerius, had only sent me the names of the notables there. They vary, of course, from time to time, and most of those I knew are now dead. In spite of that, I have written some formal letters which Valerius may use if he chooses; otherwise send me the names. I hear from Balbus that Lepidus' inaugural celebrations will last until the 29th.

I am waiting for another letter from you and hope to learn about the little matter of Torquatus. I have sent you a letter from Quintus to show how much he likes Torquatus, and how much he regrets that you do not like him.

Attica must be a very happy little girl; kiss her, please, for me.

ON DUTY

[De Officiis, 1]

You have now, son Marcus, been studying with Cratippus [1]
for a whole year and living in Athens, and so under that authoritative teacher and in that most brilliant of cities you
should be well grounded in the maxims and principles of
philosophy. Cratippus can enrich you with his learning, Athens
by the examples she offers you. However, I have always found
it useful to combine Latin studies with Greek, not only in
philosophy, but also in the practice of speaking, and I recommend you to do the same, so as to become adept in both languages. Along this line, I believe I have been of considerable
help to my countrymen; for, as a result of my efforts, some
hitherto ignorant of Greek, and even some acquainted with
it, think they have gained much, both in skill of speaking and
in clarity of thought.

Accordingly, you will continue to study under the best
philosopher of our time for as long as you wish; and you
should wish to continue as long as you think you are making
progress. But at the same time, read some of my books. My
views do not differ much from those of the Peripatetics, for
we both claim to be pupils of Socrates and Plato. For your
conclusions, however, use your own judgment. I shall not
object. But by reading my books you will certainly increase
your command of the Latin language. I do not wish you to
think I am boasting. In knowledge of philosophy there are
many better than I, but I feel justified in claiming the special

---

[1] Head of a school of Peripatetic or Aristotelian philosophy in Athens.

proficiency of an orator in speaking suitably, clearly, and gracefully, for I have devoted my life to the study of that art.

I therefore strongly advise you, my dear Marcus, to read carefully both my speeches and my philosophical writings, which are now almost as extensive. The speeches have more power of style, the philosophical essays a calm and restrained style, also worth cultivating. So far as I know, no Greek has yet succeeded in attaining excellence in both fields—in public speaking and in quiet, philosophic discourse, unless perhaps Demetrius of Phaleron [2] might be mentioned here. He was a subtle reasoner, and a charming orator, though not very forceful. You can recognize in him a pupil of Theophrastus. But let others judge my accomplishments in the two fields; I have attempted them both.

As a matter of fact, I feel confident that if Plato had cared to appear as a public speaker, he could have spoken with the greatest impressiveness and eloquence. Similarly, if Demosthenes had preserved and wished to expound what he had learned from Plato, he could have done so fluently and brilliantly. The same is true, in my opinion, of Aristotle and Isocrates,[3] each of whom, however, was absorbed in his own field and had little interest in the other.

But since I have decided to write you a letter now, and more later, I should like to start with something suited to your age and my position. Now there are important, practical problems in philosophy, which have been accurately and fully discussed by the philosophers, but their theories and teachings on duty seem to have the widest application. For no phase of life, whether public or private, political or domestic, whether

[2] Demetrius of Phaleron (345–283 B.C.) was an Athenian orator and politician until his exile in 307 when he retired to Egypt and devoted himself to literature and philosophy.
[3] Isocrates (436–338 B.C.) was one of the most famous of Attic orators.

it is a matter of yourself alone or of your dealings with others, can be without its duty, on the performance of which depends all the virtue of your life, and neglect of which is sin.

And this question of duty has been taken up by all the philosophers. For who would dare to call himself a philosopher if he failed to teach some moral code? Yet there are certain schools that by their theories of good and evil pervert the whole idea of morality. Some men define the supreme good as having no relation to virtue, and measure it by their personal advantage, instead of by a standard of honor. If such a man is consistent and does not yield at times to his own natural goodness, he will be incapable of friendship, justice, or generosity. For a man who considers pain the supreme evil can never be brave; one who calls pleasure the supreme good can never be temperate. The truth of this observation is so patent that it needs no argument; however, I have dealt with the subject elsewhere.

If these schools of thought were only consistent, they would not speak of duty at all. For a fixed, steadfast, and natural code of morals can be established only by men who believe that goodness is desirable solely or chiefly for its own sake. So the teaching of duty is the work especially of the Stoic, Academic, and Peripatetic schools. The notions of the Skeptics, and of Ariston, Pyrrho, and Erillus,[4] were refuted long ago. Yet they would have had the right to discuss duty, if they had left themselves any choice between things, so as to discover what duty is. In this discourse, at this time, I shall present mainly the Stoic view, though not as a mere translator. As in the past, I shall use my own taste and judgment, and

[4] That is, the schools that had a sound ethical basis were the Stoic, Platonic, and Aristotelian. The school of the Skeptics, which declared that all truth was unattainable, had no absolute standards by which to judge morality. Pyrrho (fourth century) was the founder of the Skeptical school. Ariston and Erillus were eccentric Stoics, of whom Cicero disapproved. See on Ariston, above, p. 235, fn. 13.

draw from the sources as much as and in the way that suits my purpose.

Since then this whole discussion is to be about duty, I should like to begin with a definition of what duty is. I am surprised to notice that Panaetius [5] neglected to define it. For any systematic treatment of a subject should begin with a definition, so that everyone may understand what is the object of the inquiry. . . .[6]

Every discussion of duty has two parts. One part deals with the question of the supreme good; the other with the rules that should guide our ordinary lives in every respect. The following are problems of the first part. Are all duties binding on us without any qualification? Is one kind of duty more important than another?—and similar questions. As for the traditional moral code, though it bears a relation to our concept of the supreme good, the relationship is not so apparent, for it seems to aim more at the regulation of everyday life. But it is this part of the subject which I shall treat at length in these books.

There is still another classification of duties. For we speak of one duty as relative and another as absolute. Absolute duty I think we may call "the right," following the Greeks, who call it "the straight," whereas relative duty they call simply "the fitting." And they define those terms as follows: whatever is right, they call an absolute duty, while a relative duty is one for the performance of which a plausible reason can be adduced.

Panaetius says there are three different ways of coming to a decision on conduct. First, men ask whether the course con-

---

[5] For Panaetius of Rhodes (c.180–111 B.C.), see p. 313.
[6] Cicero's definition may have been given here. It was probably brief. One version suggested by a modern scholar is: "We call duty any act dictated by reason."

templated is morally right or wrong. Different people often come to different conclusions on this. And then they investigate and consider how far the proposed action may contribute to their comfort and pleasure in life, to the resources and wealth, the possessions and power, by which they can help themselves and their friends. Such consideration clearly falls under the head of expediency. A third way of approach is required when the course that is expedient seems to clash with that which is right. For when expediency seems to pull one way and right to call us back to the other way, the mind is distraught in its deliberations and thrown into a state of irresolution.

There are two omissions in this classification, a serious flaw, since every classification should be exhaustive. For people often consider not only the question whether an act is morally right or wrong, but also of two proposed acts which one is the nearer right; [7] and of two proposed expediencies, which is the more expedient. Thus the question which Panaetius thought had three parts we find should be divided into five. These are, first, the question of the morally right in two forms; then, the question of the expedient in the same way; and finally, the comparison of the two contrasting groups.

From the beginning all species of living creatures have been endowed by Nature with the instinct to protect their own lives and bodies and avoid whatever seems likely to do them harm, and to find and secure whatever they need for life, such as food, shelter, and the like. Common too to all animate beings is a desire for union to produce offspring and a concern for their young.

There is, however, this great difference between man and beast. The beast, inasmuch as he is motivated solely by his

---

[7] The Stoics drew no distinction between different degrees of right and wrong.

senses, adjusts himself only to that which is present at the moment, with little thought of the past or the future. Man, on the other hand, is endowed with reason through which he observes events and their consequences. He perceives the causes of things, understands the relation of cause and effect, draws analogies, and connects and combines the present with the future. In this way, he easily visualizes the course of his whole life and prepares what he needs to carry it on. Through the same power of reason Nature links man to man, by their participation in speech and in social intercourse. Above all, she implants in him a special love for his offspring. She impels men too to meet and take part in social gatherings and festivals. Thus they are driven to provide not only for their own comfort and livelihood, but also for that of their wives, children, and all others they hold dear and feel bound to protect. This responsibility stimulates their spirits, and encourages them to greater deeds.

The thing most peculiar to the human race is its search and inquiry after truth. For, as soon as we are free from the cares of necessary business, we are eager to see, hear, and learn new things and we believe that a knowledge of the secret wonders of the world is essential to our well-being. Hence we see that the simple and unperverted truth appeals strongly to man's nature. To this craving for a sight of truth is added a desire for leadership. A mind naturally well developed is reluctant to obey anyone but a teacher of morals and wisdom, or, for practical reasons, a just and law-abiding ruler. Out of this attitude grows greatness of spirit and a disdain of human institutions.

And through his great powers of nature and reason man is the one animal with a feeling for order, propriety, and moderation in word and act. In the same way, no other animal has a sense of beauty, loveliness, and symmetry in visible things.

And nature and reason enable us to transfer these impressions from our eyes to our minds and to prize beauty, stability, and order even more in our thoughts and actions. So too, we are led to avoid any indecorous or unmanly deed, and any purely sensual thought or action. Out of these elements is formed and fashioned the goodness that is the topic of our inquiry, which is noble, though it is not a property of the nobility, and goes its way unpraised; however, I say truly that by its nature it is worthy of every praise.

Here, then, son Marcus, you will see goodness take shape, and, as it were, discern the features of her face, which, as Plato says, "if once seen by human eyes, would arouse a marvelous thirst for wisdom." [8] Now all that is good has its origin in one of four sources. It may come from perception of and careful devotion to the truth, or from concern for the maintenance of human society, and the rendering to every man of his own and the faithful fulfillment of obligations, or from the great strength of a lofty and unconquerable spirit, or from an orderly and tempered control of words and deeds, which produces moderation and sobriety.[9]

These four sources are connected and interwoven with one another, yet each one creates its own particular virtue. From the first-named source, in which we include wisdom and intelligence, comes the eager and successful search for truth; this is the special object of that virtue. For the more clearly a person perceives the essential truth in any matter and the more quickly and accurately he can see and explain the reason for it, the wiser and more farsighted he will be considered, and rightly so. Thus the material, as it were, with which the first virtue deals and on which it works, is truth.

---

[8] *Phaedrus*, 250 D.
[9] Here Cicero starts his description of goodness as composed of the four Platonic virtues, wisdom, justice, courage, and self-control or temperance.

On the three other virtues rests the obligation of acquiring and safeguarding the means for the practical conduct of life, so that human association in society may be preserved, and the excellence and greatness of man's mind may be revealed, both in the accumulation of riches and advantages for himself and his family, and, far more, in his contempt for these worldly goods. Orderliness, steadfastness, moderation and the like, are in this class of virtues, for which a certain amount of action is required, not only exertion of the mind. And by observing moderation and order in the affairs of everyday life, we shall be upholding goodness and right conduct.

The first of the four virtues into which we have divided the active nature of goodness is knowledge of the truth, a virtue that appeals especially to human nature. For we are all attracted and influenced by desire for knowledge and learning, thinking it fine to excel in this field but shocking and degrading to slip, or be mistaken, or ignorant, or misinformed. In pursuit of this virtue, natural and noble as it is, two errors must be avoided. First, we must never take the unknown as known, and thoughtlessly accept it. Whoever wants to avoid this error (as we all should), will devote both time and pains to a consideration of the evidence. The second error is that of those who concentrate too much labor and energy on the study of subjects that are obscure and difficult, and useless as well.

Provided we avoid these errors, we shall be well rewarded for all the labor and effort we spend on honest subjects, worth exploring, as, in the field of astronomy, Gaius Sulpicius [10] did, I have heard, and, in the field of geometry, Sextus Pompey [11]

---

[10] Gaius Sulpicius, consul in the year 166 B.C., was famous in his day as an astronomer. He is said to have predicted an eclipse of the moon.
[11] Sextus Pompey, a cousin of Pompey the Great, was a Stoic philosopher as well as a geometrician.

whom I knew myself. Many are outstanding in logic, more in civil law. All these professions are concerned with a search for truth. But to be drawn from such study quite away from active life is contrary to duty. For virtue is praiseworthy only in action, in which, to be sure, there may be many interruptions, and many temporary returns to study. At the same time, the working of our minds, which never stops, may keep us busy with problems of knowledge without any special exertion on our part. All our thought and mental activity, however, will then be directed either to planning for things that are right and that lead to a good and happy life, or to acquiring knowledge and learning. So much for the first source of duty.

The first principle of justice is that no one should harm another, unless provoked by an injury; the next that common possessions should be used for the common interest, and only private property for the individual's interest. There is, however, no private property so established by nature, but only what has become so through long occupancy, as when in the past men settled down on vacant land, or through conquest, as when men seized it in war, or through legal process, agreement, purchase, or allotment. On such grounds the land of Arpino is said to belong to the people of Arpino, and the land of Tusculum to the people of Tusculum; and all private property is based on similar claims. So since all private property comes from what was by nature common property, each one of us should be satisfied with whatever has been his lot. If he wants more than that, he will be violating a law of human society.

We are, as Plato beautifully says, born not for ourselves alone. Our country claims a share in our existence, and our friends a share. By Stoic doctrine the whole produce of the earth was created for the use of men, and men themselves are here for the sake of their fellow men, that they may mutually assist one another. We ought then to follow Nature here and contribute to the common good by exchanging deeds of helpfulness, both giving and receiving, and by our skill, our labor, and our talents bind more closely together the association of men with men. The foundation of justice is good faith, that is, the faithful observance of promises and agreements. Some may think I am laboring the point, but I will venture, for a moment, to follow the Stoics who make a diligent study of the derivation of words, and assert that good *faith* is so called because through it a promise becomes a *fact*.[12]

There are two different kinds of injustice, the injustice of those who inflict an injury and the injustice of those who do not, when they can, protect others who are being injured. A man who, in rage or excitement, attacks anyone else unfairly is as bad as one who lays hands on his friend. And a man who does not prevent, or resist, if he can, an injury to someone else is as much a criminal as one who deserts his parents, his friends, or his country. Many of the injuries which are inflicted on purpose to do harm start from fear; the one who plans the wrong is afraid he will himself be hurt in some way if he does not strike first. But mostly men try to injure others in order to get something they want; so for this vice greed is usually the obvious motive.

Men seek wealth both to secure the necessities of life and to enjoy its pleasures. Men of higher intelligence desire wealth for the sake of the power it brings and the ability to confer favors. Marcus Crassus [13] lately declared that no sum of money was enough for a man who aimed at leadership in the state unless on the income from it he could support an army. Some

---

12 The Latin words on whose resemblance Cicero is playing here are *fides* and *fiat*, a truly far-fetched connection.
13 The wealthy Marcus Crassus had been the partner of Pompey and Caesar in the first triumvirate.

people like a sumptuous establishment and the comforts of luxury and abundance. As a result, the thirst for money is limitless. Nevertheless, I am not against the accumulation of property that hurts no one else, but injustice in acquiring it must always be avoided.

Most men, however, are inclined to forget justice altogether, when once the craving for military power or political honors and glory has taken possession of them. Remember the saying of Ennius,

> "When crowns are at stake
> No friendship is sacred, no faith will be kept,"

—words that have a wide application. For whenever a situation is such that only one man can be on top, the competition is ordinarily so bitter that to preserve "sacred friendship" is very difficult. An example of this behavior was given just recently by the unscrupulous Julius Caesar, who disregarded all rights, divine and human, in order to attain his ill-conceived and imaginary supreme command. The misfortune in this case is that the ambition for honor, military power, authority, and glory arises usually in the hearts of the greatest and most brilliantly talented men. For this reason we should be the more on guard against wrongdoing of that sort.

In any instance of injustice it makes a great deal of difference whether the injury is committed in a state of mental excitement, which is usually transitory and brief, or deliberately and with premeditation. For offenses committed in sudden heat are less serious than those that have been planned and thought out beforehand. And now we have said enough on the topic of infliction of injuries.

The reasons for failure to perform one's duty of preventing injustice to other people are apt to be varied. Men are unwilling to incur enmity, or effort, or expense, or they are indifferent, indolent, or inert, or taken up with some interests or affairs of their own so that they leave abandoned those whom they ought to protect. I wonder therefore whether Plato's dictum about philosophers is correct,[14] that they are just, because they are engaged in the search for truth, and despise and scorn the things for which the masses long and do battle with one another. They indeed practice one kind of justice in that they inflict no injury and do no harm to anyone else, but they fall into the other kind, for, engaged in their studies, they leave unhelped those whom they should protect. In fact, Plato says [15] that philosophers will take part in public business only if compelled; yet it would be better if they did so of their own accord, for, in order to be called just, the right course should be chosen voluntarily. There are people, too, so absorbed in their own affairs or so disgusted with humanity that they profess to have their hands full with their own business, and are certain they are doing no injury to others. These men avoid one kind of injustice and fall into the other; they are deserters from the common life, for they contribute nothing to it, neither their interest, nor their labor, nor their abilities.

I have described the two types of injustice and the causes that lead up to each, and have also stated the elements that go to make up justice. So now we can easily decide what our duty is at any given moment, provided we do not love ourselves overmuch. For it really is hard to be greatly concerned about other people's affairs. Yet Terence's Chremes says [16] that nothing human is alien to him. However, we do realize and feel more deeply the prosperity or adversity that affects ourselves than we do that which affects our neighbors, which

---

[14] *Republic*, VI; see Classics Club edition, p. 368.
[15] *Republic*, I; Classics Club edition, pp. 243–246.
[16] Terence, *The Self-Tormentor* (*Heauton Timorumenos*), 1, 77.

we observe, as it were, from a long distance off. We judge their situation differently from the way we judge our own. It is sage advice, to refrain from all action in a case of doubt as to where the right and the wrong lie. For the right way shines bright by itself but doubt implies an admission of possible injustice.

There are often, however, times when the virtues normally most characteristic of a just man and one whom we call good change and become their opposites. It may on occasion, for instance, not be right to return a loan or to keep a promise, and it may be right to evade or disregard the duties of truthfulness and fidelity. We must look back to the fundamental principles of justice which I laid down at the beginning; first, to harm no one, and, second, to serve the common good. As these are affected by changing circumstances, our duty also changes and is not always the same.

It may happen, for instance, that to keep a certain promise or compact would be disadvantageous either to the one to whom the promise was made, or to him who made it. If, for example, Neptune in the story had not fulfilled his promise to Theseus, Theseus would not have lost his son, Hippolytus. For, as the tale goes, Theseus was granted three wishes, and for the third, in a fit of anger, he wished for the death of Hippolytus. The granting of that wish plunged him into the depths of grief. You should, therefore, not keep promises that would be harmful to those to whom you made them; or, if to keep them would hurt you more than it would help the other. It is no violation of duty to put the greater good ahead of the smaller.

Suppose, by way of illustration, you promised someone to appear as his attorney in court and in the meantime your son fell critically ill. It would be no breach of your duty not to do what you had promised. On the contrary, if the man you had promised complained of your desertion, he would be showing a worse concept of duty. And everyone knows that promises made under duress, intimidation, or false pretenses are not binding. Pledges of this kind are frequently declared void by a praetor's edict, sometimes by law.

People often suffer injustice through a kind of chicanery, and an over-subtle or malicious interpretation of the law, whence comes the familiar saying: "The more law, the less justice." By this means a great number of wrongs are committed in public dealings. Take, for instance, the general who made with the enemy a truce of thirty days, and then ravaged their fields by night, because the truce specified days and not nights.[17] One of our own countrymen was guilty in a similar way, if the story about Quintus Fabius Labeo, or some other person, is true. I know it only from hearsay. This man was appointed by the Senate as arbitrator in a boundary dispute between Nola and Naples. On his arrival at the spot, he conferred with each party separately, urging them not to behave greedily or graspingly, but to give up something rather than try to seize more. As both parties followed this advice, a strip of land between them was left unoccupied. He then drew the boundaries as they had agreed and awarded the strip left between to the Roman people. That was certainly cheating, not a fair judgment. Such craftiness should in all circumstances be avoided.

We have certain duties to perform even toward persons who have injured us. There are bounds to vengeance and to punishment. In fact, it is perhaps enough if the offender repents of the wrong he committed so thoroughly that he will not repeat it and will discourage others from similar misdeeds.

---

[17] The story was told of Cleomenes, king of Sparta (520–491 B.C.), in his war with Argos.

In affairs of state the laws of war must be strictly observed. There are two ways of settling a dispute, the first by discussion, the other by force. The former is peculiar to men, the latter to animals, so we should resort to that only if discussion fails. Wars should never be undertaken save to make possible a life of peace and safety, and once the victory has been won, we should spare all who have not been cruel or brutal in the fight. Thus our forefathers received into citizenship the Tusculans, Aequians, Volscians, Sabines, and Hernicians, but leveled Carthage and Numantia to the ground. I wish they had not destroyed Corinth, but I presume they had some reason for doing so—perhaps the strategic location of the city, that might some day have tempted its inhabitants to start a war again. In my opinion, we should always work for peace, but a peace that will have no tricks in it. If my advice had been followed in the matter, we should still have, if not the best, at least some form of free government, as it is, we have lost it altogether.

A conquered enemy we should treat humanely, and take under our protection those who lay down their arms relying on the good faith of our generals, even if they wait to do so until the battering ram is beating at their walls. This kind of just treatment has been so scrupulously practiced by our people that the commanders who received the surrender of cities or nations defeated in war by ancient custom became their patrons. Justice in war is sacredly provided for in the Fetial Code [18] of the Roman people. There it is stated that a war to be just may not be undertaken until after a demand has been made for restitution, warning given, and a formal declaration issued.

---

[18] The Fetial Code was the law of the Fetiales or college of four priests who acted as guardians of public faith. They conducted the ceremonious declarations of war and peace, confirmation of treaties, etc.

Popilius,[19] under whom Cato's [20] son was doing his first military service in the army, was the governor-general of a province. Popilius decided to demobilize one legion, and Cato's son, who served in that legion, was discharged. But the young man, liking warfare, stayed on with the army. So his father, Cato, wrote to Popilius and asked him, if he permitted his son to stay, to make him swear a new oath of military allegiance. For since his first oath was then void, he could not lawfully fight the enemy. So punctilious at that time was the observance of law in the conduct of war. There is a letter written by the aged Cato to his son Marcus in which he says he has heard of his discharge by the consul while serving in the Macedonian campaign against Perseus.[21] Cato warns his son accordingly not to go into battle again, for, as he puts it, a man who is not a soldier has no right to be fighting against the enemy.

I should like to point out, incidentally, that a man who should properly have been called "enemy fighter" [perduellis] was then called "foreigner" [hostis], thus softening the severity of the fact by the mildness of the word. For our ancestors used the word hostis for a person we now call foreigner [peregrinus]. The Twelve Tables speak of "the day assigned for trial of a foreigner [hostis]." Again: "In dealing with a foreigner [hostis] all rights of ownership are forever inalienable." What greater sign of humanity can there be than the use of so gentle a name for one with whom we are at war? Yet the word has become harsher with the passage of time, for it has

---

19 Popilius, consul in 172 B.C., had charge of campaigns in the province of Liguria.
20 This Cato was Marcus Porcius Cato (234–149 B.C.), the Elder, censor, orator and statesman, famous for his austerity of life and morals and his stern opposition to the introduction of Greek culture.
21 Perseus was the last king of Macedonia, conquered by the Romans at Pydna, 168 B.C.

lost its meaning of mere foreigner and become exclusively an armed enemy.

Even when men are fighting for power, or striving for glory in battle, their reasons should still be the same as those I mentioned above as just causes for war. And wars fought for glory and power should be waged with not so much bitterness. Just as in civil life we struggle in one way against an enemy and another against a simple rival. In the one case, we are fighting for our lives and our good name, and in the other for a higher position and prestige. So, the wars against the Celtiberians and the Cimbri were fought as against enemies, for the question then was not who should rule the other but who should survive. But with the Latins, Sabines, Samnites, Carthaginians, and King Pyrrhus we fought for supremacy. The Carthaginians were treaty breakers, and Hannibal was cruel, but the others were all law abiding.

We know the famous speech of Pyrrhus [22] on the exchange of prisoners,[23]

"I do not ask for gold, nor shall you pay me ransom;
We do not trade in war; we are but honest soldiers;
With sword and not with gold shall all our lives be measured.
Will Fortune bring to pass that you reign here, or I do?
Let valor answer for us! Now hear this word from me:
To those courageous men whom fate of war left living
I leave assured their freedom, committing them to you.
Take them, for I release them; and may the gods approve it!"

A royal speech was that, and worthy of Aeacus' famous race.

And if, in time of stress, a person makes a promise to the

---

[22] Pyrrhus (318–272), king of Epirus, claimed descent from the heroic Achilles and from Aeacus, son of Zeus. He led an invasion into Italy and was as brave and gallant a foe as the Romans ever encountered.
[23] Ennius, *Annals*, VI.

enemy, he must keep faith with them, as Regulus [24] did, for instance. He was taken prisoner by the Carthaginians during the First Punic War, and later sent to Rome to negotiate an exchange of prisoners, having sworn that he would return. But immediately on his arrival, he moved in the Senate that no prisoners should be sent back. Then when his friends and relatives tried to keep him at home, he chose to go back to torture at Carthage rather than break his word to the enemy.

On the other hand, during the Second Punic War, Hannibal, after the battle of Cannae, sent back to Rome ten captive Romans, whom he had bound by oath to return in case they were unable to arrange for a ransom of prisoners. They broke their pledge, and for that reason the censors deprived each of them of citizenship for life. In the same way they punished a man who was guilty of oath-breaking by a trick. He left the Carthaginian camp with Hannibal's permission, and soon afterward returned, saying he had forgotten something. When he left the camp the second time, he considered he was released from the obligation of his oath. By the letter of it he was released, but not by the spirit. Always in a pledge one must think of the meaning, not merely of the words.

Our forefathers gave an outstanding example of justice to an enemy when a deserter from Pyrrhus' army made an offer to the Senate to murder the king by poison, and the Senate, under Caius Fabricius,[25] turned the man over to Pyrrhus. Thus they expressed their disapproval of the treacherous mur-

---

[24] The story of Regulus (consul in 267 and 256 B.C.) was a favorite of the Romans. After winning many victories over the Carthaginians, he was taken prisoner by them in 255.

[25] Gaius Fabricius, called "the Just," was another of the heroes of old Rome, renowned for his dignity and uprightness of character. As consul in 278 B.C., he sent back the traitor to Pyrrhus, as related here.

der of even a powerful and aggressive enemy. We have now said enough of duties connected with war-making.

Let us remember that we must be just even to people of the lowest station in life. The lowest station and the worst fate are those of slaves, and there are good teachers who tell us to treat them like paid servants. They should be obliged to work. but they should be given their dues.

There are two ways in which wrong can be done—by force and by fraud. Fraud is to be expected of a little fox, force of a lion. Both are beneath the dignity of man, but of the two, fraud is the more detestable. Of all forms of wrongdoing none is viler than that of the scoundrel who, when he is most false, acts so as to appear honorable. With this I have said enough on the subject of justice.

Next, as suggested above, let us talk of kindliness and generosity. Nothing appeals more strongly to human nature than this virtue, but it must be exercised with considerable discretion. First of all, we must see that our kindness does not harm the very persons whom it is meant to benefit, or anyone else. Secondly, our generosity must not go beyond our means. Lastly, it must be distributed according to the merit of the receiver, for this is the foundation principle of justice, by which all deeds of kindness should be measured. For those who, to please someone they wish to help, bestow on him something harmful to him, are not kind or generous, but dangerous pamperers. And those who injure one party in order to heap kindness on another are as unjust as those who help themselves to other men's property for their own benefit.

Many people, especially those who are ambitious for grandeur and glory, take from some to enrich others, and expect to be thought benefactors of their friends, if they fill those friends' pockets, regardless of how they do it. Yet duty requires something different—precisely the opposite, in fact. Our kindness should be such that it benefits our friends, but hurts no one else. So when Sulla and Caesar took property away from its rightful owners and gave it to strangers, that should not have been considered generosity, for nothing is generous that is not also just.

Another point for caution is that your generosity does not go beyond your means. Whoever tries to be more generous than his means allow is guilty, first, of wrong to his own family, conferring on outsiders property that should justly be used for their support or left to them by bequest. Also, this kind of generosity often leads to rapacity and unjust robbing of other people in order to get the means to make large gifts. We see many people, not so much generous as coveting glory, who do many things to seem benevolent that come closer to ostentation than to true good will. Such pretense is more likely hypocrisy than genuine kindness.

Thirdly, we said that while being generous we should pay some consideration to merit. The character of the person on whom we propose to bestow our benefit should be looked into, his attitude toward us, his lifetime associates and companions, as well as the services he has already rendered to our interests. It is desirable that he have every qualification, or, if not, the more important should count for more.

Now we live with men who are neither perfect, nor conspicuously wise, but who get on quite well if they keep up a semblance of virtue. Even so, I think, we should feel that no human being should be left wholly neglected who shows any trace of goodness. And the more anyone reveals of the gentler virtues, self-control, modesty, and the justice of which we have said so much, the more he should be cherished. A bold and fearless spirit in a man neither perfect nor wise is

339

often unruly. Those other virtues seem more especially the marks of the good man. And so much for the character of the object of our kindness.

As for our reaction to kindness shown to us, we should give most gratitude to him from whom we receive most love. We should not, like the young, measure affection by the passion which accompanies it, but by its steadiness and constancy. We must be particularly careful whenever we are indebted to others, and the favor was not ours to start with but something to be returned, for no duty is more imperative than the obligation to requite kindness.

Hesiod tells us [26] that we should repay with interest, if possible, what we took for our needs. What then shall we do with unsolicited gifts? Shall we copy the fertile fields that return much more than they receive? We do not hesitate to do favors for persons we expect will be of use to us. How then ought we to treat those who have already helped us? For there are two kinds of generosity—doing a kindness and returning one. We are free in the first case to do or not, but to fail to return a favor is impossible for a good man, provided he can do it without injuring someone else.

Some distinctions have to be made between the favors received, and unquestionably the greater the favor the greater our obligation. Even so, we should weigh carefully the spirit, the ardor, the affection with which the favor was done. For there are people who do a multitude of favors for everybody, impulsively, without judgment, in a morbid or hasty burst of emotion, as unstable as the wind. Such favors should not be valued so highly as those done for us with judgment, deliberately and steadily.

However, in conferring a kindness or returning a favor,

---

[26] *Works and Days,* 349–351.

other things being equal, our first duty is to help most where help is most needed. But as a rule, people do the contrary. They do most for the one from whom they expect most, even though he does not need it. The bonds that connect members of human society will be best preserved if we show our greatest kindness to those who are nearest us.

At this point I think we should go back to the natural principles on which human society and fellowship are based. There is, first of all, the common link existing between all members of the human race. This link is the power of reason and speech which through teaching and learning, communication, discussion, and judication brings men together and unites them in a kind of natural fellowship. This faculty more than any other thing distinguishes our nature from that of animals. They, we admit, often show courage, as, for instance, horses and lions do, but we do not ascribe to them justice, fairness, and goodness, because they are not endowed with reason or speech. Those are the universal bonds that join men to men and all to all. Through them the common ownership of all things that nature has produced for man's common use should be maintained. For even though all that has been made private property by statute and civil law must be protected as the laws appoint, all other things should be treated as the Greek proverb says, "everything in common among friends."

We see the common right of all men in things of the kind described by Ennius in one passage,[27] which may be extended to cover many more.

"Whoever sets a wanderer on his way
Is like a man who lights a lamp from his.
His own shines no less bright for lighting that."

[27] The lines may come from Ennius' tragedy *Telephus*, now lost.

This illustration teaches us to give even to a stranger whatever we can spare without privation. And on this principle we base the following rules. "Shut no man off from running water." "Let anyone who asks light his fire from yours." "Give sound advice to a person in uncertainty." Such kindnesses help the recipient and involve no loss to the giver. We should therefore obey those rules and constantly contribute to the common good. But since the resources of individuals are small and the number of the needy is great, our general benevolence should be regulated by the test set by Ennius; our own lamp is to "shine no less bright"—that we may have means to be generous to our friends.

There are many degrees of connection between members of the human race. To pass beyond the universal bond, there is the closer bond of race, nation, and language, by which men are bound very tightly together. Within that are the groups of citizens of the same city who have many things in common —forum, temples, arcades, streets, statutes, laws, courts, and rights of suffrage, to say nothing of social relationships and numerous property and business associations. A still closer connection exists between groups of kinsmen.

Starting from the vast society of the human race, we have now arrived at a small and narrow circle. For since by nature all living creatures desire to produce offspring, the first bond of union is that between man and wife, then between them and their children. Then comes the household, with all its possessions in common. This is the starting point of the city, the seedbed, so to speak, of the state. After it come the bond between brothers, and then between first and second cousins who, when they can no longer find room in one house, go out to separate homes, like colonies. Marriages follow with their connections, and new relatives are thus added. With this increase of numbers and their progeny comes the beginning of the state. Blood relationship produces in men good will and affection, for it means much to share with relatives the same memories of ancestors, the same religious rites, and the same tombs.

But of all the bonds mentioned so far, none is more noble or more enduring than familiar friendship, when it unites good and congenial men. For if we discover in a fellow man that goodness of which I have said so much, we are moved to make him our friend. And while every virtue attracts us and makes us love those in whom we see them exemplified, justice and generosity do so most of all. And nothing is more conducive to love and intimacy than the similarity of character of good men. When two persons strive for the same ideals and want the same things, then each loves the other as himself, and it comes about, as Pythagoras says it should in a friendship, that from being several they become one. Another strong tie between men is created by the give and take of friendly services. As long as these are reciprocal and agreeable, they make for firm friendship between those who exchange them.

But when in a spirit of reason we survey them all, we find no bond more powerful or more dear than that which binds each one of us to our country. Parents are dear, children, relatives, and friends are dear, but our love of country embraces all other loves. For her no good citizen would hesitate to lay down his life if thereby he could serve her. The more despicable are those scoundrels who have rent their country in pieces with every form of crime, and have labored and still are laboring for her total destruction!

If we should draw up a comparison to select the ones to whom we owe our greatest duty, first would come our country and our parents, to whose charity we are most deeply indebted. Next would come our children and all our households, people who look to us as their sole support and can have no other protector. Then would come our congenial relatives, whose fortunes are for the most part the same as ours.

The necessities of life, therefore, must first of all be provided for those I have just mentioned. But companionship in life and living, counsel, conversation, encouragement, consolation, sometimes even criticism are found at their best among friends. And the friendship is happiest that is knit between like characters.

But in the discharge of all these duties we must consider what is most needed in each case, and how much each person can or cannot get without our aid. In this way we shall find that the degrees of our obligation vary with circumstances. There are duties we owe to some people more than to others. For instance, in harvesting crops, you may help your neighbor more than you do your brother or your friend. But in a case in court, you will defend your relative or your friend rather than your neighbor. These and similar questions we should consider in every line of duty and make a custom and practice of doing so, in order to become good reckoners of duties, able by adding and subtracting to see what the final sum comes to and know how much we owe to each.

But just as doctors, generals, and public speakers, however well they may know the theory of their art, can never win any very admirable success without experience and practice, so though the rules for performance of duty have been laid down, as we are stating them, the fulfillment of them is so arduous that we too need experience and practice. We have now discussed sufficiently the way in which the idea of goodness, from which duty is derived, was developed out of the elements that are present in the institutions of all human society.

We must, however, remember that though the four cardinal virtues are, as we have described them, the foundations for all good conduct and duty, the acts we call most splendid are performed by men of a great and lofty spirit, scorning the ordinary ways of men. So in taunting a person, the first thing we say, if we can, is something like this: [28]

> "You, young men, have the hearts of women,
>   This girl, that of a man!"

Or like this:

> "O son of Salmacis, your spoils should show
>   no stains of sweat and blood!" [29]

On the other hand, our most exuberant praise we give to brave and noble deeds done with a high heart. Orators dilate at length on Marathon, Salamis, Plataea, Thermopylae, and Leuctra, and on our own Cocles, the Decii, Gnaeus, and Publius Scipio, Marcellus, and countless others. The people of Rome excel above all in greatness of spirit. Their enthusiasm for military glory is shown by the fact that most of their statues wear the soldier's dress.

Yet if this same high spirit that is displayed in danger and difficulty is without regard for justice, and fights not for the common good but for its own advantage, it becomes a vice. Far from being a virtue, it is rather a barbarity revolting to all humane feeling. The Stoic philosophers are therefore right in defining courage as the virtue which makes men fight for the right. No man who won a reputation for courage through treachery and cruelty ever received much praise, for nothing can be good that is not just.

There is the famous saying of Plato,[30] "All knowledge used

---

[28] The source of these lines is uncertain.
[29] Ennius, *Ajax*. Salmacis was a nymph, whose fountain at Halicarnassus made any man who drank of it weak and cowardly.
[30] *Menexenus*, 246.

to promote injustice should be called cunning rather than wisdom. And so a spirit willing to face danger, if it is moved by selfishness and not by desire for the common good, may be styled bold, but it is not courageous." We would have our brave and stouthearted men at the same time good and sincere, friends of truth and clean of all deceit. These qualities are the glorious heart of justice.

The shame is that from this loftiness and greatness of spirit spring often stubbornness and an excessive hunger for power. Plato tells us [31] that the Spartan disposition was all fired with ambition to win. Similarly, the man most outstanding for greatness of spirit most wants to become first among his fellow citizens or rather their sole ruler. It is difficult to preserve a sense of that fairness, which is essential to justice, when you are straining to outdo everyone else. Such men accordingly are not to be held in check by argument or by any public or legal edict. In public life they are apt to become bribers and intriguers, aiming at large influence and preferring a superiority based on force to an equality with justice. Yet the more difficult the task, the more glorious its accomplishment, for under no circumstances should a man forget justice.

Hence not those who commit injustice but those who prevent it are courageous and noble-hearted. A truly wise and great spirit believes that in deeds rather than in fame is the goodness which is Nature's goal. He chooses to be a leader rather than to seem so, for a man who is dependent on the vagrant opinion of the ignorant masses cannot be counted one of the great. The more ambitious a man is, the more easily can a desire for fame lead him to acts of injustice. We are here on slippery ground, for where is the man who has faced danger and conquered difficulties who does not wish to be

[31] *Laches,* 182.

rewarded with glory for his accomplishment? A soul that is altogether brave and great is distinguished by two main characteristics. One is his indifference to externals, for he is convinced that a man should never admire, or desire, or work for anything but what is good and seemly, and should never give way to any other man or any passion or any hardship of fortune. The second characteristic is that, having trained his spirit as we have just said, he will do deeds both splendid and highly useful, as well as extremely arduous and fraught with labor and danger to his own life and to many of the things that make life worth living.

It is the second of these two characteristics that ensures for him all the glory and grandeur and usefulness to others, but the cause and the intelligence that make the man great lie in the first. That is what makes a man superior and indifferent to human things. You can see this in two ways. First, he considers goodness the only good, and second, he is free from all passion. For it takes a brave and a great mind to treat as unimportant what seems to the masses most wonderful and splendid, and to despise them on firm and fixed principles. And it requires a spirit of much strength and constancy to bear all the pains, many and various, that meet us in human life and fate without losing the natural state and dignity of a wise man. And a man who is not to be shattered by fear cannot consistently be shaken by desire, nor should one who cannot be conquered by toil be conquered by pleasure. We must therefore beware of all these things and also of greed for money. For nothing is so characteristic of a narrow and small mind as a love of money, and nothing is more honorable and magnanimous than contempt for it, if you have none, and benevolent and generous spending of it, if you have it.

We should beware, too, as I have said, of too much glory, for it deprives us of the liberty that is the prize for which all great men struggle. Nor should we desire military command. We should either refuse to accept it, or after a time resign it.

We should also keep our spirits free from all disturbances, from desire and fear, from excess of pain or pleasure, and from anger, that peace and serenity may reign in our souls, and bring with them steadfastness and dignity. There have been and still are many persons who seek to obtain this peace by withdrawing from public affairs and taking refuge in a life of quiet. Among these have been the noblest and by far the greatest philosophers and other austere and serious men, who could not endure the ways of people or of princes. Some of them went to live in the country and found happiness in the conduct of their households. Their purpose was like that of kings—to suffer no want, to be subject to no one's command, to enjoy liberty, which means to live as one pleases.

This last desire is felt both by persons ambitious for power and by the quiet retired men of whom I have just spoken. The former believe they can obtain that liberty by the acquirement of great resources; the latter are satisfied with the little they have. We should not condemn either way of thinking. The life of retirement is easier and safer and less unpleasant and troublesome to others. Whereas the career of one who devotes himself to service of the state and the management of great affairs is more useful to mankind and more apt to achieve fame and wide renown.

So perhaps we must excuse those men of brilliant ability who have not taken part in politics but devoted themselves to learning, as well as those who have retired from public life because of ill health or some other serious reason and left to others the power and the credit of governing. As for those who, without any such good reason, will have nothing to do with military commands or civil offices, so much admired by the masses: I think this is not to their credit but to their discredit. Insofar as they are scornful of glory and care nothing for it, it is hard not to commend their attitude. But actually they seem to be afraid of the work and the trouble, and also of what they regard as the disgrace and the notoriety of possible attacks and defeats. For there are people who act quite inconsistently under contrary conditions. Pleasure they denounce in severest terms, but to pain they are very sensitive. Glory means nothing to them, but they are crushed by disgrace. And even in these things they are not really consistent.

But all who have received from Nature a gift for executive action should drop their hesitations, and stand for office and take a hand in the conduct of the state, for by no other means can government be carried on or a great spirit declare itself. Statesmen no less than philosophers—perhaps even more— should possess the magnanimity and superiority to human vicissitudes of which I have often spoken, and peace and serenity of mind, if they are to live free from worry, in dignity and stability. This is easier for philosophers, since their lives are less open to the blows of fortune, their needs are fewer, and if adversity comes upon them, their fall is not so serious. Not without reason, then, are men in public life more excited than men who live in seclusion, and more eager for success. All the more do they need greatness of spirit and freedom from petty anxieties. A man, then, who plans a public career should consider not only the honor of it but whether he has the ability to succeed. In doing this, he should neither despair too soon from discouragement, nor be overconfident through ambition. In every enterprise it is best to prepare carefully before starting to undertake it.

Most people suppose that military achievements are more

important than civil, but this view ought to be amended, for wars have often been started by men too eager to become famous, men who many times were gifted with great spirits and capacity. It is particularly likely to happen with men who are able and enthusiastic soldiers. If, therefore, we are to be truthful, we shall admit that many peaceful achievements have been more important and more renowned than feats of war.

Themistocles [32] is highly praised and justly so, and his name is more famous than that of Solon. Salamis is cited constantly as witness to a most glorious victory, which is rated above Solon's wise counsel in establishing the court of the Areopagus. Yet the latter achievement should be regarded as no less illustrious than the former, for Themistocles' victory served the city once, but Solon's work will be of value always. Through his measures the laws of the Athenians and their ancestral institutions have been preserved. And while Themistocles could not say that he had done anything to assist the Areopagus, it could truthfully claim to have assisted Themistocles, for the war was carried on under the direction of this senate which Solon had set up.

The same thing may be said of Pausanias and Lysander,[33] whose deeds are said to have won for Sparta her supremacy; yet they are never to be compared with the laws and social code of Lycurgus. Rather, it was due to them that Pausanias and Lysander possessed such brave and well-disciplined armies.

---

[32] Themistocles was the brilliant general who gave Athens her fleet and by his victory off the island of Salamis saved Greece from conquest by the Persians (480 B.C.); Solon (c. 638–558) was the great lawgiver who gave Athens her constitution.
[33] Pausanias, king of Sparta, commanded the Greek army in the victory over Persia at Plataea (479); Lysander, a Spartan admiral, won the decisive naval victory over Athens that decided the outcome of the Peloponnesian War (405); Lycurgus was the lawmaker of Sparta.

I, for one, do not believe that Marcus Scaurus [34] was inferior to Gaius Marius, when I was a child, or Quintus Catulus to Pompey, when I was in public life. For arms are of little use in the field if there is no wise policy at home. So Scipio Africanus, remarkable man and general as he was, did no more for his country by destroying Numantia than was done at the same time by Publius Nasica, the private citizen, when he killed Tiberius Gracchus. That act, to be sure, was not wholly civil in character, but in a way warlike, since it was an act committed by violence. Yet it had a political motive, and was performed without an army.

The best statement is that line [35] which is criticized, I hear, by malicious and jealous persons:

"Let the sword bow to the toga, let the people's voice govern the laurels." Other instances aside, when I was at the helm of state, did not the sword bow to the toga? Never was our country in greater danger and never was a peace more profound. Through my vigilant policy the swords in the hands of the bold insurgents dropped suddenly to the ground. What military victory was ever so complete? What triumph can be compared with it? I may boast to you, my son, for you are heir to my glory, and yours is the duty to imitate it. And Gnaeus Pompey, crowned with the glories of war, before a vast audience paid me the high tribute of saying that he would have won his third triumph in vain, if, without my services to the state, he had found no place in which to celebrate it. Acts of civilian courage then are not inferior to military

---

[34] Marcus Scaurus and Quintus Catulus were both aristocratic consuls and politicians, of the senatorial party, to which Cicero belonged; Gaius Marius and Pompey were two of the famous generals of the time. On Scipio Africanus, see above, p. 19, fn. 1. Nasica was the leader of the band that attacked and killed the tribune Tiberius Gracchus for his attempt at reform of the land system in the interest of the small farmer.

[35] Poem by Cicero, *On his Times*, III.

prowess. On the contrary, the former require more devotion and more energy.

In general, the goodness we look to find in a lofty and noble mind is derived from spiritual, not physical, strength. Yet the body must be exercised and so trained that it will obey the judgments of reason in carrying out assignments and undergoing toil. But the goodness which is our subject here is a matter entirely of resolution and thought. By it the men who in civil toga guide the affairs of the republic perform as great a service as those who wage our wars. Through their wise counsels wars are often averted or brought to a close. At times, too, they start wars, as when Marcus Cato brought on the Third Punic War and influenced its conduct even after his death. Wisdom in settling a conflict is more desirable indeed than courage in fighting it out. But we must be careful not to choose peace out of desire to escape a war instead of for the public interest. Whenever a war is undertaken, clearly its sole purpose should be to secure peace.

Only a brave and steadfast spirit will remain undisturbed in times of stress and not be upset and lose sight of his goal, but keep his presence of mind and his judgment and push on in the path of reason. By reasoning to anticipate the future, and recognize beforehand what may happen in either the best or the worst contingency, and what must be done in any event, and never to have to say, "I did not think of that,"—all this requires a brave spirit and also high intelligence.

This is the conduct of a great and lofty soul, confident in his foresight and wisdom. But to dash recklessly into battle and fight the enemy sword in hand seems rather barbarous, animal behavior. Yet if circumstances demand it, we must resort to our swords and prefer death to slavery and disgrace.

When it comes to the destruction or plundering of conquered cities, great care must be taken that nothing is done wantonly or too brutally. In turbulent times it is a great man's duty to punish the guilty, but to protect the masses and maintain under all circumstances an upright and honorable course. As I said before, there are men who set achievements in war above those of peace, and so you will find many to whom dangerous and rash decisions appear more glorious and brilliant than those that are calm and well considered.

On the one hand, we must never try so hard to avoid a danger as to seem cowardly and fearful, but we must beware too of exposing ourselves to danger without due reason—than which nothing can be more stupid. So in approaching dangers we should copy the physician's method; in light cases of illness, they give mild treatments, for the seriously sick, they must use perilous and sometimes drastic remedies. Only a fool will pray for a storm in fair weather, but when a storm comes, a wise man resists it with all his power, especially when he expects to gain more by winning out than he risks by the struggle.

The dangers of political action fall at times on those who undertake it, at other times on the state itself. Some risk their lives, some their reputations and the good will of their fellow citizens. We should, however, be more ready to face perils ourselves than to endanger the community, and to fight for honor and glory harder than for other possessions. Many would willingly sacrifice their property and even their lives for their country, even though their country calls for it. Take, for instance, Callicrates,[36] who, after being admiral for the Spartans in the Peloponnesian War and doing excellent service, at the end ruined everything by refusing to heed the advice of those who thought he should withdraw his fleet from Arginusae and not try battle with the Athenians. His

---

[36] Callicrates lost both his fleet and his life at Arginusae, 406 B.C.

answer was that the Spartans, if they lost that fleet, could build another, but that he could not retreat without disgracing himself. And actually it was not a heavy blow to Sparta! But when Cleombrotus,[37] in fear of criticism, undertook to rashly fight Epaminondas, his disastrous defeat meant the collapse of Sparta's power.

How much wiser was Quintus Fabius Maximus,[38] of whom Ennius says: [39]

"One man by his delays our country has preserved,
Its safety he has put before his own fair fame,
And thus henceforth his glory brighter grows."

Misdeeds of this sort should not be committed in political life either. There are men who for fear of criticism never dare to express their opinion, excellent as it may be.

In general, political leaders should remember the two rules of Plato: [40] first, to be so careful of the people's welfare that in every act they consider that, without regard to their own advantage; second, to watch over the whole body of the citizenry, lest they betray some while protecting others. The administration of the state should be like a guardianship, conducted for the benefit of the wards, and not for that of the guardians. Those who disregard the interests of a part of the citizens, while they favor another part, introduce a pernicious influence into the state, sedition and party strife.

---

[37] Cleombrotus, son of the king of Sparta, was defeated and killed in the battle of Leuctra, 371 B.C. Thereupon Thebes, under her great general Epaminondas, became the leading city of Greece.

[38] Quintus Fabius Maximus won his victory over Hannibal in 217 B.C., by his slow and cautious strategy of seizing every opportunity to harass the enemy, but refusing battle, until the Carthaginians were so weakened that their defeat was certain.

[39] *Annals*, XII.

[40] *Republic*, I, 342; IV, 420.

As a result, some will support the popular party, others the aristocratic, but few will take thought for the nation as a whole.

As a result of such conditions, violent factions arose in Athens, and in our republic we have had not only uprisings, but calamitous civil wars. Any sincere and courageous patriot, worthy of leadership in the state, will oppose and hate this state of things and will devote himself wholly to his country, with no thought of his own wealth or power. He will safeguard it and act in the interests of all the citizens. He will not use false charges to bring odium or suspicion on anyone, but will hold so fast to justice and honesty that he will suffer any loss, however heavy, in order to be true to his principles, and suffer death rather than give them up.

We have certainly a most unfortunate way of campaigning and struggling for public offices. Plato has some fine words on that subject.[41] "People who compete with each other to see who shall administer the government act like sailors who fight to take over the helm." He also advises us to treat as enemies only those who resort to arms, not those who merely have views of their own about conduct of administration. The dispute between Publius Africanus and Quintus Metellus was like that, without bitterness.

We should pay no attention to persons who tell us that we should feel a violent hatred for our enemies, and that such passion is the sign of a brave and noble man. Nothing is more admirable and nothing more worthy of a great and extraordinary character than gentleness and tolerance. And among a free people, where all are equal before the law, we must practice amiability and what we call poise of mind. For if we are irritated with people who call on us at incon-

---

[41] *Republic*, VI, 488, 489; VIII, 567; *Laws*, IX, 856.

venient hours or make impertinent requests of us, we may fall into a state of foolish and offensive bad temper. At the same time, we must realize that courtesy and kindliness are good only if they do not interfere with strictness in the cause of the state, without which government cannot be administered. But even punishment and censure should not be insulting, nor designed for the satisfaction of the punisher or censurer, but for the best interest of the republic.

We should see to it also that the punishment is not greater than the crime, and that some are not penalized for offenses for which others are not even put on trial. Above all, there should be no anger shown in punishing. For when an angry man inflicts punishment, he never takes the middle course between too much and too little. This middle course is the doctrine of the Peripatetics,[42] a good doctrine, too, if only they would not praise anger, and call it a useful gift bestowed on us by Nature. But, in reality, we should not countenance anger under any circumstances, but should expect our political leaders to be like the laws, which punish with justice but without passion.

When we are prosperous and everything is going our way, we should take pains to avoid arrogance, haughtiness, and pride, for it is as much a mark of weakness to be overexcited by good fortune as by bad. An admirable thing it is to keep one's equanimity all through life, with always a calm face and expression, as, we hear, Socrates and Gaius Laelius [43] did. King Philip of Macedon, though outdone by his son in military achievements and glory, was his superior, I believe, in courtesy and humanity. Philip then was always a great man, while

---

[42] The Peripatetics were the followers of Aristotle. On his doctrine of the "golden mean" see his Ethics; Classics Club edition, p. 109 ff.
[43] Gaius Laelius, who served under Scipio Africanus at Carthage was a Stoic and friend of the philosopher, Panaetius, mentioned below.

Alexander was often extremely vicious. The warning seems sound, that the higher we rise, the more humbly we should walk. Panaetius [44] reports that his pupil and friend, Scipio Africanus, used to say, "When horses that have taken part in many battles become fierce, they have to be turned over to trainers to make them manageable again. And so men, unhinged by prosperity and brimful of self-confidence should be sent to the training-ring of reason and learning, to discover there the frailty of human life and the fickleness of fortune."

So at the pinnacle of our success we should listen very closely to the advice of our friends and defer even more than before to their opinions. At the same time, we must be careful not to open our ears to flatterers or listen to their blandishments. For it is easy to be deceived and we may come to think we deserve their compliments. Here is the starting point of much wrongdoing, for men, puffed up with conceit, make themselves shockingly ridiculous and commit the most outrageous errors. Enough on this subject!

To answer now our earlier question, we must admit that our greatest achievements, marks of the greatest spirit, are those accomplished by men who govern states, for their activities are most widespread and affect the largest number of people. Yet there are and have been many great souls living lives of seclusion, engaged in researches or undertakings of deep importance, who confine themselves strictly to their own work, or else stand midway between philosophers and public officials, enjoying their possessions, without trying with all their might to increase them, or shutting others out from them, but sharing them with their friends and their country, if it needs them. Their property, in the first place, will be acquired in no fraudulent or harmful way. Then it will be en-

---

[44] For Panaetius, see above, p. 313.

larged by intelligence, industry, and thrift. Lastly, it will be made available to as many people as possible, provided they are worthy, and will be used in ways of generosity and benevolence instead of sensuality and luxury. Following these rules, you may live nobly, in dignity and state, yet at the same time simply and loyally, as a true friend of man.

We must next discuss the one remaining phase of goodness, that including modesty and self-control, which are a kind of refinement of life, moderation, suppression of passions, and orderliness in things. It also includes what we call in Latin "decorum" and the Greeks call "fitness." The quality of this last cannot be distinguished from goodness, for whatever is fitting is good, and what is good is fitting. The difference between the two can be more easily felt than explained. Whatever decorum is, it is visible only after goodness has preceded it. This account of decorum applies not only to the phase of goodness we are now discussing but also to the three we discussed before. To think and speak wisely, to do what one does considerately, and to see and uphold the truth in everything is fitting. On the other hand, to be mistaken, to be led astray, to fall into error and be deceived, is as unfitting as to be insane and out of one's mind. Everything just is fitting, and everything unjust, like vice, is unfitting. The relationship of decorum to courage is similar. Whatever is done in a manly and courageous spirit is worthy of a man and fitting; what is cowardly is, like something immoral, unfitting.

So this decorum, of which I speak, is present in every aspect of goodness, and its presence is evident and requires no expert investigation. In every virtuous deed there is perceptible an element of decorum. The two can be separated theoretically, but not practically. As the charm and beauty of the body cannot be separated from its health, so this decorum is in fact inextricably mixed with virtue, but in thought and theory we distinguish them.

We may describe decorum or fitness under two heads. There is a general decorum, we know, that appears in all goodness, and another, subordinate to the first, that belongs to the several kinds of goodness. The former is commonly defined about as follows: decorum is a quality that marks human excellence in those things in which man by nature differs from other animals. The more particular type of decorum is defined as a quality in accord with nature, which produces moderation, self-control, and good manners.

That this is the accepted understanding of decorum we can see from the way the poets observe it. But of that I have said more elsewhere.[45] But poets conform, we say, to the rules of fitness when the acts and words of their characters are in accord with the nature of each individual. It would seem unfitting, for instance, if either Aeacus or Minos [46] were made to say:

> "Let them hate me, as long as they fear me,"

or:

> "The father is himself his children's tomb,"

because we have been told that those men were just. But if Atreus [47] speaks such lines they are applauded because the sentiment accords with his personality.

The poets, then, decide from each one's personality the part that is fitting for him. But Nature herself has assigned us all

---

[45] *The Orator*, XXII, 71.

[46] Aeacus, son of Zeus and legendary king of Aegina was renowned for his goodness and piety. With Minos, another noble son of Zeus and king of Crete, he was made judge of the dead in Hades.

[47] Atreus, father of Agamemnon and Menelaus, in the tale was the murderer of one brother and of the children of another.

personalities of great excellence, and souls superior to those of all other creatures. The poets choose for a large variety of characters, even bad ones, what is fitting and proper for each one, but on us Nature has imposed roles of steadfastness, moderation, self-control, and courtesy. She teaches us also to be careful in the way we treat our fellow men, that we show both that decorum that accompanies all goodness generally, and that which is to be seen in each separate type of goodness. For even as a beautiful body attracts our eyes by the fine symmetry of its members, and delights us with the graceful interplay of all its parts, so this decorum, if it appears in our daily lives, draws the praise of our fellow men for the orderliness, consistency, and moderation of all our words and acts.

We should accordingly show something like reverence toward other men, toward the best, and also the others. Not to care what others think of us is a sign not only of arrogance, but also of a lack of principle. There is a difference between justice and courtesy in our dealings with other men. Justice requires us not to wrong them, courtesy not to hurt their feelings. It is in this last respect that decorum becomes most apparent. With these remarks I think it is clear what it is that we mean by decorum.

The duty that we derive from it leads us first to the way of harmony with Nature and obedience to her laws. For following Nature as our guide, we shall never go astray, but shall be on the road to keen perception and understanding (which is wisdom), and to an ardent and courageous spirit. But the special power of decorum appears in the virtue we are now discussing (that is, moderation). For only those actions of our bodies and of our minds are to be called right that are in agreement with Nature's laws.

The activities of our minds are naturally twofold. One kind has its seat in desire—called in Greek appetite—which drives men hither and yon. The other kind is based on reason, which teaches and explains to us what we should do and what avoid. As a result, our reason controls us and our desires obey it.

We should do nothing rashly or carelessly, and nothing for which we cannot give a sound reason. This rule amounts almost to a definition of duty. We must see to it too that our desires obey our reason, and neither run ahead of it nor lazily and timidly lag behind it, but remain calm and cause no disturbance to the spirit. Thus we shall achieve a luminous steadfastness and moderation in all things. But when our desires are given free reign and break loose, so to speak, into greed or aversion, with no sufficient control by reason, they transgress glaringly all limits of decent behavior. They discard and reject all ideas of obedience to reason, although the law of Nature made them subject to it; and create disturbances not only in the mind, but in the body. We have only to look at the faces of people in a rage, or under the spell of passion or fear, or who are disporting themselves in gross pleasures. Their faces, voices, gestures, postures are all of them changed.

To return to our picture of duty, we see now that all our appetites should be restrained and kept in bounds, and we should take constant pains not to do anything rashly, haphazardly, inconsiderately, or carelessly. For Nature has not created us to behave as if we were here for play and fun, but for a serious life of earnest and important tasks. Sports and jesting we may indeed enjoy, but as we do sleep and other relaxations, after we have finished our serious and significant work. Even then, our kind of fun should not be extravagant or immodest, but decent and witty. We do not allow our children to play every kind of game, but only those compatible with good behavior; similarly our jests should be lighted by nobility of spirit.

There are, in general, two forms of jesting. One is rude,

361

coarse, vicious, and obscene; the other, refined, polite, clever, and witty. Both our poet, Plautus, and the Old Comedy at Athens, and also the books of the Socratic philosophers, are full of jests of the latter type, and many witty sayings of other men, like those that the elder Cato collected, called *Apophthegmata* [aphorisms]. It is easy to tell the decent from the improper jest. The one, if rightly timed, that is, when minds are relaxed, is suitable even for the most dignified person; the other is unfit for any free man, when the subject is foul and the language obscene. In our amusements too we should observe certain rules, so as not to go too far and be carried away by our revels and lapse into sheer debauchery. The games on our Campus Martius and hunting excursions are examples of healthy amusements.

In any discussion of duty we should keep in mind how far man is by nature superior to the cattle and other animals. They think of nothing but their own pleasure and all their instincts drive them to press toward it. Man's mind, on the other hand, is trained by learning and thinking. He is forever either investigating or doing something and delights in seeing and hearing. Even if he is too prone to run after sensual pleasures, so long as he is not in a class with beasts—for there are creatures who are men in name only, not in reality—even if he is somewhat too prone to the joys of the flesh, he hides the fact, however much they captivate him, and out of shame conceals his desires. From this we deduce that physical pleasures are not worthy of the dignity of a man, and should be despised and rejected. If, however, one should yield a bit to pleasure, one should take care to be moderate in his indulgence. Our bodily lives and comforts should be patterned on the rules of health and strength, not of pleasure. And if only we remember the excellence and dignity of our natures, we shall realize how degraded it is to abandon ourselves to

luxury and soft and voluptuous living and how right it is to
live thriftily, continently, plainly, and soberly.

We should recognize the fact that Nature has, so to speak,
endowed us with two characters. One of these we share with
all other men in that we all have reason and capacity superior
to that of animals. On this common nature we base our whole
idea of goodness and fitness, and from it we derive our way of
ascertaining our duty. The second character allotted to us is
the one peculiar to each of us as an individual. There are
great differences in bodily physique. Some persons, we see, are
swift in a race, others are powerful wrestlers; likewise, in appearance, some are dignified, others graceful. Differences in
mind are still greater. Lucius Crassus [48] and Lucius Philippus
were very witty, Gaius Caesar, the son of Lucius, even more
so, though his wit was rather studied. But at that same time
Marcus Scaurus and the young Marcus Drusus were exceptionally serious, Caius Laelius very jolly, and his intimate
friend Scipio more ambitious and sterner in his way of living.

As for the Greeks, we hear that Socrates was charming,
witty, and gay, always pretending to know nothing; the Greeks
called him "ironical." Pericles and Pythagoras, on the other
hand, acquired immense authority without being in the least
humorous. The Carthaginian Hannibal and our own general
Quintus Maximus were both shrewd and clever at concealing
their plans, holding their tongues, disguising their strategy,
and anticipating the enemy's designs. In these qualities too
the Greeks say Themistocles and Jason of Pherae [49] excelled.
And Solon was particularly sharp and crafty, when, in order to

---

[48] Lucius Crassus and Lucius Philippus were well known and admired
orators of the generation before Cicero. Gaius Caesar was also an
orator and a poet. Scaurus, Drusus, and Laelius were prominent men
of Cicero's time.

[49] Jason, ruler of Pherae in Thessaly (395–370), was considered a sagacious soldier and diplomat.

protect his own life and do a service to his country, he pretended to be insane.

Other men have entirely different characters, simple and open. They do not believe in secretiveness and plotting, but love truth and hate fraud. Others again will stop at nothing, stoop to anyone, if only they can gain their ends. Sulla and Crassus, as we saw, were of that type. But the craftiest and most persevering man of that sort was, we are told, the Spartan Lysander, whereas Callicratidas, who succeeded him as commander of the fleet, belonged to the opposite kind. Some people in very high positions make a point of appearing quite ordinary in their conversation. Catulus,[50] father and son, we saw were like that, and also Quintus Mucius. I have heard from older friends that Scipio Nasica was the same. His father,[51] on the other hand, the man who punished Tiberius Gracchus for his unscrupulous agitations, had no gracious way of talking, and for that reason became great and famous. There are countless other differences of nature and habits, no one of which is to be condemned.

Everyone should, however, hold firmly to his own characteristics, as long as they are not bad but only his own, and so maintain that fitness in things that is our object. We should act so as not to violate the universal laws of nature, but yet while obeying those follow our own peculiar bent. Even though other men's work seems better and more important, we should measure our own way by the standard set by our natures. For one gains nothing by fighting his own nature, pursuing something he can never attain. This shows still more clearly the meaning of fitness, which is, that nothing is fit if it is in opposition to Minerva, as the saying runs, or that goes

[50] On Quintus Catulus, see above, p. 351, fn. 34; on Quintus Mucius Scaevola, Cicero's old teacher, see above, p. 28, fn. 11.
[51] See above, p. 351, fn. 34.

against or contradicts one's nature. Indeed if there is such a thing as fitness or decorum at all, it lies especially in the consistency of our life as a whole and of all our individual actions. This consistency we cannot preserve by disregarding our own natures in order to imitate another's. Just as we should use our native language, and not, as some do, get ourselves deservedly ridiculed by dragging in Greek words, so our acts and our entire lives should be all of a piece.

These differences in human nature may go so deep that suicide may be right for one man and under the same circumstances wrong for another. Was Marcus Cato [52] in a different situation from those who surrendered to Caesar in Africa? For them, perhaps, it would have been a crime to kill themselves, for their mode of life had been softer and their characters were more easygoing. But Cato had been endowed by nature with a remarkably serious character, which he had strengthened by training, remaining always constant to his aim and to the course on which he had resolved. He had to choose death rather than face a tyrant.

How much Ulysses endured during his long wanderings, when he was servant to women—if Circe and Calypso can be called women—and yet he always tried in every word to be courteous and pleasant to everyone! On his return home, he submitted to the insults of his menservants and maids in order to attain at last the end for which he longed. Ajax, however, with the character ascribed to him, would have chosen to die a thousand times rather than endure such indignities. With these examples in mind we should each one of us consider well what are his own peculiar gifts, train those

[52] Marcus Cato, great grandson of the Cato of the Carthaginian wars (see p. 149, fn. 7) was one of the republicans who took Pompey's part in his war with Caesar and committed suicide after the defeat of his forces at Thapsus in North Africa.

well, and not desire to see how another man's become him. The thing that best becomes any man is that which is most his own.

We should all then learn to know our own abilities and become strict judges of our good and bad qualities, and not let the actors show more sense than we do. For they pick not the finest plays, but those most suited to them. Those who are proud of their voices take the *Epigoni* [53] or the *Medus*. Those who prefer action take the *Menalippa* or *Clytemnestra*. Rupilius, whom I remember well, always chose *Antiope*, but Aesopus rarely played Ajax. Shall the player then have an eye to what he can do best on the stage, and the wise man fail to do it in life? We shall do the best work in the fields for which we are fitted. However, if necessity ever thrusts us into some occupation for which we are not qualified, we must give to it all our efforts, thought, and pains, so as to do our work, if not handsomely, at least with as little impropriety as possible. And we should not try so hard to acquire the gifts that were not given us as to get rid of our faults.

To the two characters which, we have said, Nature has given each individual should be added a third, imposed on us by chance and circumstance, and a fourth which we deliberately assume. Royal power, military authority, nobility of birth and of office, wealth, influence, and their opposites, depend on chance and are shaped by circumstance. But it lies

---

[53] The *Epigoni* of the Latin poet Accius was a tragedy that carried on the story of the *Seven Against Thebes*, by Aeschylus. The *Medus* was a tragedy by the Latin poet Pacuvius. The hero was a son of the barbarian princess Medea, the heroine of a tragedy by Euripides. *Menalippa* was a play by Ennius, *Clytemnestra* a tragedy by Accius. *Antiope* was a play of vengeance by Pacuvius. Ennius was the author of a Latin tragedy on the tale of the Homeric Ajax. The subjects of all this early Latin drama were drawn from Greek literature. None of it has survived, except in scattered passages.

within our will to decide which role we want to play. Some turn to philosophy, others to civil law, others to oratory. And as to the virtues, one man would like to excel in one, another in another.

Men whose fathers or ancestors have been prominent in some field of distinction often try to become famous in the same field, like Quintus Mucius, for instance, son of Publius Mucius, in civil law, and Africanus, son of Paulus, in the army. Some have even added glory to the name they inherited from their fathers, as Africanus [54] did, who crowned his brilliant generalship with his eloquence. Timotheus, son of Conon, did the same, proving equal to his father in military fame and adding to that a renown for learning and intellectual brilliance. Sometimes, however, sons do not copy their fathers but follow a plan of their own. Some who come of lowly parentage and set their goals high have achieved great success.

All these things we must bear in mind and consider when we ask what is fitting for us. Above all, we must be quite sure who and what kind of person we wish to be and what kind of life we want to lead. This last is the most difficult problem of all, for it is in early youth, when we are least able to make important decisions, that we each select for ourselves the career that most takes our fancy. Thus we become involved in some course or calling in life before we can judge what is best for us.

We mortals are not given the choice which Hercules had in the story told by Prodicus [55] and repeated by Xenophon.

[54] Scipio Africanus, the younger, was the son of Aemilius Paulus, but being adopted by the son of Scipio Africanus the Elder took the name of his legal father. Timotheus, admiral of the Athenian fleet (378–356) was the son of the admiral Conon.

[55] Prodicus was a fifth-century Greek sophist, who taught at Athens. His account of the *Choice of Hercules* is to be found in Xenophon's Memorabilia, II, 1, 21–34.

"When the hero was growing into manhood, the time that Nature has appointed for deciding what path to take in life, he went out into the wilderness, and sitting down meditated for a long time. For he saw two paths open to him, one, the path of pleasure, the other, the path of virtue, and wondered which it would be better to take." This might perhaps happen to Hercules, son of Jove, but not to us. We imitate those we like, and are influenced by them to make their interests and aims our own. Often, too, we are imbued with the teachings of our parents, and fall into their habits and ways of life. Some are swayed by the popular voice and want most what looks finest to the masses. Some, however, by a stroke of luck or their own good disposition, take the right course in life without direction from their parents.

One kind of person is very rare—the man of extraordinary natural ability, or unusual learning and education, or both, who has time to reflect carefully on the career he wishes to choose. Then the decision should be based wholly on the man's character. For, whereas in all decisions we ask, as we said before, what is the suitable thing for each one's natural disposition, we must take far greater pains when it comes to planning a whole life, that we may be true to ourselves throughout all our lives and not be hampered in performing our duties.

In this decision we are influenced primarily by Nature and secondarily by fortune. Both should be considered in selecting our way of life, but Nature first. For Nature is much the stronger and more stable, so that fortune, when it comes into conflict with Nature seems like a mortal fighting a god. The man who has based his choice in life on his own better nature should hold steadfastly to it—for that is what is most fitting for him, unless by chance he discovers that his choice was a mistake. In that case—for it may happen—he must change his occupation and way of life. If circumstances are favorable, he may make the change easily and satisfactorily. Otherwise he must go slowly, step by step. Just as when a friendship no longer gives pleasure and has lost its value, a wise man thinks it more fitting to discontinue it gradually than to break it off abruptly. And once we have changed our manner of life, we should endeavor in every way to make it clear that we did it for good reason.

I said above that we should imitate our forefathers, but I must make an exception. We should not copy their faults, nor should we follow in their footsteps if our own natures do not warrant it. For example, the son of the elder Africanus, who adopted the younger Africanus, son of Paulus, was prevented by his poor health from following the career of his father, who had himself followed his father. So, if a man is unable to speak in court so as to capture the audience's attention, in the assembly, or to fight a war, he should at least practice those virtues that are within his power—justice, loyalty, generosity, modesty, and self-control, until he is able to meet most of the demands made on him. The finest inheritance that parents can leave their children, more precious than any estate, is a reputation for goodness and brave deeds. To disgrace such an inheritance should be considered a crime.

People of different ages have different duties, and those of youth are not the same as those of old age. Hence I must say a word on that subject. A young man should respect his elders, and choose the company of the best and most eminent of them so as to profit by their advice and influence. For the ignorance of youth needs to be steadied and guided by the prudent wisdom of age. Above all, the young should be kept from sensual dissipation, trained to work and endurance of mind and body, that they may be active in service whether as soldiers or as citizens. Even when they wish to relax and enjoy themselves, they should avoid excesses and remember to be modest. They will find that easier if they let their elders take part even in their pleasures.

Old men, on the other hand, should reduce the amount of their physical exertions but increase the activities of their minds. They should do their best, with wisdom and advice, to be of as much service as possible to their friends, to young people, and especially to their country. Above everything else, old men should beware of giving themselves up to feebleness and indolence. A luxurious life is bad for all ages, but most pernicious for the old, and if licentiousness is added to luxury, the harm is doubled, for age in that case not only disgraces itself, but makes youth bolder to indulge itself.

It is not inappropriate to mention here the duties of magistrates, of private citizens, and of resident foreigners. The particular duty of a magistrate is to realize the fact that he represents the state, and must uphold its dignity and honor, maintain its laws, guard the rights of the citizens, and remember that his post was given to him in trust. A private citizen should live in fairness and justice with his fellow men, neither servile and abject nor domineering. In public affairs he should stand for peace and decency. A man of this sort we judge and call a good citizen. A foreigner or resident alien has merely the duty of minding his own business, not inquiring into other people's affairs, and not meddling in the politics of a country not his own.

We should now have ready a fair idea of duty, when we are asked what is fitting and right for any individual, occasion, or age. The most fitting or decorous conduct is always to be consistent in the things we do and the plans we make.

This decorum shows itself in all our deeds and words, and in the very motions and postures of our bodies. It manifests itself in three ways, in beauty, in orderliness, and in good taste, difficult things to explain in words, sufficiently easy to understand. In three ways too we reveal our anxiety to be approved by the persons with whom we live. Accordingly we should say a few words about them.

To begin with, Nature herself seems to have had a marvelous plan for the structure of our bodies. Our faces and the other parts of our physique that are agreeable to look at she has made plainly visible, while the parts that are given to us to serve our natural needs and would appear unsightly and ugly she has covered up and hidden away. Human modesty follows this careful design of Nature. For all healthy-minded persons keep out of sight the parts that Nature has concealed, and perform their necessary operations as privately as they can. The functions of these parts of the body are indeed necessary, but neither the parts nor the functions are called by their proper names. There is nothing wrong in performing these functions, if it is done in private, but to talk about them is indecent. So both the open performance of such acts and frequent mention of them are indecencies.

We should pay no heed to the Cynics or to those Stoics who are almost Cynics, who criticize and ridicule us for thinking it improper to speak of some things that are not themselves wrong and calling by their names other things that are wrong. Robbery, fraud, and adultery are surely crimes, yet there is nothing indecent in talking about them. To beget children is a good act, but to speak of it is indecent. Along these lines, they attack on many points our ideas of modesty. Let us, however, follow Nature and shun everything displeasing to our eyes and ears. So whether standing or walking, sitting, or lying down, in face, in eyes, in the movements of our hands, let us maintain this kind of decorum.

In this connection we should avoid two pitfalls, be neither effeminate and soft, nor callous and boorish. Nor should we expect this rule to apply to actors and public speakers, and not to us. The custom of the stage with its tradition of discipline is so modest that no actor steps out on the stage without a loincloth, for fear that he might accidentally expose parts of his body that it would be indecorous to see. With us grown sons do not customarily bathe with their fathers, or sons-in-law with their fathers-in-law. We should then preserve this kind of modesty, especially since Nature herself is our teacher and guide.

As for beauty, there are two types. In one loveliness is the dominant feature, in the other, dignity. Loveliness we consider more appropriate for women, dignity for men. A man should, therefore, keep off his person any apparel that diminishes his dignity and guard against similar faults in his bearing and movements. The behavior taught in the gymnasium is often grotesque, and the bearing of some actors is quite unsuitable. And in both gymnasium and theater good and simple manners win the praise. Dignity of appearance is enhanced by a good complexion, and a good complexion is the result of physical exercise. We must also be neat, not in an unpleasant, exaggerated way, but enough so to avoid uncivilized and underbred slovenliness. Our dress should follow the same rules. Here, as in most other matters, the best is the golden mean. We should be careful too in walking not to saunter along languidly, like bearers in a procession, or hurry ahead too fast. When we do that we get out of breath, our expression is altered, our features distorted, demonstrating plainly our lack of poise.

However, it is much more important to keep the workings of our minds harmonious with Nature, and this we shall achieve if we avoid giving way to over-excitement or depression, and fix our attention on maintaining a true decorum. Our minds work in two different ways, in thinking and in feeling. Thought centers on the search for truth; feeling impels us to act. Accordingly, we should spend our thinking on the noblest subjects and keep our feelings under the control of our intellect.

The power of speech is great and it appears in two forms, oratory and conversation. Oratory is to be used in arguments in court, in the people's assemblies, and in the Senate. Conversation takes place in social gatherings and discussions, at meetings of friends, and may be introduced at dinner parties. Rules for oratory are laid down by the rhetoricians. There are none for conversation, though I do not know why there could not be. For wherever there are students eager to learn, instructors are found to teach them; but no one is interested in learning how to converse, while the classrooms of the rhetoricians are crowded. However, the rules that govern the choice of words and structure of sentences in oratory are the same too for conversation.

Our organ of speech is the voice, in using which we should aim at two things, to be clear and to be melodious. Both are gifts to be sought for from Nature, yet clarity may be increased by practice, and melodiousness by imitating those who speak softly and pleasantly. There was nothing about the two Catuli to make one think them particularly rare judges of literature, although they were men of good education. But so too were others. These two men, however, were considered perfect masters of the Latin tongue. Their pronunciation was delightful. They neither overstressed nor mumbled their syllables. They were neither indistinct nor affected. Their voices were neither strained nor weak, nor yet shrill. Lucius Crassus was a more fluent speaker, and no less adept, but the reputation of the Catuli for eloquence was as great as his. When it came to wit and humor, the brother of the elder Catulus,

Caesar,[56] surpassed them all. Even in court he would with his informal style defeat his opponents with their elaborate oratory. So, if we wish to serve decorum under all conditions, we must pay some attention to all these points.

In the art of conversation, Socratics were pastmasters. The talk should be easy, not insistent, but lively. No individual should shut out others from speaking, as if he had a monopoly of the conversation, but here, as in other things, he should realize that turn about is fair play. One should note first the subject of the conversation; if it is serious, one should approach it soberly; if trivial, lightly. One should be especially careful not to let his talk suggest something wrong in his own character, as happens often when people in jest or earnest set themselves to disparaging the absent with malicious slander.

The topics of conversation are ordinarily domestic matters, or politics, or the practice of arts or learning. If the talk begins to drift away to other subjects, one should bring it back but without hurting the feelings of those present. For we are not all interested in the same things at all times or to the same extent. One should watch too to see how far the conversation is still enjoyed, and as it had a reason for beginning, so it should come to a proper end.

Just as for every phase of life we have the excellent rule to avoid excitement, that is, passions that are too strong and do not obey reason, so our conversation should be free from such emotions. We should not display anger, or greed, or indolence, or callousness, or anything of the sort. Most of all, we should aim to show respect and consideration for those with whom we are talking.

It may sometimes, however, be necessary to express disapproval. On such occasions we should perhaps use a sharper

---

[56] This Caesar was known as "the orator."

tone of voice and sterner expressions, and even put on an appearance of anger. But we should resort to this kind of reproof seldom, and with reluctance, as we do to cautery and amputation, and never unless it is necessary, and no other remedy can be found. And there must be no real anger, for that prevents all fair, considered action. In most cases a mild reproof is enough, but gravely administered, so as to show its seriousness, and avoiding insult to the feelings. We must make it plain too that whatever harshness there was in our reproof was intended only for the good of the person reproved.

In disputes with our bitterest enemies, even while we hear ourselves insulted, the right thing is to remain calm and restrain our anger. For action taken in excitement cannot be steadily consistent and will not be approved by the witnesses. It is bad taste to talk about oneself, especially to say what is not true, and before a derisive audience to imitate the "boastful soldier."

Now, since we are surveying the subject in all its aspects (at least that is our aim), we should say something about the kind of house suitable for a distinguished and prominent citizen. The main object of a house is usefulness, and to meet this purpose the plan of the building should be designed. At the same time, some pains should be taken to make it comfortable and dignified.

Gnaeus Octavius,[57] the first of his family to become consul, had distinguished himself, we are told, by building on the Palatine Hill a beautiful and impressive house. Crowds came to see it, and it was thought that it won votes for its owner. a new man in politics, and helped bring about his election to the consulship. Scaurus tore down that house and built on the site an addition to his own palace. So Octavius first

[57] Gnaeus Octavius, who commanded a fleet in the Macedonian war, was consul in 165 B.C.

brought to his house the honor of the consulship, while Scaurus, son of a great and eminent gentleman, brought to a much enlarged house, not only defeat but disgrace and ruin.[58] One's standing may be enhanced by the house one lives in, but it must not all depend on the house. The house should be honored for its owner, not the owner for his house.

As in everything else, one should consider not only one's own wants, but also the needs of others. The house of a prominent citizen, therefore, in which many guests are to be entertained and large crowds of every sort of visitors received, must be spacious. Under other circumstances a large house may be a discredit to its owner, if it looks lonely, and especially if under another owner, it once was full of people. It is disagreeable to hear passersby remarking:

"O, poor old house, alack, how different an owner owns you now!" Nowadays the same can be said of many a house.[59]

Particularly in building one's own house one should take care not to go beyond one's limit in expense and grandeur. Much harm can be done along this line simply by setting a bad example. For many people follow eagerly the lead of the great, especially in this direction. Who, for instance, thinks of copying the virtues of noble Lucius Lucullus? [60] But how many there are who imitate the magnificence of his villas! Some limit should certainly be set to such expenditures and an effort made to return to moderation. The same moderation should be shown in all usages and modes of living. But enough now on this subject.

---

[58] Marcus Scaurus, the younger, a stepson of Sulla, made a great fortune out of plundering the island of Sardinia during his terms there as governor, 56 B.C. Four years later he was condemned and banished from Rome.

[59] Adherents of Caesar were at this time living in many of the great houses that had belonged to members of Pompey's party.

[60] The consul Lucullus was famous for giving magnificent banquets.

In undertaking any enterprise, we should hold in mind three rules. First, our reason should be master of our desires, for there is no better way to make sure we adhere to our duty. Secondly, we should see clearly just how important is the thing we wish to accomplish so as to spend neither more nor less pains and labor on it than the case calls for. Thirdly, we should be careful to maintain moderation in everything connected with a gentleman's appearance and dignity. This can best be done by staying within the bounds of the decorum we discussed above, and not going beyond it. But of these three rules, the most important is to control our desires by our reason.

The next topic to be discussed is orderliness in things and seasonableness of occasion. These qualities are included by the Greeks in the property they call "right organization"—not the word we translate as "moderation," but rather one that means preservation of order. Making use, however, of our word "moderation," the Stoics define it this way: "Moderation is the art of giving its proper place to whatever we do or say." Orderliness and proper placing thus seem to have the same meaning, for the Stoics define orderliness as the "arrangement of things in their appropriate and convenient places." The place for an action is, according to them, its seasonable time. The seasonable time for an act the Greeks call the "right moment," the Latins "occasion." So moderation, as we define it here, is, as I have said, the art of doing the right thing at the suitable time.

Prudence, too, of which we spoke at the beginning, can be defined in the same way. Here, however, we are discussing temperance, self-control, and similar virtues. The characteristics of prudence we mentioned in their proper connection. We are now, as we have been for some time, talking of these other virtues that have to do with respect for and ways of winning the approval of our fellow men.

We should be so orderly in our conduct that everything in our lives is as well organized and harmonious as words in a set speech. It is shocking and highly reprehensible to introduce in a serious conversation jokes appropriate only at a dinner party or in other frivolous talk. Once when Pericles had the poet Sophocles as his colleague in office, and they were conferring about their common duties, a handsome boy chanced to pass by, and Sophocles exclaimed, "Look Pericles; what a beautiful boy!" And Pericles rightly reproved him by saying, "But, Sophocles, a general should keep not only his hands, but his eyes too under control!" Yet if Sophocles had made the same remark at an athletic competition, he could not have been justly blamed. So great is the importance of time and place. If, for example, a man preparing to defend a case in court, memorizes his speech while traveling or on a walk, or thinks intently about something else, no one criticizes him. But if he does the same thing at a dinner party, he is considered rude, for ignoring the nature of the occasion.

Flagrant violations of good manners, as singing in the street or other bad misbehavior, are obviously wrong and do not much need our admonition and instruction. We should be more on our guard against faults that seem small, and that may pass unobserved by many. As when a harp or a flute is only slightly out of tune, the expert still notices it, so we must see to it that nothing in our lives is out of tune, and all the more as a harmony of deeds is deeper and better than a harmony of sounds.

And as the ear of a musician detects even slight dissonances in the tone of a harp, we—if we want to be sharp and constant observers of faults in conduct—will often discover important things by means of trifles. From a glance of the eye, a con-

378

traction or lift of the eyebrows, an air of gloom, a burst of
hilarity, a laugh, a word, a silence, a raising or lowering of the
voice, and other signs of the sort, we shall readily tell what is
a proper action and what a violation of a duty or of Nature. In
this connection it is not a bad idea to learn what is right or
wrong to do by the behavior of others so that what is obnoxious in them we may avoid in ourselves. For it is somehow
a fact that we see faults in other people more easily than we
do in ourselves. So pupils in school are quickest to correct
their faults, when their masters imitate them to teach them
better.

And when we are in doubt which course to choose, it is
proper to consult men of learning or practical experience, to
find out what they think on any point of duty. Most men tend
to drift in the direction their nature takes them. If we consult
someone else we should take into consideration not only what
he says, but also what he thinks and why he thinks as he does.
Painters, sculptors, and poets, too, like to have their work inspected by the public, so that they can improve whatever is
most criticized. Both by themselves and from others they try
to find out where they have failed. So we are helped by other
people's judgment to know what to do and what not to do,
what to alter and what to correct.

No rules are required for our attitude toward common usage
and civic regulations. For they are themselves rules, and no
one should make the mistake of imagining that because
Socrates and Aristippus [61] did or said something contrary to
the ways and customs of their city, he has a right to do the
same. For these men earned their privilege by their great and

---

[61] Aristippus (c. 370 B.C.) was a pupil of Socrates who founded a
philosophic school of his own. He taught that pleasure was the chief
aim of man.

godlike virtue. We must reject altogether the Cynics' manner of reasoning,[62] for it is opposed to any sense of reverence, without which nothing can be right and nothing good.

We should respect and honor all those whose lives have been noted for good and important accomplishments, the true patriots who have served and are serving their country just as much as if they held positions of civil and military authority. We should also show great respect to the aged, give precedence to public officials, make some distinction between a citizen and a foreigner, and in the case of foreigners between those who have come on private and on public business. To sum up, without going into details, we should respect, uphold, and preserve the common bonds of unity and association that exist between all the members of the human race.

Now with regard to trades and other modes of earning a living, as to which are to be considered gentlemanly and which vulgar, our instructors taught us as follows.[63] First, no occupation is desirable that makes other people hate us, such as tax collecting and usury. Unworthy too and vulgar are the occupations of all hired workmen, whom we pay for physical labor and not for artistry, for in their case their wages are a mark of slavery. Vulgar too we must call the business of those who buy from other merchants to sell by retail immediately, for all their profits are due to plain lying, and nothing is more contemptible than deceit. Mechanics all have a vulgar profession, for nothing noble can be found in a workshop. At the bottom of the list come trades that cater to luxurious living—"the fishmongers, butchers, and cooks, the poulterers, and

---

[62] The Cynics in their lives and in their teachings expressed a contemptuous indifference to convention and ordinary standards of decency.
[63] Cicero's stipulations as to acceptable occupations and behavior are thought to have been the most important influence in shaping the concept of the "English gentleman."

fishmen," as Terence says.[64] You can add to them, if you wish, the perfumers, dancers and all the slapstick comedians.

Professions that either require a higher intelligence, or perform a considerable service for the community, like medicine, architecture, and good teaching, are right for those whose social standing makes them possible. Trade, when conducted on a small scale, should be called vulgar, but when carried on on a large scale, like wholesale importing from all over the world and distribution to many without fraud, it is not so much to be disdained. As a matter of fact, those successful traders, who, satiated or at any rate satisfied with their fortunes, as once they sailed from the high seas into harbor proceed now from the harbor to country estates inland, deserve much approbation. Of all the gainful occupations, however, none is better than agriculture, none more profitable, none more agreeable, and none more worthy of a free man. But that subject I have discussed already in my *Cato the Elder.* You will find there material on that point.

I have now, I think, explained fully enough how all our duties are derived from the four divisions of goodness. Yet, often a conflict and a rivalry arise between actions that are themselves good, as to which of the two good acts is the better—a problem that Panaetius ignored. Now the four divisions of all goodness are, first, wisdom; second, respect for one's fellow men; third, courage; and fourth, temperance. Hence in making a choice between duties, it is often necessary to compare the importance of these virtues.

In my opinion, the duties based on ties with our fellow men are closer to our natural instinct than those that are matters of the intellect. I can support this view by the following argument. Suppose a wise man were granted a life of complete

---

[64] Terence, *The Eunuch,* II, 2, 26.

affluence so that in perfect comfort he might study and reflect on everything worth knowing; even so, if he were left so solitary that he could never see another human being, he would die. Now the highest of all virtues is the understanding which the Greeks call "wisdom," for by "prudence," which they call "sagacity," we mean something else, namely, a practical knowledge of what to avoid. But the wisdom which I shall call the supreme virtue is the knowledge of things divine and human, among which are included the bonds of relationship between God and man and the fellowship of man with man. If this wisdom is really the highest virtue as it undoubtedly is, then the duty based on ties with our fellow men must be the most important. For the contemplation and understanding of Nature would be somehow incomplete and defective if it led to no practical action. Such action is especially concerned with the furthering of man's welfare. It is of interest therefore to the whole of human society and should be valued accordingly above any mere speculation.

All the best men agree on this point, and prove it by their behavior. For who is so engrossed in the investigation and study of the universe, that if, in the midst of his most important studies and deliberations, he were informed of some sudden danger or crisis in his country that he could relieve or help, would not drop everything, even though he thought he might be about to count the stars or measure the size of the world? He would do the same to help a parent or friend, or to save them from danger. Hence we may conclude that duties required by justice should take precedence over pursuit of knowledge and duties connected with it. For the former promote the well-being of mankind and nothing should be more sacred than that to any man.

However, the men who have devoted all their lives and efforts to the search for knowledge have not failed to contribute to the improvement of the welfare and safety of man-kind. For they have taught many to be better citizens and more useful to their communities. So, for instance, the Pythagorean Lysis [65] taught the Theban Epaminondas, Plato Dion of Syracuse, and many others have done likewise. As for myself and whatever I have done for my country, if it has been anything at all, I came to my career trained and equipped by teachers who taught me well. And not only while they are living and here with us do those wise men teach and enlighten those who wish to learn, but after their death their literary works go on performing the same service.

Nor did they overlook any subject that was a part of legal, moral, or political science. It seems indeed as if they had devoted all their leisure time to aiding us with our public responsibilities. So those men dedicated to the study of learning and wisdom have used their foresight and understanding wonderfully to help mankind. For this reason those who say much, provided they do it wisely, are of greater value than those who speculate most profoundly but never put it into words. For mere speculation centers on itself, while speech takes in our fellow members in society.

As the bees do not assemble in swarms for the sake of making honeycombs, but make their honeycombs because they are gregarious by nature, so—and much more—do men exercise their genius together in thought and action because they are naturally gregarious. And so, if the virtue that consists of safeguarding humanity, that is, maintaining human society, does not accompany the search for knowledge, knowl-

---

[65] Lysis, a Pythagorean philosopher, expelled from Italy, went to Greece and became there a teacher of Epaminondas, the great Theban patriot and general. Dion, a relative of the more famous Dionysius of Syracuse, studied under Plato both at Athens and at Syracuse. He was tyrant of Syracuse from 356 to 353 B.C.

edge comes to seem self-centered and fruitless. Courage, too, if not guided by concern for human society and human fellowship, degenerates into a kind of brutality and ferocity. Wherefore a care for human society and relationships is more important than the pursuit of theoretical knowledge.

Nor is it true, as some people say, that human society and fellowship were first established to meet the needs of daily life, because without the help of others we could not obtain or provide the things our nature demands. If this were so, and if, by some magic wand, as the story goes, everything necessary for our livelihood and comfort were supplied us, then surely every man of brilliant intellect would drop all his other business and immerse himself altogether in learning and scholarship. But that is not true. He would try to avoid loneliness and look for company in his studies. He would want to teach and to learn, to listen and to talk. Every duty then that promotes the maintenance of human society and fellowship should be given preference over one that has to do with learning and study only.

Another question should perhaps be raised in this connection. Should our obligation to our fellow men be always considered more important than temperance and moderation? I do not think so. For there are some acts either so repulsive or so wicked that no wise man would perform them even to save his country. Posidonius [66] collected a long list of such crimes, and some of them are so vile and indecent that it seems a sin even to mention them. A wise man will not do such things even for the sake of his country, nor will his country want him to do them for her. But this problem easily resolves itself, for a time cannot come when it would be to a country's advantage to have a wise man commit any of those crimes.

---

[66] See p. 124, fn. 5.

We may take it, therefore, as settled that in choosing between duties that conflict, those demanded by the interests of society should be given precedence. Any well-considered action indeed is the result of knowledge and forethought, but such action is more important than mere wise speculation. This is enough to say on this point. For I have explained the matter so that it should not be hard to tell in a dilemma concerning duties which should be chosen in preference to another. Yet within the class of obligations to our fellows there are grades of duty, and one must know their order of importance. Our first debt is to the immortal gods, our second to our country, our third to our parents, and thereafter in descending scale to other people.

From this brief discussion we see that men are often in doubt not only as to what is right and wrong, but also between two good courses of action as to which is better. This problem, as I said before, was overlooked by Panaetius. But let us go on now to the rest of our subject.